Supreme Court
Watch—1998

Other Books by David M. O'Brien

STORM CENTER:
THE SUPREME COURT IN AMERICAN POLITICS
FOURTH EDITION

CONSTITUTIONAL LAW AND POLITICS:
Vol. 1, STRUGGLES FOR POWER AND GOVERNMENTAL
ACCOUNTABILITY

Vol. 2, CIVIL RIGHTS AND CIVIL LIBERTIES
THIRD EDITION

ABORTION AND AMERICAN POLITICS
(co-authored)

JUDICIAL ROULETTE

WHAT PROCESS IS DUE?
COURTS AND SCIENCE-POLICY DISPUTES

VIEWS FROM THE BENCH:
THE JUDICIARY AND CONSTITUTIONAL POLITICS
(co-authored)

THE POLITICS OF TECHNOLOGY ASSESSMENT:
INSTITUTIONS, PROCESSES, AND POLICY DISPUTES
(co-authored)

THE PUBLIC'S RIGHT TO KNOW:
THE SUPREME COURT AND THE FIRST AMENDMENT

PRIVACY, LAW, AND PUBLIC POLICY

THE POLITICS OF AMERICAN GOVERNMENT
SECOND EDITION
(co-authored)

TO DREAM OF DREAMS:
RELIGIOUS FREEDOM AND CONSTITUTIONAL POLITICS
IN POSTWAR JAPAN

JUDGES ON JUDGING

SUPREME COURT WATCH—1998

Highlights of the 1996–1998 Terms
Preview of the 1998–1999 Term

DAVID M. O'BRIEN

UNIVERSITY OF VIRGINIA

W. W. NORTON & COMPANY

New York   London

ISBN 0-393-97355-7 (pbk.)

W. W. Norton & Company, Inc., 500 Fifth Avenue, New York, N.Y. 10110
http://www.wwnorton.com
W. W. Norton & Company Ltd., 10 Coptic Street, London WC1A 1PU

1 2 3 4 5 6 7 8 9 0

CONTENTS

Cases in italics only are excerpted; cases within brackets are discussed and extensively quoted in the chapter introductions.

VOLUME TWO

PREFACE

Supreme Court Watch—1998 examines the changes and decisions made during the Supreme Court's 1996 and 1997 terms. Besides highlighting the major constitutional rulings in excerpts from leading cases, I discuss in section-by-section introductions other important decisions and analyze recent developments in various areas of constitutional law. The important cases that the Court has granted review and will decide in its 1998–1999 term are also previewed here. To offer even more information in an efficient format, I have included special boxes titled "The Development of Law" and "Inside the Court."

The favorable reception of and comments received on previous editions of the *Watch* have been gratifying, and I hope that this 1998 edition will further contribute to students' understanding of constitutional law, politics, and history, as well as to their appreciation for how the politics of constitutional interpretation turns on differing interpretations of constitutional politics. I am also most grateful to Sarah Caldwell and to Deborah Gerish for doing a terrific and expeditious job of copyediting.

D.M.O.
July 4, 1998

VOLUME ONE

2

LAW AND POLITICS IN THE SUPREME COURT: JURISDICTION AND DECISION-MAKING PROCESS

A. JURISDICTION AND JUSTICIABLE CONTROVERSIES

The Rehnquist Court avoided ruling on a major controversy over whether states may require public employees to speak only English by finding the case *Arizonans for Official English v. Arizona*, 117 S.Ct. 1055 (1997), to have become moot. More than twenty states have enacted laws making English the official language. In 1988, Arizona voters approved a state constitutional amendment making English the official language and requiring all government workers to do business only in English. At that time, Maria-Kelly Yniguez, a state employee handing malpractice claims, challenged the constitutionality of that law as a violation of her First Amendment right of free speech to speak Spanish to malpractice claimants, who often could not understand English. But in 1990, a few months after the federal district court handed down its initial ruling, Ms. Yniguez resigned and went to work in the private sector. The district court found the English-only amendment to be overly broad and rejected the state attorney general's narrower interpretation of the law. When Arizona's governor decided not to appeal that ruling, two newcomers, the Arizonans for Official English Committee (AOE) and Robert Park, AOE's chair, moved to intervene on the ground that they had sponsored the ballot initiative that resulted in the amendment. The district court denied them standing to intervene. But the Court of Appeals for the Ninth Circuit viewed the matter differently and permitted AOE and Park to proceed as the appellants. Subsequently, a three-judge panel held that Arizona's English-only law violated public employees' First Amendment rights and by a six-to-five vote the Ninth Circuit *en banc* affirmed that decision and rejected the contention that the case had become moot when Ms. Yniguez left public employment. Writing for a unanimous Court, Justice Ginsburg vacated that decision and ordered the case dismissed because it had become moot and the AOE and Park, who were not government employees, lacked standing to intervene in the suit.

The Court also, initially, avoided ruling on the merits of the controversy over the constitutionality of Congress's giving the President the power of a line-item veto of appropriations bills. But the Court did for the first time rule on the issue of standing for legislators to challenge the constitutionality of laws that they voted against. In *Raines v. Byrd* (excerpted below), Chief Justice Rehnquist denied standing to six members of Congress trying to challenge the constitutionality of the Line Item Veto Act, but held out the possibility of other challenges to the law. Dissenting Justices Stevens and Breyer would have granted standing and reached the merits of the case.

Raines v. Byrd
117 S.Ct. 2312 (1997)

On April 4, 1996, President Clinton signed the Line Item Veto Act into law, which went into effect on January 1, 1997. That law gives the President the authority to "cancel" individual spending and tax benefit provisions contained in a bill after signing the bill into law. Because of the controversy over the constitutionality of Congress's giving the President the power of a line-item veto, the law also provided that any member of Congress "adversely affected" by the law could file a suit in federal district court, with direct expedited appeal to the Supreme Court. The day after the law went into effect, four Senators and two members of the 104th Congress (1995–1996) who had voted against the act filed a suit in the District Court for the District of Columbia against Frederick Raines (the director of the Office of Management and Budget) and the secretary of the Treasury. The district court held that the members of Congress had standing to sue, that the controversy was ripe even though the President had not yet used the "cancellation" authority granted him, and that the law was unconstitutional. Eight days after that ruling, an appeal was made to the Supreme Court, which granted expedited briefing and oral arguments in May 1997.

The Court's decision was seven to two and its opinion delivered by Chief Justice Rehnquist. Justice Souter filed a concurring opinion, which Justice Ginsburg joined. Justices Stevens and Breyer filed dissenting opinions.

CHIEF JUSTICE REHNQUIST delivered the opinion of the Court.

Under Article III, Section 2 of the Constitution, the federal courts have jurisdiction over this dispute between appellants and appellees only if it is a "case" or "controversy." This is a "bedrock requirement." *Valley Forge Christian College v. Americans United for Separation of Church and State, Inc.*, 454 U.S. 464 (1982).

One element of the case-or-controversy requirement is that appellees, based on their complaint, must establish that they have standing to sue. The standing inquiry focuses on whether the plaintiff is the proper party to bring this suit, although that inquiry "often turns on the nature and source of the claim asserted," *Warth v. Seldin*, 422 U.S. 490 (1975). To meet the standing requirements of Article III, "[a] plaintiff must allege personal injury fairly traceable to the defendant's allegedly unlawful conduct and likely to be redressed by the requested relief." *Allen v. Wright*, 468 U.S. 737 (1984). We have consistently stressed that a plaintiff's complaint must establish that he has a "personal stake" in the alleged dispute, and that the alleged injury suffered is particularized as to him.

We have also stressed that the alleged injury must be legally and judicially cognizable. This requires, among other things, that the plaintiff have suffered "an invasion of a legally protected interest which is . . . concrete and particularized," *Lujan v. Defenders of Wildlife*, 504 U.S. 555 (1992), and that the dispute is "traditionally thought to be capable of resolution through the judicial process," *Flast v. Cohen*, 392 U.S. 83 (1968).

We have always insisted on strict compliance with this jurisdictional standing requirement. And our standing inquiry has been especially rigorous when reaching the merits of the dispute would force us to decide whether an action taken by one of the other two branches of the Federal Government was unconstitutional. . . .

We have never had occasion to rule on the question of legislative standing presented here. In *Powell v. McCormack*, 395 U.S. 486 (1969), we held that a Member of Congress' constitutional challenge to his exclusion from the House of Representatives (and his consequent loss of salary) presented an Article III case or controversy. But *Powell* does not help appellees. First, appellees have not been singled out for specially unfavorable treatment as opposed to other Members of their respective bodies. Their claim is that the Act causes a type of institutional injury (the diminution of legislative power), which necessarily damages all Members of Congress and both Houses of Congress equally. Second, appellees do not claim that they have been deprived of something to which they personally are entitled—such as their seats as Members of Congress after their constituents had elected them. Rather, appellees' claim of standing is based on a loss of political power, not loss of any private right, which would make the injury more concrete. Unlike the injury claimed by Congressman Adam Clayton Powell, the injury claimed by the Members of Congress here is not claimed in any private capacity but solely because they are Members of Congress. If one of the Members were to retire tomorrow, he would no longer have a claim; the claim would be possessed by his successor instead. The claimed injury thus runs (in a sense) with the Member's seat, a seat which the Member holds (it may quite arguably be said) as trustee for his constituents, not as a prerogative of personal power.

The one case in which we have upheld standing for legislators (albeit state legislators) claiming an institutional injury is *Coleman v. Miller*, 307 U.S. 433 (1939). Appellees, relying heavily on this case, claim that they, like the state legislators in *Coleman*, "have a plain, direct and adequate interest in maintaining the effectiveness of their votes" sufficient to establish standing. In *Coleman,* 20 of Kansas' 40 State Senators voted not to ratify the proposed "Child Labor Amendment" to the Federal Constitution. With the vote deadlocked 20–20, the amendment ordinarily would not have been ratified. However, the State's Lieutenant Governor, the presiding officer of the State Senate, cast a deciding vote in favor of the amendment, and it was deemed ratified (after the State House of Representatives voted to ratify it). The 20 State Senators who had voted against the amendment, joined by a 21st State Senator and three State House Members, filed an action in the Kansas Supreme Court seeking a writ of *mandamus* that would compel the appropriate state officials to recognize that the legislature had not in fact ratified the amendment. That court held that the members of the legislature had standing to bring their *mandamus* action, but ruled against them on the merits.

This Court affirmed. By a vote of 5–4, we held that the members of the legislature had standing. In explaining our holding, we repeatedly emphasized that if these legislators (who were suing as a bloc) were correct on the merits, then their votes not to ratify the amendment were deprived of all validity. . . .

[O]ur holding in *Coleman* stands (at most) for the proposition that legislators whose votes would have been sufficient to defeat (or enact) a specific legislative act have standing to sue if that legislative action goes into effect (or does not go into effect), on the ground that their votes have been completely nullified.

It should be equally obvious that appellees' claim does not fall within our holding in *Coleman*, as thus understood. They have not alleged that they voted for a specific bill, that there were sufficient votes to pass the bill, and that the bill was nonetheless deemed defeated. In the vote on the Line Item Veto Act, their votes were given full effect. They simply lost that vote. . . .

Not only do appellees lack support from precedent, but historical practice appears to cut against them as well. It is evident from several episodes in our history that in analogous confrontations between one or both Houses of Congress and the Executive Branch, no suit was brought on the basis of claimed injury to official authority or power. The Tenure of Office Act, passed by Congress over the veto of President Andrew Johnson in 1867, was a thorn in the side of succeeding Presidents until it was finally repealed at the behest of President Grover Cleveland in 1887. . . .

Similarly, in *INS v. Chadha*, 462 U.S. 919 (1983), the Attorney General would have had standing to challenge the one-House veto provision because it rendered his authority provisional rather than final. By parity of reasoning, President Gerald Ford could have sued to challenge the appointment provisions of the Federal Election Campaign Act which were struck down in *Buckley v. Valeo*, 424 U.S. 1 (1976), and a Member of Congress could have challenged the validity of President Coolidge's pocket veto that was sustained in *The Pocket Veto Case*, 279 U.S. 655 (1929).

There would be nothing irrational about a system which granted standing in these cases; some European constitutional courts operate under one or another variant of such a regime. But it is obviously not the regime that has obtained under our Constitution to date. Our regime contemplates a more restricted role for Article III courts, well expressed by Justice Powell in his concurring opinion in *United States v. Richardson*, 418 U.S. 166 (1974):

"The irreplaceable value of the power articulated by Mr. Chief Justice Marshall [in *Marbury v. Madison*, 1 Cranch 137 (1803)] lies in the protection it has afforded the constitutional rights and liberties of individual citizens and minority groups against oppressive or discriminatory government action. It is this role, not some amorphous general supervision of the operations of government, that has maintained public esteem for the federal courts and has permitted the peaceful coexistence of the countermajoritarian implications of judicial review and the democratic principles upon which our Federal Government in the final analysis rests."

In sum, appellees have alleged no injury to themselves as individuals (contra *Powell*), the institutional injury they allege is wholly abstract and widely dispersed (contra *Coleman*), and their attempt to litigate this dispute at this time and in this form is contrary to historical experience. . . . We also note that our conclusion neither deprives Members of Congress of an adequate remedy (since they may repeal the Act or exempt appropriations bills from its reach), nor forecloses the Act from constitutional challenge (by someone who suffers judicially cognizable injury as a result of the Act). Whether the case would be different if any of these circumstances were different we need not now decide.

We therefore hold that these individual members of Congress do not have a sufficient "personal stake" in this dispute and have not alleged a sufficiently concrete injury to have established Article III standing. The judgment of the District Court is vacated, and the case is remanded with instructions to dismiss the complaint for lack of jurisdiction.

Justice SOUTER, concurring in the judgment, with whom Justice GINSBURG joins, concurring.

Under our precedents, it is fairly debatable whether this injury is sufficiently "personal" and "concrete" to satisfy the requirements of Article III. . . . Because it is fairly debatable whether appellees' injury is sufficiently personal and concrete to give them standing, it behooves us to resolve the question under more general separation-of-powers principles underlying our standing requirements. Although the contest here is not formally between the political branches (since Congress passed the bill augmenting Presidential power and the President signed it), it is in substance an interbranch controversy about calibrating the legislative and executive powers, as well as an intrabranch dispute between segments of Congress itself. Intervention in such a controversy would risk damaging the public confidence that is vital to the functioning of the Judicial Branch by embroiling the federal courts in a power contest nearly at the height of its political tension. . . .

The virtue of waiting for a private suit is only confirmed by the certainty that another suit can come to us. The parties agree, and I see no reason to question, that if the President "cancels" a conventional spending or tax provision pursuant to the Act, the putative beneficiaries of that provision will likely suffer a cognizable injury and thereby have standing under Article III. By depriving beneficiaries of the money to which they would otherwise be entitled, a cancellation would produce an injury that is "actual," "personal and individual," and involve harm to a "legally protected interest," *Lujan v. Defenders of Wildlife*, 504 U.S. 555 (1992); assuming the canceled provision would not apply equally to the entire public, the injury would be "concrete"; and it would be "fairly traceable to the challenged action of the" executive officials involved in the cancellation, as well as probably "redressable by a favorable decision."

I therefore conclude that appellees' alleged injuries are insufficiently personal and concrete to satisfy Article III standing requirements of personal and concrete harm. Since this would be so in any suit under the conditions here, I accordingly find no cognizable injury to appellees.

Justice STEVENS, dissenting.

The Line Item Veto Act purports to establish a procedure for the creation of laws that are truncated versions of bills that have been passed by the Congress and presented to the President for signature. If the procedure were valid, it would deny every Senator and every Representative any opportunity to vote for or against the truncated measure that survives the exercise of the President's cancellation authority. Because the opportunity to cast such votes is a right guaranteed by the text of the Constitution, I think it clear that the persons who are deprived of that right by the Act have standing to challenge its constitutionality. Moreover, because the impairment of that constitutional right has an immediate impact on their official powers, in my judgment they need not wait until after the President has exercised his cancellation authority to bring suit. Finally, the same reason that the respondents have standing provides a sufficient basis for concluding that the statute is unconstitutional.

Article I, Sec. 7, of the Constitution provides that every Senator and every Representative has the power to vote on "Every Bill . . . before it become a law" either as a result of its having been signed by the President or as a result of its "Reconsideration" in the light of the President's "Objections." In contrast, the Line Item Veto Act establishes a mechanism by which bills passed by both Houses of Congress will eventually produce laws that have not passed either House of Congress and that have not been voted on by any Senator or Representative.

Assuming for the moment that this procedure is constitutionally permissible, and that the President will from time to time exercise the power to cancel portions of a just-enacted law, it follows that the statute deprives every Senator and every Representative of the right to vote for or against measures that may become law. The appellees cast their challenge to the constitutionality of the Act in a slightly different way. Their complaint asserted that the Act "alters the legal and practical effect of all votes they may cast on bills containing such separately vetoable items" and "divests them of their constitutional role in the repeal of legislation." These two claimed injuries are at base the same as the injury on which I rest my analysis. The reason the complaint frames the issues in the way that it does is related to the Act's technical operation. Under the Act, the President would receive and sign a bill exactly as it passed both Houses, and would exercise his partial veto power only after the law had been enacted. The appellees thus articulated their claim as a combination of the diminished effect of their initial vote and the circumvention of their right to participate in the subsequent repeal. Whether one looks at the claim from this perspective, or as a simple denial of their right to vote on the precise text that will ultimately become law, the basic nature of the injury caused by the Act is the same.

In my judgment, the deprivation of this right—essential to the legislator's office—constitutes a sufficient injury to provide every Member of Congress with standing to challenge the constitutionality of the statute. If the dilution of an individual voter's power to elect representatives provides that voter with standing—as it surely does—the deprivation of the right possessed by each Senator and Representative to vote for or against the precise text of any bill before it becomes law must also be a sufficient injury to create Article III standing for them. . . .

Accordingly, I would affirm the judgment of the District Court.

Justice BREYER, dissenting.

[T]he interests that the parties assert are genuine and opposing, and the parties are therefore truly adverse.

Nonetheless, there remains a serious constitutional difficulty due to the fact that this dispute about lawmaking procedures arises between government officials and is brought by legislators. The critical question is whether or not this dispute, for that reason, is so different in form from those "matters that were the traditional concern of the courts at Westminster" that it falls outside the scope of Article III's judicial power. Justice FRANKFURTER explained this argument in his dissent in *Coleman*, saying that courts traditionally

> "leave intra-parliamentary controversies to parliaments and outside the scrutiny of law courts. The procedures for voting in legislative assemblies—who are members, how and when they should vote, what is the requisite number of votes for different phases of legislative activity, what votes were cast and how they were counted—surely are matters that not merely concern political action, but are of the very essence of political action, if 'political' has any connotation at all. . . . In no sense are they matters of 'private damage.' They pertain to legislators not as individuals but as political representatives executing the legislative process. To open the law courts to such controversies is to have courts sit in judgment on the manifold disputes engendered by procedures for voting in legislative assemblies."

Justice FRANKFURTER dissented because, in his view, the "political" nature of the case, which involved legislators, placed the dispute outside the scope of Article III's "case" or "controversy" requirement. Nonetheless, the *Coleman* Court rejected his argument.

Although the majority today attempts to distinguish *Coleman*, I do not believe that Justice FRANKFURTER's argument or variations on its theme can carry the day here. First, as previously mentioned, the jurisdictional statute before us eliminates all but constitutional considerations, and the circumstances mentioned above remove all but the "political" or "intragovernmental" aspect of the constitutional issue.

Second, the Constitution does not draw an absolute line between disputes involving a "personal" harm and those involving an "official" harm. Justice FRANKFURTER himself said that this Court had heard cases involving injuries suffered by state officials in their official capacities. *Coleman* itself involved injuries in the plaintiff legislators' official capacity. . . .

Third, Justice FRANKFURTER's views were dissenting views, and the dispute before us, when compared to *Coleman*, presents a much stronger claim, not a weaker claim, for constitutional justiciability. The law-makers in *Coleman* complained of a lawmaking procedure that, at worst, improperly counted Kansas as having ratified one proposed constitutional amendment, which had been ratified by only 5 other States, and rejected by 26, making it unlikely that it would ever become law. The lawmakers in this case complain of a lawmaking procedure that threatens the validity of many laws (for example, all appropriations laws) that Congress regularly and frequently enacts. The systematic nature of the harm immediately affects the legislators' ability to do their jobs. The harms here are more serious, more pervasive, and more immediate than the harm at issue in *Coleman*.

The majority finds a difference in the fact that the validity of the legislators' votes was directly at issue in *Coleman*. But since many of the present plaintiffs will likely vote in the majority for at least some appropriations bills that are then subject to presidential cancellation, I think that—on their view of the law—their votes are threatened with nullification too. . . .

In sum, I do not believe that the Court can find this case nonjusticiable without overruling *Coleman*. Since it does not do so, I need not decide whether the systematic nature, seriousness, and immediacy of the harm would make this dispute constitutionally justiciable even in *Coleman*'s absence. Rather, I can and would find this case justiciable on *Coleman*'s authority. [B]ecause the majority has . . . expressed no view on the merits of the appeal, I shall not discuss the merits either, but reserve them for future argument.

THE DEVELOPMENT OF LAW

Other Important Rulings on Standing

Case	Vote	Ruling
Bennett v. Spear, 117 S.Ct. 1154 (1997)	9:0	Held that property owners, no less than environmentalists, may assert standing to bring

"citizen suits" under the Endangered Species Act, and thereby challenge proposed environmental regulations. Writing for the Court, Justice Scalia ruled that the act's permitting "any person" to sue should be broadly interpreted because "the overall subject matter of this legislation is the environment . . . a matter in which it is common to think all persons have an interest." As a result, landowners have new legal standing to challenge environmental regulations.

B. THE COURT'S DOCKET AND SCREENING CASES

The Supreme Court's docket over the last few decades has continued to grow rather steadily, reaching over 8,000 cases in the 1994 term and falling slightly to 7,602 cases in the 1996 term. Over the last decade, the largest growth has been in unpaid, or *in forma pauperis*, cases, which tend to be filed by prison inmates. (For further discussion see Vols. 1 or 2, Ch. 2.[1]) In the 1996–1997 term, for instance, there were 5,165 unpaid cases filed, compared with only 2,430 paid cases.

In spite of the growth in its docket, the Court has granted plenary consideration—that is, briefing on the merits of a case and oral arguments—to a smaller number and percentage of cases. As illustrated below, only about 1 percent of the cases coming to the Court are now given plenary consideration.[2] By comparison, in 1953, the first year of Chief Justice Earl Warren's tenure, the Court had only 1,463 cases on its docket and decided 76 (or 5.1 percent) by written opinion. Sixteen years later, in 1969, in Chief Justice Warren Burger's first year on the bench, the Court faced a docket of 4,202 cases and decided 108 (or 2.5 percent). But in Chief Justice Burger's last term the Court had a docket of 5,158 cases and decided 171 (or 3.3 percent). In 1986, when Justice William H. Rehnquist was elevated to chief justice, the Court had a docket of 5,123 cases and heard oral arguments in 175 (or 3.4 percent). Ten years later, in the 1995–1996 term, the Court decided only 90 (or 1.1 percent) of the cases on its docket. Figure 1 on the next page shows this trend in greater detail.

Even some justices are "amazed" by the trend. Prior to arriving at the Court at the start of the 1990 term, Justice Souter noticed that the number had "come down significantly from the historical highs," which reached 184 decisions in the 1981 and 1983 terms. On the high bench, he found there had not been a conscious decision to reduce the number. "It had in fact just happened," in his words; "nobody set a quota; nobody sits at the conference table and says, 'We've taken too much. We must pull back.' . . . It simply has happened."

During his remarks at a 1995 circuit conference, Justice Souter considered a number of possible explanations for the declining plenary docket. All were factors external to the Court. Presidential vetoes of legislation by Ronald Reagan and George Bush may have resulted in "a diminishing supply of new statutes . . . that cried out for some immediate and speedy" interpretation. Under those two Republican administrations, there was neither "much antitrust work" coming from the Department of Justice nor a great

---

[1] References to Vols. 1 and 2 are to the author's two-volume *Constitutional Law and Politics* (Norton, 3d ed., 1997).

[2] This discussion draws on the author's more extensive analysis in "Join-3 Votes, the Rule of Four, the *Cert.* Pool, and the Supreme Court's Shrinking Plenary Docket," 13 *Journal of Law and Politiics* 779–808 (1997).

deal of civil rights litigation, except for voting rights cases. Finally, he agreed with some Court-watchers that, after twelve years of Republican judicial appointments, Reagan's and Bush's lower-court appointees may have produced "a diminished level of philosophical division within the federal courts from which so much of the conflicting opinions tend to arise."

FIGURE 1
Percentage of Docket Granted Review, 1968–1995

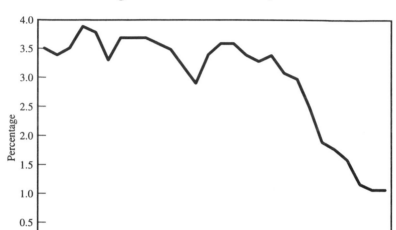

Other external factors may have played a part as well. Notably, the Court's discretionary jurisdiction was expanded with the 1988 Act to Improve the Administration of Justice. Virtually all nondiscretionary appellate jurisdiction was eliminated, except for appeals in reapportionment cases and suits under Civil Rights and Voting Rights acts, antitrust laws, and the Presidential Election Campaign Fund Act. But, as Figure 2 shows, the plenary docket started diminishing prior to that jurisdictional change.

Factors internal to the Court, however, undoubtedly also contributed in decisive ways. More specifically, the fluctuation in the plenary docket registers changes in the Court's decision-making process *and* changes in its composition. As Figure 2 shows, the plenary docket jumped in the 1971 term to over 170 cases and remained in that range for the rest of the decade. Beginning in the 1981 term, the docket reached its peak of over 180 cases per term. Following the retirements of Chief Justice Burger at the end of the 1985 term and Justice Lewis F. Powell, Jr., at the end of the 1986 term, however, the plenary docket gradually declined and then fell sharply in the 1990s.

The increase in the number of cases granted plenary consideration in the 1970s appears directly related to changes in the Court's operation made early in Chief Justice Burger's tenure. One important change he persuaded the others to make was in the oral argument calendar. Prior to 1970, attorneys in cases granted oral argument were each given one hour to present their arguments. In 1970, the time allotted each side was reduced to thirty minutes, which in turn permitted the Court to hear more cases. Instead of hearing 12 cases during a two-week oral argument session, the Burger Court went to hearing 12 cases in three days. Not surprisingly, the number of orally argued cases rose from 144 to 151 to 177 during the 1969, 1970, and 1971 terms, respectively.

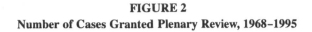

FIGURE 2
Number of Cases Granted Plenary Review, 1968–1995

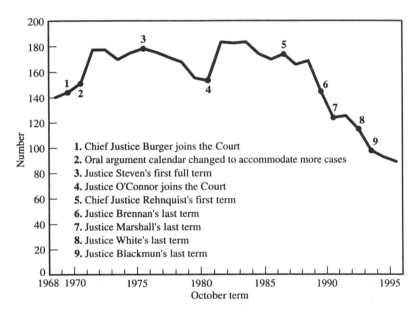

1. Chief Justice Burger joins the Court
2. Oral argument calendar changed to accommodate more cases
3. Justice Steven's first full term
4. Justice O'Connor joins the Court
5. Chief Justice Rehnquist's first term
6. Justice Brennan's last term
7. Justice Marshall's last term
8. Justice White's last term
9. Justice Blackmun's last term

In addition to the increase in the space on the oral argument calendar came another change—a change in the justices' voting practice in granting cases. In the early 1970s Chief Justice Burger and some other justices began casting "Join-3" votes, rather than simply voting to grant or deny petitions for *certiorari*. Because earlier in this century the Court adopted the informal so-called Rule of Four—namely, that at least four justices must agree that a case merits review—a Join-3 vote is a vote to provide a fourth vote if others vote to grant review, but is otherwise considered as voting to deny. The introduction of Join-3 votes arguably contributed to the Court's taking more cases by lowering the threshold for granting review established by the Rule of Four.

Based on an examination of Justice Thurgood Marshall's papers for the 1979 to 1990 terms, it is clear that some justices cast an extraordinary share of such votes, whereas others rarely do, if ever. Justice Harry Blackmun led in Join-3 votes. By comparison, Justice Stevens never casts such votes. Other justices' Join-3 votes fall somewhere between these two extremes. Of the cases granted during those terms, Join-3 votes were cast in 26 percent. More significantly, 12 percent were placed on the plenary docket on the basis of less than four votes to grant plus one or more Join-3 votes; some cases were even granted on the basis of only two votes to grant and two or more Join-3 votes. In short, Join-3 votes clearly lowered the threshold for granting cases and contributed to the inflation of the plenary docket. Put differently, had the Rule of Four been maintained, the Burger Court could have reduced its plenary docket by at least 12 percent and possibly by as much as 26 percent.

The key to the Court's "incredibly shrinking" docket in the 1990s, therefore, may be found in the Burger Court's responses to its rising docket and inflated plenary docket in the 1970s and early 1980s. Besides enlarging the plenary docket by changing the oral argument calendar, the Burger Court no longer strictly adhered to the Rule of Four, thereby sacrificing some control over what and how much to decide. As Figure 2 indicates, after an initial increase in 1971, the number of cases annually decided rose again following the 1981 appointment of Justice O'Connor, who cast a fair number of Join-3 votes (less than Justice Blackmun but more than the others). With several justices casting Join-3 votes, by the 1980s the numbers granted reached "historical highs." Following the retirements of Chief Justice Burger and Justice Powell, the plenary docket shrank slowly. Neither Justice Scalia nor Justice Kennedy is as inclined as those two or most other former members of the Burger Court to cast Join-3 votes. The decline continued after the retirements of Justices Brennan and Marshall at the end of the 1989 and 1990 terms, respectively, and then fell further after the retirements of Justices White and Blackmun at the end of the 1992 and 1993 terms. In sum, the inflation of the plenary docket in the 1970s and early 1980s, as well as the docket's contraction in the late 1980s and 1990s, basically registers changes in the Court's composition and case selection process, specifically the predisposition of certain justices to cast Join-3 votes and to vote to grant review.

In addition, Justice Stevens emphasizes that the justices' greater reliance in the 1990s on their law clerks' recommendations on whether to grant cases may have contributed to the declining plenary docket. All the justices, except Stevens, now receive a single memo on each petition from the *"cert. pool,"* their shared law clerks, whereas in the 1970s and 1980s fewer justices participated in the *cert.* pool and relied on their or their own clerks' independent review of each petition. According to Stevens, the clerks have become more cautious about recommending the granting of cases. "You stick your neck out as a clerk when you recommend to grant a case," observes Justice Stevens. "The risk-averse thing to do is to recommend not to take a case. I think it accounts for the lessening of the docket."[3]

---

[3] Interview quoted by Tony Mauro, "Justices Give Pivotal Role to Novice Lawyers," *USA Today* A1, A2 (March 13–15, 1998).

In historical perspective, the Rehnquist Court's shrinking docket is doubly ironic. First, although recognized for his interest in judicial administration, Chief Justice Burger failed to fully appreciate that the crisis brought about by the Court's rising caseload did not comport with the justices' "workload problem." While promoting judicial reforms that would have created an additional federal appellate court above the thirteen courts of appeals, his Court's "workload problem" was one of its own making. Second, in the 1980s Justice Rehnquist sided with Chief Justice Burger in lamenting the workload of the Court's expanded plenary docket. As he repeatedly observed, "For better or for worse—and I happen to think it is better—I think the Supreme Court is committed to hearing and deciding somewhere in the neighborhood of 150 cases each term." Yet as chief justice he has presided for a decade over a Court with a sharply diminishing plenary docket.

Although the Rehnquist Court has been giving plenary consideration to fewer and fewer cases, it has not abandoned its responsibility to supervise the lower federal courts. The Court generally takes only cases with nationwide importance, especially to resolve conflicting rulings rendered by lower courts or to reverse decisions of lower federal and state courts. The Court's affirmance and reversal of lower court decisions in its 1997–1998 term is indicated below.

The Court's Disposition of Appeals in the 1997–1998 Term

	Affirmed	Reversed or Vacated
First Circuit	2	3
Second Circuit	2	
Third Circuit	3	1
Fourth Circuit	1	3
Fifth Circuit	6	5
Sixth Circuit		3
Seventh Circuit	3	4
Eighth Circuit	5	9
Ninth Circuit	4	12
Tenth Circuit	1	
Eleventh Circuit		2
Federal Circuit	1	1
District of Columbia Circuit	4	4
Other Federal Courts	1	2
State Courts and Other	3	8
Total	36	57

INSIDE THE COURT

The Business of the Supreme Court in the 1997–1998 Term[*]

Subject of Court Opinions[*]	Summary	Plenary
Admiralty		1
Antitrust		1
Bankruptcy		4
Bill of Rights (other than		
rights of accused) and equal protection		5
Commerce clause		
1. Constitutionality and construction		
of federal regulation		
2. Constitutionality of state regulation		
Common law		1
Miscellaneous statutory construction	1	29
Due process		
1. Economic interests		2
2. Procedure and rights of accused	1	14
3. Substantive due process (non-economic)		
Impairment of contract and just compensation		
International law, war, and peace		
Jurisdiction, procedure, and practice	1	16
Land legislation		1
Native Americans		6
Patents, copyright, and trademarks		
Other suits against the government	1	6
Suits by states		
Taxation (federal and state)	1	3
Totals	5	89

[*] The classification of cases is that of the author and necessarily invites differences of opinion as to the dominant issue in some cases.

Included are opinions in cases whether decided summarily or given plenary consideration, but not cases summarily disposed of by simple orders, dissents from the denial of review, and those in dismissing cases as improvidently granted.

H. OPINION DAYS AND COMMUNICATING DECISIONS

INSIDE THE COURT

Opinion Writing during the 1997–1998 Term[*]

Opinions	Majority	Concurring	Dissenting	Separate	Totals
Per curiam	2				2
Rehnquist	11	2	1	2	16
Stevens	7	6	15	3	31
O'Connor	12	2	2	1	17
Scalia	10	11	12	1	34
Kennedy	10	6	1	1	18
Souter	10	6	4	1	21
Thomas	10	1	4	1	16
Ginsburg	12	5	8		25
Breyer	10	6	7	1	24
Totals	94	45	54	11	204

[*] Court opinions disposing of two or more companion cases are counted only once here. In addition, this table includes cases disposed of either summarily or upon plenary consideration, but does not include orders dismissing or remanding cases, nor concurring or dissenting opinions from the denial of *certiorari*.

Voting Alignments in the Rehnquist Court, 1986–1996 Terms

	Rehnquist	White	Blackmun	Stevens	O'Connor	Scalia	Kennedy	Souter	Thomas	Brennan	Marshall	Ginsburg	Breyer
Rehnquist	--	80.8	55.2	52.2	79.5	79.1	81.2	69.9	79.2	47.6	46.4	66.7	61.9
White	80.8	--	62.2	60.4	72.5	69.8	75.7	73.5	67.7	52.9	52.9		
Blackmun	55.2	62.2	--	72.0	58.4	49.1	57.6	64.8	44.4	77.4	77.0	68.2	
Stevens	52.2	60.4	72.0	--	56.9	47.8	58.2	65.9	43.0	69.9	71.6	75.6	74.2
O'Connor	79.5	72.5	58.4	56.9	--	71.6	77.8	73.9	69.2	49.4	47.9	68.0	72.0
Scalia	79.1	69.8	49.1	47.8	71.6	--	77.2	63.6	87.9	47.5	45.0	59.4	55.7
Kennedy	81.2	75.7	57.6	58.2	77.8	77.2	--	74.3	72.8	53.7	51.2	71.0	68.5
Souter	69.9	73.5	64.8	65.9	73.9	63.6	74.3	--	59.2		54.6	79.9	82.7
Thomas	79.2	67.7	44.4	43.0	69.2	87.9	72.8	59.2	--		55.0	55.0	53.1
Brennan	47.6	52.9	77.4	69.9	49.4	47.5	53.7			--	95.0		
Marshall	46.4	52.9	77.0	71.6	47.9	45.0	51.2	54.6	55.0	95.0	--		
Ginsburg	66.7		68.2	75.6	68.0	59.4	71.0	79.9	55.0			--	79.6
Breyer	61.9			74.2	72.0	55.7	68.5	82.7	53.1			79.6	--

Note: The above are average percentages. The percentages for each term are from Table 1B) of the *Harvard Law Review*'s annual review of the Supreme Court's term in volumes 101–111 (1988–1997).

I. THE IMPACT OF SUPREME COURT DECISIONS: COMPLIANCE AND IMPACT

THE DEVELOPMENT OF LAW

Other Recent State Supreme Court Decisions Declining to Follow the U.S. Supreme Court's Rulings

Case	Vote	Ruling
American Academy of Pediatrics v. Lungren, 940 P.2d 797 (1997)	4–3	By a vote of four to three, the Supreme Court of California refused to follow the U.S.

Supreme Court's rulings upholding state restrictions on minors seeking abortions by requiring them to obtain the permission of their parents or a judge. Here, the court invalidated the parental consent and judicial bypass requirement for infringing on minors' right of privacy under the California Constitution.

4

THE PRESIDENT AS
CHIEF EXECUTIVE
IN DOMESTIC AFFAIRS

C. LEGISLATIVE POWERS IN THE
ADMINISTRATIVE STATE

After avoiding a ruling on the constitutionality of congressional delega-tion to the President of the power of line-item veto in *Raines v. Byrd* (1997) (excerpted in Chapter 2), the Court struck down the Line Item Veto Act of 1996 in *Clinton v. City of New York* (1998) (excerpted below). As in *INS v. Chadha*, 462 U.S. 919 (1983) (excerpted in Vol. 1, Ch. 4), striking down one-house legislative vetoes of administrative decisions, the Court ruled in *Clinton v. City of New York* that the power of line-item veto violates the presentment clause of Article I, Section 7, Clause 2.

Clinton v. City of New York
118 S.Ct. 2091 (1998)

The pertinent facts are discussed by Justice Stevens in his opinion for the Court. The Court's decision was six to three and its opinion announced by Justice Stevens. Justice Kennedy filed a concurring opinion. Justice Scalia filed an opinion concurring in part and dissenting in part, which Justice O'Connor joined. Justice Breyer filed a dissenting opinion, which Justices O'Connor and Scalia joined in part.

Justice STEVENS delivered the opinion of the Court.

The Line Item Veto Act (Act) was enacted in April 1996 and became effective on January 1, 1997. The following day, six Members of Congress who had voted against the Act brought suit in the District Court for the District of Columbia challenging its constitutionality. On April 10, 1997, the District Court entered an order holding that the Act is unconstitutional. We determined, however, that the Members of Congress did not have standing to sue because they had not "alleged a sufficiently concrete injury to have established Article III standing," *Raines v. Byrd*, [117 S.Ct. 2312] (1997). . . .

Less than two months after our decision in that case, the President exercised his authority to cancel one provision in the Balanced Budget Act of 1997, and two provisions in the Taxpayer Relief Act of 1997. Appellees, claiming that they had been injured by two of those cancellations, filed these cases in the District Court. That Court again held the statute invalid and we again expedited our review. We now hold that these appellees have standing to challenge the constitutionality of the Act and, reaching the merits, we agree that the cancellation procedures set forth in the Act violate the Presentment Clause, Art. I, Sec. 7, cl. 2, of the Constitution. . . .

Appellees filed two separate actions against the President and other federal officials challenging these two cancellations. The plaintiffs in the first case are the City of New York, two hospital associations, one hospital, and two unions representing health care employees. The plaintiffs in the second are a farmers' cooperative [Snake River Cooperative] consisting of about 30 potato growers in Idaho and an individual farmer who is a member and officer of the cooperative. The District Court consolidated the two cases and determined that at least one of the plaintiffs in each had standing under Article III of the Constitution. . . .

On the merits, the District Court held that the cancellations did not conform to the constitutionally mandated procedures for the enactment or repeal of laws in two respects. First, the laws that resulted after the cancellations "were different from those consented to by both Houses of Congress." Moreover, the President violated Article I "when he unilaterally canceled provisions of duly enacted statutes." As a separate basis for its decision, the District Court also held that the Act "impermissibly disrupts the balance of powers among the three branches of government."

As in the prior challenge to the Line Item Veto Act, we initially confront jurisdictional questions. . . . In both the New York and the Snake River cases, the Government argues that the appellees are not actually injured because the claims are too speculative and, in any event, the claims are advanced by the wrong parties. We find no merit in the suggestion that New York's injury is merely speculative because HHS has not yet acted on the State's waiver requests. The State now has a multibillion-dollar contingent liability that had been eliminated by Section 4722(c) of the Balanced Budget Act of 1997. The District Court correctly concluded that the State, and the appellees, "suffered an immediate, concrete injury the moment that the President used the Line Item Veto to cancel section 4722(c) and deprived them of the benefits of that law." The self-evident significance of the contingent liability is confirmed by the fact that New York lobbied Congress for this relief, that Congress decided that it warranted statutory attention, and that the President selected for cancellation only this one provision in an act that occupies 536 pages of the Statutes-at-Large. His action was comparable to the judgment of an appellate court setting aside a verdict for the defendant and remanding for a new trial of a multibillion-dollar damages claim. . . .

The Snake River farmers' cooperative also suffered an immediate injury when the President canceled the limited tax benefit that Congress had enacted to facilitate the acquisition of processing plants. Three critical facts identify the specificity and the importance of that injury. First, Congress enacted Section 968 for the specific purpose of providing a benefit to a defined category of potential purchasers of a defined category of assets. The members of that statutorily defined class received the equivalent of a statutory "bargaining chip" to use in carrying out the congressional plan to facilitate their purchase of such assets. Second, the President selected Section 968 as one of only two tax benefits in the Taxpayer Relief Act of 1997 that should be canceled. The cancellation rested on his determination that the use of those bargaining chips would have a significant impact on the Federal budget deficit. Third, the Snake River cooperative was organized for the very purpose of acquiring processing facilities, it had concrete plans to utilize the benefits of Section 968, and it was engaged in ongoing negotiations with the owner of a processing plant who had expressed an interest in structuring a tax-deferred sale when the President canceled Section 968. . . . By depriving them of their statutory bargaining chip, the cancellation inflicted a sufficient likelihood of economic injury to establish standing under our precedents. . . .

The Line Item Veto Act gives the President the power to "cancel in whole" three types of provisions that have been signed into law: "(1) any dollar amount of discretionary budget authority; (2) any item of new direct spending; or (3) any limited tax benefit." It is undisputed that the New York case involves an "item of new direct spending" and that the Snake River case involves a "limited tax benefit" as those terms are defined in the Act. It is also undisputed that each of those provisions had been signed into law pursuant to Article I, Section 7, of the Constitution before it was canceled.

The Act requires the President to adhere to precise procedures whenever he exercises his cancellation authority. In identifying items for cancellation he must consider the legislative history, the purposes, and other relevant information about the items. He must determine, with respect to each cancellation, that it will "(i) reduce the Federal budget deficit; (ii) not impair any essential Government functions; and (iii) not harm the national interest." Moreover, he must transmit a special message to Congress notifying it of each cancellation within five calendar days (excluding Sundays) after the enactment of the canceled provision. It is undisputed that the President meticulously followed these procedures in these cases.

A cancellation takes effect upon receipt by Congress of the special message from the President. If, however, a "disapproval bill" pertaining to a special message is enacted into law, the cancellations set forth in that message become "null and void." The Act sets forth a detailed expedited procedure for the consideration of a "disapproval bill," but no such bill was passed for either of the cancellations involved in these cases. A majority vote of both Houses is sufficient to enact a disapproval bill. The Act does not grant the President the authority to cancel a disapproval bill, but he does, of course, retain his constitutional authority to veto such a bill. . . .

There are important differences between the President's "return" of a bill pursuant to Article I, Section 7, and the exercise of the President's cancellation authority pursuant to the Line Item Veto Act. The constitutional return takes place before the bill becomes law; the statutory cancellation occurs after the bill becomes law. The constitutional return is of the entire bill; the statutory cancellation is of only a part. Although the Constitution expressly authorizes the President to play a role in the process of enacting statutes, it is silent on the subject of unilateral Presidential action that either repeals or amends parts of duly enacted statutes.

There are powerful reasons for construing constitutional silence on this profoundly important issue as equivalent to an express prohibition. The procedures governing the enactment of statutes set forth in the text of Article I were the product of the great debates and compromises that produced the Constitution itself. Familiar historical materials provide abundant support for the conclusion that the power to enact statutes may only "be exercised in accord with a single, finely wrought and exhaustively considered, procedure." [*INS v.*] *Chadha*, 462 U.S. [919 (1983)]. Our first President understood the text of the Presentment Clause as requiring that he either "approve all the parts of a Bill, or reject it in toto." What has emerged in these cases from the President's exercise of his statutory cancellation powers, however, are truncated versions of two bills that passed both Houses of Congress. They are not the product of the "finely wrought" procedure that the Framers designed. . . .

The Government advances two related arguments to support its position that despite the unambiguous provisions of the Act, cancellations do not amend or repeal properly enacted statutes in violation of the Presentment Clause. First, relying primarily on *Field v. Clark*, 143 U.S. 649 (1892), the Government contends that the cancellations were merely exercises of discretionary authority granted to the President by the Balanced Budget Act and the Taxpayer Relief Act read in light of the previously enacted Line Item Veto Act. Second, the Government submits that the substance of the authority to cancel tax and spending items "is, in practical effect, no more and no less than the power to 'decline to spend' specified sums of money, or to 'decline to implement' specified tax measures." Neither argument is persuasive. . . .

[In *Field v. Clark*, the Court identified] three critical differences between the power to suspend the exemption from import duties and the power to cancel portions of a duly enacted statute. First, the exercise of the suspension power was contingent upon a condition that did not exist when the Tariff Act was passed: the imposition of "reciprocally unequal and unreasonable" import duties by other countries. In contrast, the exercise of the cancellation power within five days after the enactment of the Balanced Budget and Tax Reform Acts necessarily was based on the same conditions that Congress evaluated when it passed those statutes. Second, under the Tariff Act, when the President determined that the contingency had arisen, he had a duty to suspend; in contrast, while it is true that the President was required by the Act to make three determinations before he canceled a provision, those determinations did not qualify his discretion to cancel or not to cancel. Finally, whenever the President suspended an exemption under the Tariff Act, he was executing the policy that Congress had embodied in the statute. In contrast, whenever the President cancels an item of new direct spending or a limited tax benefit he is rejecting the policy judgment made by Congress and relying on his own policy judgment. Thus, the conclusion in *Field v. Clark* that the suspensions mandated by the Tariff Act were not exercises of legislative power does not undermine our opinion that cancellations pursuant to the Line Item Veto Act are the functional equivalent of partial repeals of Acts of Congress that fail to satisfy Article I, Section 7. . . .

Neither are we persuaded by the Government's contention that the President's authority to cancel new direct spending and tax benefit items is no greater than his traditional authority to decline to spend appropriated funds. . . . It is argued that the Line Item Veto Act merely confers comparable discretionary authority over the expenditure of appropriated funds. The critical difference between this statute and all of its predecessors, however, is that unlike any of them, this Act gives the President the unilateral power to change the text of duly enacted statutes. None of the Act's predecessors could even arguably have been construed to authorize such a change.

Although they are implicit in what we have already written, . . . it is appropriate to emphasize three points.

First, we express no opinion about the wisdom of the procedures authorized by the Line Item Veto Act. Many members of both major political parties who have served in the Legislative and the Executive Branches have long advocated the enactment of such procedures for the purpose of "ensuring greater fiscal accountability in Washington." . . . We do not lightly conclude that their action was unauthorized by the Constitution. We have, however, twice had full argument and briefing on the question and have concluded that our duty is clear.

Second, . . . because we conclude that the Act's cancellation provisions violate Article I, Section 7, of the Constitution, we find it unnecessary to consider the District Court's alternative holding that the Act "impermissibly disrupts the balance of powers among the three branches of government."

Third, our decision rests on the narrow ground that the procedures authorized by the Line Item Veto Act are not authorized by the Constitution. . . .

If there is to be a new procedure in which the President will play a different role in determining the final text of what may "become a law," such change must come not by legislation but through the amendment procedures set forth in Article V of the Constitution. *Cf. U.S. Term Limits, Inc. v. Thornton*, 514 U.S. 779 (1995).

The judgment of the District Court is affirmed.

It is so ordered.

Justice KENNEDY, concurring.

I write to respond to my colleague Justice BREYER, who observes that the statute does not threaten the liberties of individual citizens, a point on which I disagree. The argument is related to his earlier suggestion that our role is lessened here because the two political branches are adjusting their own powers between themselves. To say the political branches have a somewhat free hand to reallocate their own authority would seem to require acceptance of two premises: first, that the public good demands it, and second, that liberty is not at risk. The former premise is inadmissible. The Constitution's structure requires a stability which transcends the convenience of the moment. The latter premise, too, is flawed. Liberty is always at stake when one or more of the branches seek to transgress the separation of powers.

Separation of powers was designed to implement a fundamental insight: concentration of power in the hands of a single branch is a threat to liberty. *The Federalist* states the axiom in these explicit terms: "The accumulation of all powers, legislative, executive, and judiciary, in the same hands . . . may justly be pronounced the very definition of tyranny." *The Federalist* No. 47. So convinced were the Framers that liberty of the person inheres in structure that at first they did not consider a Bill of Rights necessary. It was at Madison's insistence that the First Congress enacted the Bill of Rights. It would be a grave mistake, however, to think a Bill of Rights in Madison's scheme then or in sound constitutional theory now renders separation of powers of lesser importance.

In recent years, perhaps, we have come to think of liberty as defined by that word in the Fifth and Fourteenth Amendments and as illuminated by the other provisions of the Bill of Rights. The conception of liberty embraced by the Framers was not so confined. They used the principles of separation of powers and federalism to secure liberty in the fundamental political sense of the term, quite in addition to the idea of freedom from intrusive governmental acts. The idea and the promise were that when the people delegate some degree of control to a remote central authority, one branch of government ought not possess the power to shape their destiny without a sufficient check from the other two. In this vision, liberty demands limits on the ability of any one branch to influence basic political decisions. . . .

It follows that if a citizen who is taxed has the measure of the tax or the decision to spend determined by the Executive alone, without adequate control by the citizen's Representatives in Congress, liberty is threatened. Money is the instrument of policy and policy affects the lives of citizens. The individual loses liberty in a real sense if that instrument is not subject to traditional constitutional constraints. . . .

Separation of powers helps to ensure the ability of each branch to be vigorous in asserting its proper authority. In this respect the device operates on a horizontal axis to secure a proper balance of legislative, executive, and judicial authority. Separation of powers operates on a vertical axis as well, between each branch and the citizens in whose interest powers must be exercised. The citizen has a vital interest in the regularity of the exercise of governmental power. If this point was not clear before *Chadha*, it should have been so afterwards. Though *Chadha* involved the deportation of a person, while the case before us involves the expenditure of money or the grant of a tax exemption, this circumstance does not mean that the vertical operation of the separation of powers is irrelevant here. By increasing the power of the President beyond what the Framers envisioned, the statute compromises the political liberty of our citizens, liberty which the separation of powers seeks to secure. . . .

Justice BREYER, with whom Justice O'CONNOR and Justice SCALIA join as to Part III, dissenting.

II

I approach the constitutional question before us with three general considerations in mind. First, the Act represents a legislative effort to provide the President with the power to give effect to some, but not to all, of the expenditure and revenue-diminishing provisions contained in a single massive appropriations bill. And this objective is constitutionally proper.

When our Nation was founded, Congress could easily have provided the President with this kind of power. In that time period, our population was less than four million, federal employees numbered fewer than 5,000, annual federal budget outlays totaled approximately $4 million, and the entire operative text of Congress's first general appropriations law read as follows:

"Be it enacted . . . that there be appropriated for the service of the present year, to be paid out of the monies which arise, either from the requisitions heretofore made upon the several states, or from the duties on import and tonnage, the following sums, viz. A sum not exceeding two hundred and sixteen thousand dollars for defraying the expenses of the civil list, under the late and present government; a sum not exceeding one hundred and thirty-seven thousand dollars for defraying the expenses of the department of war; a sum not exceeding one hundred and ninety thousand dollars for discharging the warrants issued by the late board of treasury, and remaining unsatisfied; and a sum not exceeding ninety-six thousand dollars for paying the pensions to invalids."

At that time, a Congress, wishing to give a President the power to select among appropriations, could simply have embodied each appropriation in a separate bill, each bill subject to a separate Presidential veto.

Today, however, our population is about 250 million, the Federal Government employs more than four million people, the annual federal budget is $1.5 trillion, and a typical budget appropriations bill may have a dozen titles, hundreds of sections, and spread across more than 500 pages of the Statutes at Large. Congress cannot divide such a bill into thousands, or tens of thousands, of separate appropriations bills, each one of which the President would have to sign, or to veto, separately. Thus, the question is whether the Constitution permits Congress to choose a particular novel means to achieve this same, constitutionally legitimate, end.

Second, the case in part requires us to focus upon the Constitution's generally phrased structural provisions, provisions that delegate all "legislative" power to Congress and vest all "executive" power in the President. The Court, when applying these provisions, has interpreted them generously in terms of the institutional arrangements that they permit. . . .

Third, we need not here referee a dispute among the other two branches. . . .

These three background circumstances mean that, when one measures the literal words of the Act against the Constitution's literal commands, the fact that the Act may closely resemble a different, literally unconstitutional, arrangement is beside the point. To drive exactly 65 miles per hour on an interstate highway closely resembles an act that violates the speed limit. But it does not violate that limit, for small differences matter when the question is one of literal violation of law. No more does this Act literally violate the Constitution's words.

The background circumstances also mean that we are to interpret nonliteral Separation of Powers principles in light of the need for "workable government." *Youngstown Sheet and Tube Co.* [*v. Sawyer*, 343 U.S. 579 (1952)] (JACKSON, J., concurring). If we apply those principles in light of that objective, as this Court has applied them in the past, the Act is constitutional.

III

The Court believes that the Act violates the literal text of the Constitution. A simple syllogism captures its basic reasoning:

Major Premise: The Constitution sets forth an exclusive method for enacting, repealing, or amending laws.

Minor Premise: The Act authorizes the President to "repeal or amend" laws in a different way, namely by announcing a cancellation of a portion of a previously enacted law.

Conclusion: The Act is inconsistent with the Constitution.

I find this syllogism unconvincing, however, because its Minor Premise is faulty. When the President "canceled" the two appropriation measures now before us, he did not repeal any law nor did he amend any law. He simply followed the law, leaving the statutes, as they are literally written, intact. . . .

Because one cannot say that the President's exercise of the power the Act grants is, literally speaking, a "repeal" or "amendment," the fact that the Act's procedures differ from the Constitution's exclusive procedures for enacting (or repealing) legislation is beside the point. The Act itself was enacted in accordance with these procedures, and its failure to require the President to satisfy those procedures does not make the Act unconstitutional.

IV

Because I disagree with the Court's holding of literal violation, I must consider whether the Act nonetheless violates Separation of Powers principles—principles that arise out of the Constitution's vesting of the "executive Power" in "a President," U.S. Const., Art. II, Sec. 1, and "all legislative Powers" in "a Congress," Art. I, Sec. 1. There are three relevant Separation of Powers questions here: (1) Has Congress given the President the wrong kind of power, i.e., "non-Executive" power? (2) Has Congress given the President the power to "encroach" upon Congress' own constitutionally reserved territory? (3) Has Congress given the President too much power, violating the doctrine of "nondelegation?" These three limitations help assure "adequate control by the citizen's representatives in Congress," upon which Justice KENNEDY properly insists. And with respect to this Act, the answer to all these questions is "no."

Viewed conceptually, the power the Act conveys is the right kind of power. It is "executive." As explained above, an exercise of that power "executes" the Act. Conceptually speaking, it closely resembles the kind of delegated authority—to spend or not to spend appropriations, to change or not to change tariff rates—that Congress has frequently granted the President, any differences being differences in degree, not kind.

The fact that one could also characterize this kind of power as "legislative," say, if Congress itself (by amending the appropriations bill) prevented a provision from taking effect, is beside the point. . . .

If there is a Separation of Powers violation, then, it must rest, not upon purely conceptual grounds, but upon some important conflict between the Act and a significant Separation of Powers objective.

The Act does not undermine what this Court has often described as the principal function of the Separation of Powers, which is to maintain the tripartite structure of the Federal Government—and thereby protect individual liberty—by providing a "safeguard against the encroachment or aggrandizement of one branch at the expense of the other." *Buckley v. Valeo*, 424 U.S. 1 (1976). . . .

[O]ne cannot say that the Act "encroaches" upon Congress' power, when Congress retained the power to insert, by simple majority, into any future appropriations bill, into any section of any such bill, or into any phrase of any section, a provision that says the Act will not apply. Congress also retained the power to "disapprove," and thereby reinstate, any of the President's cancellations. And it is Congress that drafts and enacts the appropriations statutes that are subject to the Act in the first place—and thereby defines the outer limits of the President's cancellation authority. Thus this Act is not the sort of delegation "without . . . sufficient check" that concerns Justice KENNEDY. Indeed, the President acts only in response to, and on the terms set by, the Congress.

Nor can one say that the Act's basic substantive objective is constitutionally improper, for the earliest Congresses could have, and often did, confer on the President this sort of discretionary authority over spending. And, if an individual Member of Congress, who say, favors aid to Country A but not to Country B, objects to the Act on the ground that the President may "rewrite" an appropriations law to do the opposite, one can respond, "But a majority of Congress voted that he have that power; you may vote to exempt the relevant appropriations provision from the Act; and if you command a majority, your appropriation is safe." Where the burden of overcoming legislative inertia lies is within the power of Congress to determine by rule. Where is the encroachment?

Nor can one say the Act's grant of power "aggrandizes" the Presidential office. The grant is limited to the context of the budget. It is limited to the power to spend, or not to spend, particular appropriated items, and the power to permit, or not to permit, specific limited exemptions from generally applicable tax law from taking effect. . . .

The "nondelegation" doctrine represents an added constitutional check upon Congress' authority to delegate power to the Executive Branch. And it raises a more serious constitutional obstacle here. The Constitution permits Congress to "seek assistance from another branch" of Government, the "extent and character" of that assistance to be fixed "according to common sense and the inherent necessities of the governmental co-ordination." *J. W. Hampton, Jr. & Co. v. United States*, 276 U.S. [394 (1928)]. But there are limits on the way in which Congress can obtain such assistance; it "cannot delegate any part of its legislative power except under the limitation of a prescribed standard." *United States v. Chicago, M., St. P. & P.R. Co.*, 282 U.S. 311 (1931). Or, in Chief Justice TAFT's more familiar words, the Constitution permits only those delegations where Congress "shall lay down by legislative act an intelligible principle to which the person or body authorized to [act] is directed to conform." *J. W. Hampton.*

The Act before us seeks to create such a principle in three ways. The first is procedural. The Act tells the President that, in "identifying dollar amounts [or] . . . items. . . for cancellation" (which I take to refer to his selection of the amounts or items he will "prevent from having legal force or effect"), he is to "consider," among other things, "the legislative history, construction, and purposes of the law which contains [those amounts or items, and] . . . any specific sources of information referenced in such law or . . . the best available information. . . ."

The second is purposive. The clear purpose behind the Act, confirmed by its legislative history, is to promote "greater fiscal accountability" and to "eliminate wasteful federal spending and . . . special tax breaks."

The third is substantive. The President must determine that, to "prevent" the item or amount "from having legal force or effect" will "reduce the Federal budget deficit; . . . not impair any essential Government functions; and . . . not harm the national interest."

The resulting standards are broad. But this Court has upheld standards that are equally broad, or broader. . . .

V

In sum, I recognize that the Act before us is novel. In a sense, it skirts a constitutional edge. But that edge has to do with means, not ends. The means chosen do not amount literally to the enactment, repeal, or amendment of a law. Nor, for that matter, do they amount literally to the "line item veto" that the Act's title announces. Those means do not violate any basic Separation of Powers principle. They do not improperly shift the constitutionally foreseen balance of power from Congress to the President. Nor, since they comply with Separation of Powers principles, do they threaten the liberties of individual citizens. They represent an experiment that may, or may not, help representative government work better. The Constitution, in my view, authorizes Congress and the President to try novel methods in this way. Consequently, with respect, I dissent.

Justice SCALIA, with whom Justice O'CONNOR joins, and with whom Justice BREYER joins as to Part III, concurring in part and dissenting in part.

III

I do not believe that Executive cancellation of this item of direct spending violates the Presentment Clause.

The Presentment Clause requires, in relevant part, that "every Bill which shall have passed the House of Representatives and the Senate, shall, before it becomes a Law, be presented to the President of the United States; If he approve he shall sign it, but if not he shall return it." There is no question that enactment of the Balanced Budget Act complied with these requirements: the House and Senate passed the bill, and the President signed it into law. It was only after the requirements of the Presentment Clause had been satisfied that the President exercised his authority under the Line Item Veto Act to cancel the spending item. Thus, the Court's problem with the Act is not that it authorizes the President to veto parts of a bill and sign others into law, but rather that it authorizes him to "cancel"—prevent from "having legal force or effect"—certain parts of duly enacted statutes.

Article I, Sec. 7 of the Constitution obviously prevents the President from canceling a law that Congress has not authorized him to cancel. Such action cannot possibly be considered part of his execution of the law, and if it is legislative action, as the Court observes, "repeal of statutes, no less than enactment, must conform with Art. I." But that is not this case. It was certainly arguable, as an original matter, that Art. I, Sec. 7 also prevents the President from canceling a law which itself authorizes the President to cancel it. But as the Court acknowledges, that argument has long since been made and rejected. In 1809, Congress passed a law authorizing the President to cancel trade restrictions against Great Britain and France if either revoked edicts directed at the United States. Joseph STORY regarded the conferral of that authority as entirely unremarkable in *The Orono*, 18 F.Cas. 830 (CCD Mass. 1812). The Tariff Act of 1890 authorized the President to "suspend, by proclamation to that effect" certain of its provisions if he determined that other countries were imposing "reciprocally unequal and unreasonable" duties. This Court upheld the constitutionality of that Act in *Field v. Clark*, reciting the history since 1798 of statutes conferring upon the President the power to "discontinue the prohibitions and restraints hereby enacted and declared," "suspend the operation of the aforesaid act," and "declare the provisions of this act to be inoperative." . . .

I turn, then, to the crux of the matter: whether Congress's authorizing the President to cancel an item of spending gives him a power that our history and traditions show must reside exclusively in the Legislative Branch. I may note, to begin with, that the Line Item Veto Act is not the first statute to authorize the President to "cancel" spending items. In *Bowsher v. Synar*, 478 U.S. 714 (1986), we addressed the constitutionality of the Balanced Budget and Emergency Deficit Control Act of 1985, which required the President, if the federal budget deficit exceeded a certain amount, to issue a "sequestration" order mandating spending reductions specified by the Comptroller General. The effect of sequestration was that "amounts sequestered . . . shall be permanently cancelled." We held that the Act was unconstitutional, not because it impermissibly gave the Executive legislative power, but because it gave the Comptroller General, an officer of the Legislative Branch over whom Congress retained removal power, "the ultimate authority to determine the budget cuts to be made," "functions . . . plainly entailing execution of the law in constitutional terms." The President's discretion under the Line Item Veto Act is certainly broader than the Comptroller General's discretion was under the 1985 Act, but it is no broader than the discretion traditionally granted the President in his execution of spending laws. . . .

Certain Presidents have claimed Executive authority to withhold appropriated funds even absent an express conferral of discretion to do so. In 1876, for example, President Grant reported to Congress that he would not spend money appropriated for certain harbor and river improvements, because "under no circumstances [would he] allow expenditures upon works not clearly national," and in his view, the appropriations were for "works of purely private or local interest, in no sense national." President Franklin D. Roosevelt impounded funds appropriated for a flood control reservoir and levee in Oklahoma. President Truman ordered the impoundment of hundreds of millions of dollars that had been appropriated for military aircraft. President Nixon, the Mahatma Gandhi of all impounders, asserted at a press conference in 1973 that his "constitutional right" to impound appropriated funds was "absolutely clear." Our decision two years later in *Train v. City of New York*, 420 U.S. 35 (1975), proved him wrong, but it implicitly confirmed that Congress may confer discretion upon the executive to withhold appropriated funds, even funds appropriated for a specific purpose. The statute at issue in *Train* authorized spending "not to exceed" specified sums for certain projects, and directed that such "sums authorized to be appropriated . . . shall be allotted" by the Administrator of the Environmental Protection Agency.

Upon enactment of this statute, the President directed the Administrator to allot no more than a certain part of the amount authorized. This Court held, as a matter of statutory interpretation, that the statute did not grant the Executive discretion to withhold the funds, but required allotment of the full amount authorized.

The short of the matter is this: Had the Line Item Veto Act authorized the President to "decline to spend" any item of spending contained in the Balanced Budget Act of 1997, there is not the slightest doubt that authorization would have been constitutional. What the Line Item Veto Act does instead—authorizing the President to "cancel" an item of spending—is technically different. But the technical difference does not relate to the technicalities of the Presentment Clause, which have been fully complied with; and the doctrine of unconstitutional delegation, which is at issue here, is preeminently not a doctrine of technicalities. The title of the Line Item Veto Act, which was perhaps designed to simplify for public comprehension, or perhaps merely to comply with the terms of a campaign pledge, has succeeded in faking out the Supreme Court. The President's action it authorizes in fact is not a line-item veto and thus does not offend Art. I, Sec. 7; and insofar as the substance of that action is concerned, it is no different from what Congress has permitted the President to do since the formation of the Union. . . .

For the foregoing reasons, I respectfully dissent.

D. ACCOUNTABILITY AND IMMUNITIES

In *Clinton v. Jones* (excerpted below), the Court unanimously rejected President William (Bill) Clinton's claim of immunity while in the Oval Office from a civil suit filed by Paula Jones, who sought $700,000 in damages for sexual harassment by then-governor Clinton in 1991.

Clinton v. Jones
117 S.Ct. 1636 (1997)

The facts are discussed in the excerpt below. The Court's decision was unanimous and its opinion announced by Justice Stevens. Justice Breyer filed a concurring opinion.

Justice STEVENS delivered the opinion of the Court.

This case raises a constitutional and a prudential question concerning the Office of the President of the United States. Respondent, a private citizen, seeks to recover damages from the current occupant of that office based on actions allegedly taken before his term began. The President submits that in all but the most exceptional cases the Constitution requires federal courts to defer such

litigation until his term ends and that, in any event, respect for the office warrants such a stay. Despite the force of the arguments supporting the President's
submissions, we conclude that they must be rejected.

Petitioner, William Jefferson Clinton, was elected to the Presidency in 1992,
and re-elected in 1996. His term of office expires on January 20, 2001. In 1991
he was the Governor of the State of Arkansas. Respondent, Paula Corbin Jones,
is a resident of California. In 1991 she lived in Arkansas, and was an employee
of the Arkansas Industrial Development Commission.

On May 6, 1994, she commenced this action in the United States District
Court for the Eastern District of Arkansas by filing a complaint naming petitioner and Danny Ferguson, a former Arkansas State Police officer, as defendants. The complaint alleges two federal claims, and two state law claims over
which the federal court has jurisdiction because of the diverse citizenship of the
parties. As the case comes to us, we are required to assume the truth of the
detailed—but as yet untested—factual allegations in the complaint.

Those allegations principally describe events that are said to have occurred on
the afternoon of May 8, 1991, during an official conference held at the Excelsior
Hotel in Little Rock, Arkansas. The Governor delivered a speech at the conference;
respondent—working as a state employee—staffed the registration desk. She
alleges that Ferguson persuaded her to leave her desk and to visit the Governor
in a business suite at the hotel, where he made "abhorrent" sexual advances that
she vehemently rejected. She further claims that her superiors at work subsequently dealt with her in a hostile and rude manner, and changed her duties to
punish her for rejecting those advances. Finally, she alleges that after petitioner
was elected President, Ferguson defamed her by making a statement to a reporter
that implied she had accepted petitioner's alleged overtures, and that various persons authorized to speak for the President publicly branded her a liar by denying
that the incident had occurred.

In response to the complaint, petitioner promptly advised the District Court
that he intended to file a motion to dismiss on grounds of Presidential immunity,
and requested the court to defer all other pleadings and motions until after the
immunity issue was resolved. Relying on our cases holding that immunity questions should be decided at the earliest possible stage of the litigation, our recognition of the " 'singular importance of the President's duties,'" (quoting *Nixon v.
Fitzgerald*, 457 U.S. 731 (1982)), and the fact that the question did not require
any analysis of the allegations of the complaint, the court granted the request.
Petitioner thereupon filed a motion "to dismiss . . . without prejudice and to toll
any statutes of limitation [that may be applicable] until he is no longer President,
at which time the plaintiff may refile the instant suit."

The District Judge denied the motion to dismiss on immunity grounds and ruled
that discovery in the case could go forward, but ordered any trial stayed until the
end of petitioner's Presidency. Although she recognized that a "thin majority" in
Nixon v. Fitzgerald had held that "the President has absolute immunity from civil
damage actions arising out of the execution of official duties of office," she was
not convinced that "a President has absolute immunity from civil causes of
action arising prior to assuming the office." She was, however, persuaded by
some of the reasoning in our opinion in *Fitzgerald* that deferring the trial if one
were required would be appropriate. Relying in part on the fact that respondent
had failed to bring her complaint until two days before the 3-year period of limitations expired, she concluded that the public interest in avoiding litigation that

might hamper the President in conducting the duties of his office outweighed any demonstrated need for an immediate trial.

Both parties appealed. A divided panel of the Court of Appeals affirmed the denial of the motion to dismiss, but because it regarded the order postponing the trial until the President leaves office as the "functional equivalent" of a grant of temporary immunity, it reversed that order. Writing for the majority, Judge Bowman explained that "the President, like all other government officials, is subject to the same laws that apply to all other members of our society," that he could find no "case in which any public official ever has been granted any immunity from suit for his unofficial acts," and that the rationale for official immunity "is inapposite where only personal, private conduct by a President is at issue." . . .

The President, represented by private counsel, filed a petition for *certiorari.* The Solicitor General, representing the United States, supported the petition, arguing that the decision of the Court of Appeals was "fundamentally mistaken" and created "serious risks for the institution of the Presidency." In her brief in opposition to *certiorari*, respondent argued that this "one-of-a-kind case is singularly inappropriate" for the exercise of our *certiorari* jurisdiction because it did not create any conflict among the Courts of Appeals, it "does not pose any conceivable threat to the functioning of the Executive Branch," and there is no precedent supporting the President's position. . . .

Petitioner's principal submission—that "in all but the most exceptional cases," the Constitution affords the President temporary immunity from civil damages litigation arising out of events that occurred before he took office—cannot be sustained on the basis of precedent.

Only three sitting Presidents have been defendants in civil litigation involving their actions prior to taking office. Complaints against Theodore Roosevelt and Harry Truman had been dismissed before they took office; the dismissals were affirmed after their respective inaugurations. Two companion cases arising out of an automobile accident were filed against John F. Kennedy in 1960 during the Presidential campaign. After taking office, he unsuccessfully argued that his status as Commander in Chief gave him a right to a stay under the Soldiers' and Sailors' Civil Relief Act of 1940. The motion for a stay was denied by the District Court, and the matter was settled out of court. Thus, none of those cases sheds any light on the constitutional issue before us.

The principal rationale for affording certain public servants immunity from suits for money damages arising out of their official acts is inapplicable to unofficial conduct. In cases involving prosecutors, legislators, and judges we have repeatedly explained that the immunity serves the public interest in enabling such officials to perform their designated functions effectively without fear that a particular decision may give rise to personal liability. We explained in *Ferri v. Ackerman*, 444 U.S. 193 (1979): "As public servants, the prosecutor and the judge represent the interest of society as a whole. The conduct of their official duties may adversely affect a wide variety of different individuals, each of whom may be a potential source of future controversy. The societal interest in providing such public officials with the maximum ability to deal fearlessly and impartially with the public at large has long been recognized as an acceptable justification for official immunity. The point of immunity for such officials is to forestall an atmosphere of intimidation that would conflict with their resolve to perform their designated functions in a principled fashion." That rationale provided the principal basis for our holding that a former President of the United

States was "entitled to absolute immunity from damages liability predicated on his official acts," *Fitzgerald.* Our central concern was to avoid rendering the President "unduly cautious in the discharge of his official duties."

This reasoning provides no support for an immunity for unofficial conduct. As we explained in *Fitzgerald,* "the sphere of protected action must be related closely to the immunity's justifying purposes." Because of the President's broad responsibilities, we recognized in that case an immunity from damages claims arising out of official acts extending to the "outer perimeter of his authority." But we have never suggested that the President, or any other official, has an immunity that extends beyond the scope of any action taken in an official capacity.

Moreover, when defining the scope of an immunity for acts clearly taken within an official capacity, we have applied a functional approach. "Frequently our decisions have held that an official's absolute immunity should extend only to acts in performance of particular functions of his office." As our opinions have made clear, immunities are grounded in "the nature of the function performed, not the identity of the actor who performed it."

Petitioner's effort to construct an immunity from suit for unofficial acts grounded purely in the identity of his office is unsupported by precedent. . . .

Petitioner's strongest argument supporting his immunity claim is based on the text and structure of the Constitution. He does not contend that the occupant of the Office of the President is "above the law," in the sense that his conduct is entirely immune from judicial scrutiny. The President argues merely for a postponement of the judicial proceedings that will determine whether he violated any law. His argument is grounded in the character of the office that was created by Article II of the Constitution, and relies on separation of powers principles that have structured our constitutional arrangement since the founding.

As a starting premise, petitioner contends that he occupies a unique office with powers and responsibilities so vast and important that the public interest demands that he devote his undivided time and attention to his public duties. He submits that—given the nature of the office—the doctrine of separation of powers places limits on the authority of the Federal Judiciary to interfere with the Executive Branch that would be transgressed by allowing this action to proceed.

We have no dispute with the initial premise of the argument. Former presidents, from George Washington to George Bush, have consistently endorsed petitioner's characterization of the office. . . . It does not follow, however, that separation of powers principles would be violated by allowing this action to proceed. The doctrine of separation of powers is concerned with the allocation of official power among the three co-equal branches of our Government. The Framers "built into the tripartite Federal Government . . . a self-executing safeguard against the encroachment or aggrandizement of one branch at the expense of the other." *Buckley v. Valeo,* 424 U.S. [1 (1976)]. Thus, for example, the Congress may not exercise the judicial power to revise final judgments, or the executive power to manage an airport. Similarly, the President may not exercise the legislative power to authorize the seizure of private property for public use. *Youngstown* [*Sheet & Tube Co. v. Sawyer,* 343 U.S. 579 (1952)]. And, the judicial power to decide cases and controversies does not include the provision of purely advisory opinions to the Executive, or permit the federal courts to resolve nonjusticiable questions.

Of course the lines between the powers of the three branches are not always neatly defined. But in this case there is no suggestion that the Federal Judiciary is being asked to perform any function that might in some way be described as "executive." Respondent is merely asking the courts to exercise their core Article III jurisdiction to decide cases and controversies. Whatever the outcome of this case, there is no possibility that the decision will curtail the scope of the official powers of the Executive Branch. The litigation of questions that relate entirely to the unofficial conduct of the individual who happens to be the President poses no perceptible risk of misallocation of either judicial power or executive power.

Rather than arguing that the decision of the case will produce either an aggrandizement of judicial power or a narrowing of executive power, petitioner contends that—as a by-product of an otherwise traditional exercise of judicial power—burdens will be placed on the President that will hamper the performance of his official duties. We have recognized that "even when a branch does not arrogate power to itself . . . the separation-of-powers doctrine requires that a branch not impair another in the performance of its constitutional duties." As a factual matter, petitioner contends that this particular case—as well as the potential additional litigation that an affirmance of the Court of Appeals judgment might spawn—may impose an unacceptable burden on the President's time and energy, and thereby impair the effective performance of his office.

Petitioner's predictive judgment finds little support in either history or the relatively narrow compass of the issues raised in this particular case. As we have already noted, in the more than 200-year history of the Republic, only three sitting Presidents have been subjected to suits for their private actions. If the past is any indicator, it seems unlikely that a deluge of such litigation will ever engulf the Presidency. As for the case at hand, if properly managed by the District Court, it appears to us highly unlikely to occupy any substantial amount of petitioner's time. . . .

In sum, "it is settled law that the separation-of-powers doctrine does not bar every exercise of jurisdiction over the President of the United States." *Fitzgerald*. If the Judiciary may severely burden the Executive Branch by reviewing the legality of the President's official conduct, and if it may direct appropriate process to the President himself, it must follow that the federal courts have power to determine the legality of his unofficial conduct. The burden on the President's time and energy that is a mere by-product of such review surely cannot be considered as onerous as the direct burden imposed by judicial review and the occasional invalidation of his official actions. We therefore hold that the doctrine of separation of powers does not require federal courts to stay all private actions against the President until he leaves office. . . .

[W]e are persuaded that it was an abuse of discretion for the District Court to defer the trial until after the President leaves office. Such a lengthy and categorical stay takes no account whatever of the respondent's interest in bringing the case to trial. The complaint was filed within the statutory limitations period— albeit near the end of that period—and delaying trial would increase the danger of prejudice resulting from the loss of evidence, including the inability of witnesses to recall specific facts, or the possible death of a party. . . .

The Federal District Court has jurisdiction to decide this case. Like every other citizen who properly invokes that jurisdiction, respondent has a right to an orderly disposition of her claims. Accordingly, the judgment of the Court of Appeals is affirmed.

It is so ordered.

Justice BREYER, concurring in the judgment.

I agree with the majority that the Constitution does not automatically grant the President an immunity from civil lawsuits based upon his private conduct. . . . In my view, however, once the President sets forth and explains a conflict between judicial proceeding and public duties, the matter changes. At that point, the Constitution permits a judge to schedule a trial in an ordinary civil damages action (where postponement normally is possible without overwhelming damage to a plaintiff) only within the constraints of a constitutional principle—a principle that forbids a federal judge in such a case to interfere with the President's discharge of his public duties. I have no doubt that the Constitution contains such a principle applicable to civil suits, based upon Article II's vesting of the entire "executive Power" in a single individual, implemented through the Constitution's structural separation of powers, and revealed both by history and case precedent. . . .

6

CONGRESS:
LEGISLATIVE, TAXING,
AND SPENDING POWERS

C. FROM THE NEW DEAL CRISIS TO
THE ADMINISTRATIVE STATE

In a major and controversial ruling bearing upon congressional power, the separation of powers, federalism, and the First Amendment's guarantee for religious freedom, the Court struck down the Religious Freedom Restoration Act of 1993 (RFRA; see Vol. 2, Ch. 6). Congress enacted that law following the Supreme Court's ruling *Employment Division, Department of Human Resources of Oregon v. Smith*, 494 U.S. 872 (1990) (in Vol. 2, Ch. 6) and established as a matter of statutory law the pre-*Smith* test for balancing claims to religious freedom against governmental interests in other generally applicable laws. Writing for the majority in *City of Boerne v. Flores*, 117 S.Ct. 2157 (1997) (excerpted below in Vol. 2, Ch. 6), Justice Kennedy held that Congress exceeded its power under Section 5 of the Fourteenth Amendment in enacting the RFRA. That statute swept too broadly and, according to Justice Kennedy, exceeded Congress's power under Section 5, which the Court held was remedial and did not authorize Congress to expand the scope of constitutional rights. Justices O'Connor, Breyer, and Souter dissented.

City of Boerne v. Flores
117 S.Ct. 2157 (1997)

(This decision is excerpted below in Vol. 2, Ch. 6.)

7

THE STATES AND AMERICAN FEDERALISM

A. STATES' POWER OVER COMMERCE AND REGULATION

THE DEVELOPMENT OF LAW

Rulings on State Regulatory Powers
in the Absence of Federal Legislation

Case	Vote	Ruling
General Motors Corporation v. Tracy, Tax Commissioner of Ohio, 117 S.Ct. 383 (1997)	8:1	Ohio imposes general sales and use taxes on natural gas purchases from all sellers, whether in state or out of state,

including state-regulated utilities but not independent producers and marketers. In an appeal of a challenge to the constitutionality of that distinction, Justice Souter held that Ohio's differential tax treatment of natural gas sales does not violate the dormant commerce clause. Justice Stevens dissented.

Camps Newfound/Owatonna, Inc. v. Town of Harrison, 117 S.Ct. 1590 (1997)	5:4	Writing for a bare majority, Justice Stevens struck down Maine's statute governing tax exemptions for charitable in-

stitutions that gave more limited benefits to institutions serving primarily nonresidents as a violation of the dormant commerce clause. Chief Justice Rehnquist and Justices Scalia, Thomas, and Ginsburg dissented.

B. THE TENTH AMENDMENT AND THE STATES

In two cases challenging congressional power, a bare majority struck down a key provision of the Brady Handgun Violence Prevention Act of

1993, requiring state and local law enforcement officials to conduct background checks on gun purchasers. The Court's decision will affect twenty-three states, but some will voluntarily continue the checks and in 1998 the federal government is scheduled to implement its own system of checking gun purchasers' backgrounds. Eighteen states were not subject to the law because they already had laws requiring background checks and another nine states adopted similar laws after the enactment of the Brady law. Still, the ruling in *Printz v. United States* and *Mack v. United States* (excerpted below) was significant and split the Court five to four. The ruling also continued a recent trend in a line of decisions invalidating federal laws for impinging on state authority. See *New York v. United States*, 505 U.S. 144 (1992) (in Vol. 1, Ch. 7); *United States v. Lopez*, 514 U.S. 549 (1995), and *Seminole Tribe of Florida v. Florida*, 116 S.Ct. 1114 (1996) (both excerpted in Vol. 1, Ch. 6); and *City of Boerne v. Flores*, 117 S.Ct. 2157 (1997) (excerpted below in Vol. 2, Ch. 6).

Printz v. United States
and
Mack v. United States
117 S.Ct. 2365 (1997)

In 1993, after seven years of debate, Congress enacted the Brady Handgun Violence Prevention Act as an amendment to the Gun Control Act of 1968. The law was named after James S. Brady, who was disabled in the 1981 assassination attempt on President Ronald Reagan. Among other provisions, the law required state and local law enforcement officials to conduct background checks on prospective handgun purchasers. That provision was challenged by two chief law enforcement officers, Jay Printz of Ravalli County, Montana, and Richard Mack of Graham County, Arizona. They argued that the federal provision was unconstitutional because Congress has no authority to require state and local officials to carry out federal laws. Besides claiming that the law was an unfunded federal mandate, they claimed that the law was burdensome and diverted resources and time from their investigative responsibilities. A federal district court agreed but the Court of Appeals for the Ninth Circuit reversed and Printz and Mack, supported by the National Rifle Association, appealed.

The Court's decision was five to four and its opinion delivered by Justice Scalia. Justices O'Connor and Thomas filed concurring opinions. Justice Stevens filed a dissenting opinion, which was joined by Justices Souter, Ginsburg, and Breyer. Justices Souter and Breyer also filed separate dissenting opinions.

Justice SCALIA delivered the opinion of the Court.

The question presented in these cases is whether certain interim provisions of the Brady Handgun Violence Prevention Act, commanding state and local law enforcement officers to conduct background checks on prospective handgun purchasers and to perform certain related tasks, violate the Constitution. . . .

[T]he Brady Act purports to direct state law enforcement officers to participate, albeit only temporarily, in the administration of a federally enacted regulatory scheme. Regulated firearms dealers are required to forward Brady Forms not to a federal officer or employee, but to the CLEOs [chief law enforcement officers], whose obligation to accept those forms is implicit in the duty imposed upon them to make "reasonable efforts" within five days to determine whether the sales reflected in the forms are lawful. While the CLEOs are subjected to no federal requirement that they prevent the sales determined to be unlawful (it is perhaps assumed that their state-law duties will require prevention or apprehension), they are empowered to grant, in effect, waivers of the federally prescribed 5-day waiting period for handgun purchases by notifying the gun dealers that they have no reason to believe the transactions would be illegal.

The petitioners here object to being pressed into federal service, and contend that congressional action compelling state officers to execute federal laws is unconstitutional.

Because there is no constitutional text speaking to this precise question, the answer to the CLEOs' challenge must be sought in historical understanding and practice, in the structure of the Constitution, and in the jurisprudence of this Court. We treat those three sources in that order. . . .

The Government observes that statutes enacted by the first Congresses required state courts to record applications for citizenship, to transmit abstracts of citizenship applications and other naturalization records to the Secretary of State, and to register aliens seeking naturalization and issue certificates of registry. It may well be, however, that these requirements applied only in States that authorized their courts to conduct naturalization proceedings. Other statutes of that era apparently or at least arguably required state courts to perform functions unrelated to naturalization, such as resolving controversies between a captain and the crew of his ship concerning the seaworthiness of the vessel, hearing the claims of slave owners who had apprehended fugitive slaves and issuing certificates authorizing the slave's forced removal to the State from which he had fled, taking proof of the claims of Canadian refugees who had assisted the United States during the Revolutionary War, and ordering the deportation of alien enemies in times of war.

These early laws establish, at most, that the Constitution was originally understood to permit imposition of an obligation on state judges to enforce federal prescriptions, insofar as those prescriptions related to matters appropriate for the judicial power. That assumption was perhaps implicit in one of the provisions of the Constitution, and was explicit in another. In accord with the so-called Madisonian Compromise, Article III, Sec. 1, established only a Supreme Court, and made the creation of lower federal courts optional with the Congress—even though it was obvious that the Supreme Court alone could not hear all federal cases throughout the United States. And the Supremacy Clause, Art. VI, cl. 2, announced that "the Laws of the United States . . . shall be the supreme Law of the Land; and the Judges in every State shall be bound thereby." It is understandable why courts should have been viewed distinctively in this regard; unlike legislatures and executives, they applied the law of other sovereigns all the time. The principle underlying so-called "transitory" causes of action was that laws which operated elsewhere created obligations in justice that courts of the forum state would enforce. The Constitution itself, in the Full Faith and Credit Clause, Art. IV, Sec. 1, generally required such enforcement with respect to obligations arising in other States

For these reasons, we do not think the early statutes imposing obligations on state courts imply a power of Congress to impress the state executive into its service. Indeed, it can be argued that the numerousness of these statutes, contrasted with the utter lack of statutes imposing obligations on the States' executive (notwithstanding the attractiveness of that course to Congress), suggests an assumed absence of such power. The only early federal law the Government has brought to our attention that imposed duties on state executive officers is the Extradition Act of 1793, which required the "executive authority" of a State to cause the arrest and delivery of a fugitive from justice upon the request of the executive authority of the State from which the fugitive had fled. That was in direct implementation, however, of the Extradition Clause of the Constitution itself, see Art. IV, Sec. 2.

Not only do the enactments of the early Congresses, as far as we are aware, contain no evidence of an assumption that the Federal Government may command the States' executive power in the absence of a particularized constitutional authorization, they contain some indication of precisely the opposite assumption. On September 23, 1789—the day before its proposal of the Bill of Rights—the First Congress enacted a law aimed at obtaining state assistance of the most rudimentary and necessary sort for the enforcement of the new Government's laws: the holding of federal prisoners in state jails at federal expense. Significantly, the law issued not a command to the States' executive, but a recommendation to their legislatures. . . . Moreover, when Georgia refused to comply with the request, Congress's only reaction was a law authorizing the marshal in any State that failed to comply with the Recommendation of September 23, 1789, to rent a temporary jail until provision for a permanent one could be made.

In addition to early legislation, the Government also appeals to other sources we have usually regarded as indicative of the original understanding of the Constitution. It points to portions of *The Federalist* which reply to criticisms that Congress's power to tax will produce two sets of revenue officers—for example, "Brutus's" assertion in his letter to the *New York Journal* of December 13, 1787, that the Constitution "opens a door to the appointment of a swarm of revenue and excise officers to prey upon the honest and industrious part of the community, eat up their substance, and riot on the spoils of the country." "Publius" responded that Congress will probably "make use of the State officers and State regulations, for collecting" federal taxes, *The Federalist* No. 36 (A. Hamilton), and predicted that "the eventual collection [of internal revenue] under the immediate authority of the Union, will generally be made by the officers, and according to the rules, appointed by the several States," No. 45 (J. Madison). The Government also invokes *The Federalist*'s more general observations that the Constitution would "enable the [national] government to employ the ordinary magistracy of each [State] in the execution of its laws," No. 27 (A. Hamilton), and that it was "extremely probable that in other instances, particularly in the organization of the judicial power, the officers of the States will be clothed in the correspondent authority of the Union," No. 45 (J. Madison). But none of these statements necessarily implies—what is the critical point here—that Congress could impose these responsibilities without the consent of the States. They appear to rest on the natural assumption that the States would consent to allowing their officials to assist the Federal Government. . . .

Justice SOUTER contends that his interpretation of *Federalist* No. 27 is "supported by No. 44," written by Madison, wherefore he claims that "Madison and Hamilton" together stand opposed to our view. In fact, *Federalist* No. 44 quite clearly contradicts Justice SOUTER's reading. In that Number, Madison justifies the requirement that state officials take an oath to support the Federal Constitution on the ground that they "will have an essential agency in giving effect to the federal Constitution." If the dissent's reading of *Federalist* No. 27 were correct (and if Madison agreed with it), one would surely have expected that "essential agency" of state executive officers (if described further) to be described as their responsibility to execute the laws enacted under the Constitution. Instead, however, *Federalist* No. 44 continues with the following description: "The election of the President and Senate will depend, in all cases, on the legislatures of the several States. And the election of the House of Representatives will equally depend on the same authority in the first instance; and will, probably, forever be conducted by the officers and according to the laws of the States." It is most implausible that the person who labored for that example of state executive officers' assisting the Federal Government believed, but neglected to mention, that they had a responsibility to execute federal laws. If it was indeed Hamilton's view that the Federal Government could direct the officers of the States, that view has no clear support in Madison's writings, or as far as we are aware, in text, history, or early commentary elsewhere.

To complete the historical record, we must note that there is not only an absence of executive-commandeering statutes in the early Congresses, but there is an absence of them in our later history as well, at least until very recent years. The Government points to the Act of August 3, 1882, which enlisted state officials "to take charge of the local affairs of immigration in the ports within such State, and to provide for the support and relief of such immigrants therein landing as may fall into distress or need of public aid"; to inspect arriving immigrants and exclude any person found to be a "convict, lunatic, idiot," or indigent; and to send convicts back to their country of origin "without compensation." The statute did not, however, mandate those duties, but merely empowered the Secretary of the Treasury "to enter into contracts with such State . . . officers as may be designated for that purpose by the governor of any State." . . .

The constitutional practice we have examined above tends to negate the existence of the congressional power asserted here, but is not conclusive. We turn next to consideration of the structure of the Constitution, to see if we can discern among its "essential postulates," *Principality of Monaco v. Mississippi*, 292 U.S. 313 (1934), a principle that controls the present cases.

It is incontestable that the Constitution established a system of "dual sovereignty." *Gregory v. Ashcroft*, 501 U.S. 452 (1991). Although the States surrendered many of their powers to the new Federal Government, they retained "a residuary and inviolable sovereignty," *The Federalist* No. 39 (J. Madison). This is reflected throughout the Constitution's text, including (to mention only a few examples) the prohibition on any involuntary reduction or combination of a

State's territory, Art. IV, Sec. 3; the Judicial Power Clause, Art. III, Sec. 2, and the Privileges and Immunities Clause, Art. IV, Sec. 2, which speak of the "Citizens" of the States; the amendment provision, Article V, which requires the votes of three-fourths of the States to amend the Constitution; and the Guarantee Clause, Art. IV, Sec. 4, which "presupposes the continued existence of the states and . . . those means and instrumentalities which are the creation of their sovereign and reserved rights," *Helvering v. Gerhardt*, 304 U.S. 405 (1938). Residual state sovereignty was also implicit, of course, in the Constitution's conferral upon Congress of not all governmental powers, but only discrete, enumerated ones, Art. I, Sec. 8, which implication was rendered express by the Tenth Amendment's assertion that "the powers not delegated to the United States by the Constitution, nor prohibited by it to the States, are reserved to the States respectively, or to the people."

The Framers' experience under the Articles of Confederation had persuaded them that using the States as the instruments of federal governance was both ineffectual and provocative of federal–state conflict. Preservation of the States as independent political entities being the price of union, and "the practicality of making laws, with coercive sanctions, for the States as political bodies" having been, in Madison's words, "exploded on all hands" of the Federal Convention of 1787, the Framers rejected the concept of a central government that would act upon and through the States, and instead designed a system in which the state and federal governments would exercise concurrent authority over the people— who were, in Hamilton's words, "the only proper objects of government," *The Federalist* No. 15. We have set forth the historical record in more detail elsewhere, see *New York v. United States*, [505 U.S. 144 (1992),] and need not repeat it here. It suffices to repeat the conclusion: "The Framers explicitly chose a Constitution that confers upon Congress the power to regulate individuals, not States." The great innovation of this design was that "our citizens would have two political capacities, one state and one federal, each protected from incursion by the other"—"a legal system unprecedented in form and design, establishing two orders of government, each with its own direct relationship, its own privity, its own set of mutual rights and obligations to the people who sustain it and are governed by it." *U.S. Term Limits, Inc. v. Thornton*, 514 U.S. 779 (1995) (KENNEDY, J., concurring). The Constitution thus contemplates that a State's government will represent and remain accountable to its own citizens. See *New York*; *United States v. Lopez*, 514 U.S. 549 (1995) (KENNEDY, J., concurring). As Madison expressed it: "The local or municipal authorities form distinct and independent portions of the supremacy, no more subject, within their respective spheres, to the general authority than the general authority is subject to them, within its own sphere." *The Federalist* No. 39.

We have thus far discussed the effect that federal control of state officers would have upon the first element of the "double security" alluded to by Madison: the division of power between State and Federal Governments. It would also have an effect upon the second element: the separation and equilibration of powers between the three branches of the Federal Government itself. The Constitution does not leave to speculation who is to administer the laws enacted by Congress; the President, it says, "shall take Care that the Laws be faithfully executed," Art. II, Sec. 3, personally and through officers whom he appoints (save for such inferior officers as Congress may authorize to be appointed by the "Courts of Law" or by "the Heads of Departments" who are themselves presidential appointees),

Art. II, Sec. 2. The Brady Act effectively transfers this responsibility to thousands of CLEOs in the 50 States, who are left to implement the program without meaningful Presidential control (if indeed meaningful Presidential control is possible without the power to appoint and remove). The insistence of the Framers upon unity in the Federal Executive—to insure both vigor and accountability—is well known. That unity would be shattered, and the power of the President would be subject to reduction, if Congress could act as effectively without the President as with him, by simply requiring state officers to execute its laws.

The dissent of course resorts to the last, best hope of those who defend *ultra vires* congressional action, the Necessary and Proper Clause. It reasons that the power to regulate the sale of handguns under the Commerce Clause, coupled with the power to "make all Laws which shall be necessary and proper for carrying into Execution the foregoing Powers," Art. I, Sec. 8, conclusively establishes the Brady Act's constitutional validity, because the Tenth Amendment imposes no limitations on the exercise of delegated powers but merely prohibits the exercise of powers "not delegated to the United States." What destroys the dissent's Necessary and Proper Clause argument, however, is not the Tenth Amendment but the Necessary and Proper Clause itself. When a "Law . . . for carrying into Execution" the Commerce Clause violates the principle of state sovereignty reflected in the various constitutional provisions we mentioned earlier, it is not a "Law . . . proper for carrying into Execution the Commerce Clause," and is thus, in the words of *The Federalist*, "merely [an] act of usurpation" which "deserves to be treated as such." *The Federalist* No. 33 (A. Hamilton). We in fact answered the dissent's Necessary and Proper Clause argument in *New York*: "Even where Congress has the authority under the Constitution to pass laws requiring or prohibiting certain acts, it lacks the power directly to compel the States to require or prohibit those acts. . . . The Commerce Clause, for example, authorizes Congress to regulate interstate commerce directly; it does not authorize Congress to regulate state governments' regulation of interstate commerce." . . .

Finally, and most conclusively in the present litigation, we turn to the prior jurisprudence of this Court. Federal commandeering of state governments is such a novel phenomenon that this Court's first experience with it did not occur until the 1970s, when the Environmental Protection Agency promulgated regulations requiring States to prescribe auto emissions testing, monitoring and retrofit programs, and to designate preferential bus and carpool lanes. . . . [O]pinions of ours have made clear that the Federal Government may not compel the States to implement, by legislation or executive action, federal regulatory programs. In *Hodel v. Virginia Surface Mining & Reclamation Assn., Inc.*, 452 U.S. 264 (1981), and *FERC v. Mississippi*, 456 U.S. 742 (1982), we sustained statutes against constitutional challenge only after assuring ourselves that they did not require the States to enforce federal law. . . .

When we were at last confronted squarely with a federal statute that unambiguously required the States to enact or administer a federal regulatory program, our decision should have come as no surprise. At issue in *New York v. United States*, 505 U.S. 144 (1992), were the so-called "take title" provisions of the Low-Level Radioactive Waste Policy Amendments Act of 1985, which required States either to enact legislation providing for the disposal of radioactive waste generated within their borders, or to take title to, and possession of the waste—effectively requiring the States either to legislate pursuant to Congress's directions, or to implement an administrative solution. We concluded that Congress could constitutionally require the States to do neither. "The Federal Government," we held, "may not compel the States to enact or administer a federal regulatory program." . . .

Finally, the Government puts forward a cluster of arguments that can be grouped under the heading: "The Brady Act serves very important purposes, is most efficiently administered by CLEOs during the interim period, and places a minimal and only temporary burden upon state officers." There is considerable disagreement over the extent of the burden, but we need not pause over that detail. Assuming all the mentioned factors were true, they might be relevant if we were evaluating whether the incidental application to the States of a federal law of general applicability excessively interfered with the functioning of state governments. But where, as here, it is the whole object of the law to direct the functioning of the state executive, and hence to compromise the structural framework of dual sovereignty, such a "balancing" analysis is inappropriate. It is the very principle of separate state sovereignty that such a law offends, and no comparative assessment of the various interests can overcome that fundamental defect. . . .

What we have said makes it clear enough that the central obligation imposed upon CLEOs by the interim provisions of the Brady Act—the obligation to "make a reasonable effort to ascertain within 5 business days whether receipt or possession [of a handgun] would be in violation of the law, including research in whatever State and local recordkeeping systems are available and in a national system designated by the Attorney General"—is unconstitutional. Extinguished with it, of course, is the duty implicit in the background-check requirement that the CLEO accept notice of the contents of, and a copy of, the completed Brady Form, which the firearms dealer is required to provide to him. . . .

We held in *New York* that Congress cannot compel the States to enact or enforce a federal regulatory program. Today we hold that Congress cannot circumvent that prohibition by conscripting the State's officers directly. The Federal Government may neither issue directives requiring the States to address particular problems, nor command the States' officers, or those of their political subdivisions, to administer or enforce a federal regulatory program. It matters not whether policymaking is involved, and no case-by-case weighing of the burdens or benefits is necessary; such commands are fundamentally incompatible with our constitutional system of dual sovereignty. Accordingly, the judgment of the Court of Appeals for the Ninth Circuit is reversed.

Justice O'CONNOR, concurring.

Our precedent and our Nation's historical practices support the Court's holding today. The Brady Act violates the Tenth Amendment to the extent it forces States and local law enforcement officers to perform background checks on prospective handgun owners and to accept Brady Forms from firearms dealers. Our holding, of course, does not spell the end of the objectives of the Brady Act. States and chief law enforcement officers may voluntarily continue to participate in the federal program. Moreover, the directives to the States are merely interim provisions scheduled to terminate November 30, 1998. Congress is also free to amend the interim program to provide for its continuance on a contractual basis with the States if it wishes, as it does with a number of other federal programs. . . .

Justice THOMAS, concurring.

The Court today properly holds that the Brady Act violates the Tenth Amendment in that it compels state law enforcement officers to "administer or enforce a federal regulatory program." Although I join the Court's opinion in full, I write separately to emphasize that the Tenth Amendment affirms the undeniable notion that under our Constitution, the Federal Government is one of enumerated, hence limited, powers. Accordingly, the Federal Government may act only where the Constitution authorizes it to do so. *New York v. United States*, 505 U.S. 144 (1992). . . .

Justice STEVENS, with whom Justice SOUTER, Justice GINSBURG, and Justice BREYER join, dissenting.

When Congress exercises the powers delegated to it by the Constitution, it may impose affirmative obligations on executive and judicial officers of state and local governments as well as ordinary citizens. This conclusion is firmly supported by the text of the Constitution, the early history of the Nation, decisions of this Court, and a correct understanding of the basic structure of the Federal Government.

These cases do not implicate the more difficult questions associated with congressional coercion of state legislatures addressed in *New York v. United States*, 505 U.S. 144 (1992). Nor need we consider the wisdom of relying on local officials rather than federal agents to carry out aspects of a federal program, or even the question whether such officials may be required to perform a federal function on a permanent basis. The question is whether Congress, acting on behalf of the people of the entire Nation, may require local law enforcement officers to perform certain duties during the interim needed for the development of a federal gun control program. It is remarkably similar to the question, heavily debated by the Framers of the Constitution, whether the Congress could require state agents to collect federal taxes. Or the question whether Congress could impress state judges into federal service to entertain and decide cases that they would prefer to ignore.

Indeed, since the ultimate issue is one of power, we must consider its implications in times of national emergency. Matters such as the enlistment of air raid wardens, the administration of a military draft, the mass inoculation of children to forestall an epidemic, or perhaps the threat of an international terrorist, may require a national response before federal personnel can be made available to respond. If the Constitution empowers Congress and the President to make an appropriate response, is there anything in the Tenth Amendment, "in historical understanding and practice, in the structure of the Constitution, [or] in the jurisprudence of this Court" that forbids the enlistment of state officers to make that response effective? More narrowly, what basis is there in any of those sources for concluding that it is the Members of this Court, rather than the elected representatives of the people, who should determine whether the Constitution contains the unwritten rule that the Court announces today?

Perhaps today's majority would suggest that no such emergency is presented by the facts of these cases. But such a suggestion is itself an expression of a policy judgment. And Congress' view of the matter is quite different from that implied by the Court today. . . .

The text of the Constitution provides a sufficient basis for a correct disposition of this case.

Article I, Sec. 8, grants the Congress the power to regulate commerce among the States. Putting alongside the revisionist views expressed by Justice THOMAS in his concurring opinion in *United States v. Lopez*, 514 U.S. 549 (1995), there can be no question that that provision adequately supports the regulation of commerce in handguns effected by the Brady Act. Moreover, the additional grant of authority in that section of the Constitution "to make all Laws which shall be necessary and proper for carrying into Execution the foregoing Powers" is surely adequate to support the temporary enlistment of local police officers in the process of identifying persons who should not be entrusted with the possession of handguns. In short, the affirmative delegation of power in Article I provides ample authority for the congressional enactment.

Unlike the First Amendment, which prohibits the enactment of a category of laws that would otherwise be authorized by Article I, the Tenth Amendment imposes no restriction on the exercise of delegated powers. Using language that plainly refers only to powers that are "not" delegated to Congress, it provides: "The powers not delegated to the United States by the Constitution, nor prohibited by it to the States, are reserved to the States respectively, or to the people." U.S. Const., Amdt. 10. The Amendment confirms the principle that the powers of the Federal Government are limited to those affirmatively granted by the Constitution, but it does not purport to limit the scope or the effectiveness of the exercise of powers that are delegated to Congress. Thus, the Amendment provides no support for a rule that immunizes local officials from obligations that might be imposed on ordinary citizens. Indeed, it would be more reasonable to infer that federal law may impose greater duties on state officials than on private citizens because another provision of the Constitution requires that "all executive and judicial Officers, both of the United States and of the several States, shall be bound by Oath or Affirmation, to support this Constitution." U.S. Const., Art. VI, cl. 3.

There is not a clause, sentence, or paragraph in the entire text of the Constitution of the United States that supports the proposition that a local police officer can ignore a command contained in a statute enacted by Congress pursuant to an express delegation of power enumerated in Article I.

Under the Articles of Confederation the National Government had the power to issue commands to the several sovereign states, but it had no authority to govern individuals directly. Thus, it raised an army and financed its operations by issuing requisitions to the constituent members of the Confederacy, rather than by creating federal agencies to draft soldiers or to impose taxes.

That method of governing proved to be unacceptable, not because it demeaned the sovereign character of the several States, but rather because it was cumbersome and inefficient. Indeed, a confederation that allows each of its members to determine the ways and means of complying with an overriding requisition is obviously more deferential to state sovereignty concerns than a national government that uses its own agents to impose its will directly on the citizenry. The basic change in the character of the government that the Framers conceived was designed to enhance the power of the national government, not to provide some new, unmentioned immunity for state officers. Because indirect control over individual citizens ("the only proper objects of government") was ineffective under the Articles of Confederation, Alexander Hamilton explained that "we must extend the authority of the Union to the persons of the citizens." *The Federalist* No. 15.

Indeed, the historical materials strongly suggest that the Founders intended to enhance the capacity of the federal government by empowering it—as a part of the new authority to make demands directly on individual citizens—to act through local officials. Hamilton made clear that the new Constitution, "by extending the authority of the federal head to the individual citizens of the several States, will enable the government to employ the ordinary magistracy of each, in the execution of its laws." *The Federalist* No. 27. Hamilton's meaning was unambiguous; the federal government was to have the power to demand that local officials implement national policy programs. As he went on to explain: "It is easy to perceive that this will tend to destroy, in the common apprehension, all distinction between the sources from which [the state and federal governments] might proceed; and will give the federal government the same advantage for securing a due obedience to its authority which is enjoyed by the government of each State."

More specifically, during the debates concerning the ratification of the Constitution, it was assumed that state agents would act as tax collectors for the federal government. Opponents of the Constitution had repeatedly expressed fears that the new federal government's ability to impose taxes directly on the citizenry would result in an overbearing presence of federal tax collectors in the States. Federalists rejoined that this problem would not arise because, as Hamilton explained, "the United States . . . will make use of the State officers and State regulations for collecting" certain taxes. No. 36. Similarly, Madison made clear that the new central government's power to raise taxes directly from the citizenry would "not be resorted to, except for supplemental purposes of revenue . . . and that the eventual collection, under the immediate authority of the Union, will generally be made by the officers . . . appointed by the several States." No. 45. . . .

The Court's response to this powerful historical evidence is weak. The majority suggests that "none of these statements necessarily implies . . . Congress could impose these responsibilities without the consent of the States." No fair reading of these materials can justify such an interpretation. As Hamilton explained, the power of the government to act on "individual citizens"—including "employing the ordinary magistracy" of the States—was an answer to the problems faced by a central government that could act only directly "upon the States in their political or collective capacities." *The Federalist*, No. 27. The new Constitution would avoid this problem, resulting in "a regular and peaceable execution of the law of the Union." . . .

Bereft of support in the history of the founding, the Court rests its conclusion on the claim that there is little evidence the National Government actually exercised such a power in the early years of the Republic. This reasoning is misguided in principle and in fact. While we have indicated that the express consideration and resolution of difficult constitutional issues by the First Congress in particular "provides 'contemporaneous and weighty evidence' of the Constitution's meaning since many of [its] Members . . . 'had taken part in framing that instrument,'" *Bowsher v. Synar*, 478 U.S. 714 (1986), we have never suggested that the failure of the early Congresses to address the scope of federal power in a particular area or to exercise a particular authority was an argument against its existence. That position, if correct, would undermine most of our post-New Deal Commerce Clause jurisprudence. As Justice O'CONNOR quite properly noted in *New York*, "the Federal Government undertakes activities today that would have been unimaginable to the Framers."

More importantly, the fact that Congress did elect to rely on state judges and the clerks of state courts to perform a variety of executive functions is surely evidence of a contemporary understanding that their status as state officials did not immunize them from federal service. The majority's description of these early statutes is both incomplete and at times misleading. . . .

We are far truer to the historical record by applying a functional approach in assessing the role played by these early state officials. The use of state judges and their clerks to perform executive functions was, in historical context, hardly unusual. And, of course, judges today continue to perform a variety of functions that may more properly be described as executive. The majority's insistence that this evidence of federal enlistment of state officials to serve executive functions is irrelevant simply because the assistance of "judges" was at issue rests on empty formalistic reasoning of the highest order. . . .

The Court concludes its review of the historical materials with a reference to the fact that our decision in *INS v. Chadha*, 462 U.S. 919 (1983), invalidated a large number of statutes enacted in the 1970s, implying that recent enactments by Congress that are similar to the Brady Act are not entitled to any presumption of validity. But in *Chadha*, unlike this case, our decision rested on the Constitution's express bicameralism and presentment requirements, not on judicial inferences drawn from a silent text and a historical record that surely favors the congressional understanding. Indeed, the majority's opinion consists almost entirely of arguments against the substantial evidence weighing in opposition to its view; the Court's ruling is strikingly lacking in affirmative support. Absent even a modicum of textual foundation for its judicially crafted constitutional rule, there should be a presumption that if the Framers had actually intended such a rule, at least one of them would have mentioned it.

The Court's "structural" arguments are not sufficient to rebut that presumption. The fact that the Framers intended to preserve the sovereignty of the several States simply does not speak to the question whether individual state employees may be required to perform federal obligations, such as registering young adults for the draft, creating state emergency response commissions designed to manage the release of hazardous substances, collecting and reporting data on underground storage tanks that may pose an environmental hazard, and reporting traffic fatalities, and missing children to a federal agency.

As we explained in *Garcia v. San Antonio Metropolitan Transit Authority*, 469 U.S. 528 (1985): "The principal means chosen by the Framers to ensure the role of the States in the federal system lies in the structure of the Federal Government itself. It is no novelty to observe that the composition of the Federal Government was designed in large part to protect the States from overreaching by Congress." Given the fact that the Members of Congress are elected by the people of the several States, with each State receiving an equivalent number of Senators in order to ensure that even the smallest States have a powerful voice in the legislature, it is quite unrealistic to assume that they will ignore the sovereignty concerns of their constituents. It is far more reasonable to presume that their decisions to impose modest burdens on state officials from time to time reflect a considered judgment that the people in each of the States will benefit therefrom. . . .

Finally, the Court advises us that the "prior jurisprudence of this Court" is the most conclusive support for its position. That "prior jurisprudence" is *New York v. United States*. The case involved the validity of a federal statute that provided the States with three types of incentives to encourage them to dispose of radioactive wastes generated within their borders. The Court held that the first two sets of incentives were authorized by affirmative grants of power to Congress, and therefore "not inconsistent with the Tenth Amendment." That holding, of course, sheds no doubt on the validity of the Brady Act. . . .

The provision of the Brady Act that crosses the Court's newly defined constitutional threshold is more comparable to a statute requiring local police officers to report the identity of missing children to the Crime Control Center of the Department of Justice than to an offensive federal command to a sovereign state. If Congress believes that such a statute will benefit the people of the Nation, and serve the interests of cooperative federalism better than an enlarged federal bureaucracy, we should respect both its policy judgment and its appraisal of its constitutional power.

Accordingly, I respectfully dissent.

Justice SOUTER, dissenting.

I join Justice STEVENS's dissenting opinion, but subject to the following qualifications. While I do not find anything dispositive in the paucity of early examples of federal employment of state officers for executive purposes, for the reason given by Justice STEVENS, neither would I find myself in dissent with no more to go on than those few early instances in the administration of naturalization laws, for example, or such later instances as state support for federal emergency action.

In deciding these cases, which I have found closer than I had anticipated, it is *The Federalist* that finally determines my position. I believe that the most straightforward reading of No. 27 is authority for the Government's position here, and that this reading is both supported by No. 44 and consistent with Nos. 36 and 45.

Hamilton in No. 27 first notes that because the new Constitution would authorize the National Government to bind individuals directly through national law, it could "employ the ordinary magistracy of each [State] in the execution of its laws." Were he to stop here, he would not necessarily be speaking of anything beyond the possibility of cooperative arrangements by agreement. But he then addresses the combined effect of the proposed Supremacy Clause, and state officers' oath requirement, U.S. Const., Art. VI, cl. 3, and he states that "the Legislatures, Courts and Magistrates of the respective members will be incorporated into the operations of the national government, as far as its just and constitutional authority extends; and will be rendered auxiliary to the enforcement of its laws." *The Federalist* No. 27. The natural reading of this language is not merely that the officers of the various branches of state governments may be employed in the performance of national functions; Hamilton says that the state governmental machinery "will be incorporated" into the Nation's operation, and because the "auxiliary" status of the state officials will occur because they are "bound by the sanctity of an oath," I take him to mean that their auxiliary functions will be the products of their obligations thus undertaken to support federal law, not of their own, or the States', unfettered choices. Madison in No. 44 supports this reading in his commentary on the oath requirement. He asks why state magistrates should have to swear to support the National Constitution, when national officials will not be required to oblige themselves to support the state counterparts. His answer is that national officials "will have no agency in carrying the State Constitutions into effect. The members and officers of the State Governments, on the contrary, will have an essential agency in giving effect to the Federal Constitution." *The Federalist* No. 44 (J. Madison). He then describes the state legislative "agency" as action necessary for selecting the President, see U.S. Const., Art. II, Sec. 1, and the choice of Senators, see U.S. Const., Art. I, Sec. 3 (repealed by Amendment XVII). The Supremacy Clause itself, of course, expressly refers to the state judges' obligations under federal law, and other numbers of *The Federalist* give examples of state executive "agency" in the enforcement of national revenue laws. . . .

In the light of all these passages, I cannot persuade myself that the statements from No. 27 speak of anything less than the authority of the National Government, when exercising an otherwise legitimate power (the commerce power, say), to require state "auxiliaries" to take appropriate action. To be sure, it does not follow that any conceivable requirement may be imposed on any state official. I continue to agree, for example, that Congress may not require a state legislature to enact a regulatory scheme and that *New York v. United States*, 505 U.S. 144 (1992) was rightly decided (even though I now believe its dicta went too far toward immunizing state administration as well as state enactment of such a scheme from congressional mandate); after all, the essence of legislative power, within the limits of legislative jurisdiction, is a discretion not subject to command. But insofar as national law would require nothing from a state officer inconsistent with the power proper to his branch of tripartite state government (say, by obligating a state judge to exercise law enforcement powers), I suppose that the reach of federal law as Hamilton described it would not be exceeded, cf. *Garcia v. San Antonio Metropolitan Transit Authority*, 469 U.S. 528 (1985) (without precisely delineating the outer limits of Congress's Commerce Clause power, finding that the statute at issue was not "destructive of state sovereignty"). . . .

Justice BREYER, with whom Justice STEVENS joins, dissenting.

I would add to the reasons Justice STEVENS sets forth the fact that the United States is not the only nation that seeks to reconcile the practical need for a central authority with the democratic virtues of more local control. At least some other countries, facing the same basic problem, have found that local control is better maintained through application of a principle that is the direct opposite of the principle the majority derives from the silence of our Constitution. The federal systems of Switzerland, Germany, and the European Union, for example, all provide that constituent states, not federal bureaucracies, will themselves implement many of the laws, rules, regulations, or decrees enacted by the central "federal" body. They do so in part because they believe that such a system interferes less, not more, with the independent authority of the "state," member nation, or other subsidiary government, and helps to safeguard individual liberty as well.

Of course, we are interpreting our own Constitution, not those of other nations, and there may be relevant political and structural differences between their systems and our own. But their experience may nonetheless cast an empirical light on the consequences of different solutions to a common legal problem—in this case the problem of reconciling central authority with the need to preserve the liberty-enhancing autonomy of a smaller constituent governmental entity. And that experience here offers empirical confirmation of the implied answer to a question Justice STEVENS asks: Why, or how, would what the majority sees as a constitutional alternative—the creation of a new federal gun-law bureaucracy, or the expansion of an existing federal bureaucracy—better promote either state sovereignty or individual liberty?

As comparative experience suggests, there is no need to interpret the Constitution as containing an absolute principle—forbidding the assignment of virtually any federal duty to any state official. Nor is there a need to read the Brady Act as permitting the Federal Government to overwhelm a state civil service. The statute uses the words "reasonable effort"—words that easily can encompass the considerations of, say, time or cost, necessary to avoid any such result.

Regardless, as Justice STEVENS points out, the Constitution itself is silent on the matter. Precedent supports the Government's position here. And the fact that there is not more precedent—that direct federal assignment of duties to state officers is not common—likely reflects, not a widely shared belief that any such assignment is incompatible with basic principles of federalism, but rather a widely shared practice of assigning such duties in other ways. Thus, there is neither need nor reason to find in the Constitution an absolute principle, the inflexibility of which poses a surprising and technical obstacle to the enactment of a law that Congress believed necessary to solve an important national problem.

C. JUDICIAL FEDERALISM

In a splintered ruling the Court stopped just short of jettisoning much of *Ex parte Young*, 209 U.S. 123 (1908). Although the Eleventh Amendment's provision for the states' "sovereign immunity" generally bars suits against states in federal courts, *Ex parte Young* held that state officials may be sued and enjoined from enforcing state laws that are said to be unconstitutional, even though those laws have not yet been ruled invalid. At issue in *Idaho v. Coeur d'Alene Tribe*, 117 S.Ct. 2028 (1997), was whether the state could be sued in federal court in a dispute over ownership of a lake bed, part of which is on an Indian reservation. The Court of Appeals for the Ninth Circuit allowed the lawsuit to proceed based on the doctrine of *Ex parte Young*. But a bare majority—including Chief Justice Rehnquist and Justices Kennedy, O'Connor, Scalia, and Thomas—reversed and held that the suit bore too directly and intrusively on Idaho's "sovereign interest in its lands and waters." Portions of Justice Kennedy's opinion for the Court that would have replaced the *Ex parte Young* doctrine with a case-by-case balancing test, however, were joined only by the chief justice, and Justice O'Connor in a concurring opinion expressly refused to go along with that approach. Justice Souter filed a dissenting opinion, which was joined by Justices Breyer, Ginsburg, and Stevens.

8

REPRESENTATIVE GOVERNMENT, VOTING RIGHTS, AND ELECTORAL POLITICS

B. VOTING RIGHTS AND THE REAPPORTIONMENT REVOLUTION

THE DEVELOPMENT OF LAW

Other Rulings Interpreting the Voting Rights Act

Case	Vote	Ruling
Young v. Fordice, 117 S.Ct. 1228 (1997)	9:0	Held that Mississippi was required under Section 5 of the Voting Rights Act to ob-

tain the Department of Justice's preclearance approval before implementing the federal Motor Voter law of 1995 in a way which would make it the only state with separate registration procedures for federal and state elections. Writing for the Court, Justice Breyer observed that the dual registration system "contains numerous examples of new, significantly different administrative practices" that posed "a potential for discriminatory impact" on minority voters.

Reno v. Bossier Parish School Board, 117 S.Ct. 1491 (1997)	7:2	Writing for the majority, Justice O'Connor rejected the Department of Justice's decade-old policy of deny-

ing preclearance under Section 5 of the Voting Rights Act to changes in electoral redistricting in the nine Southern states, not only when they would weaken the position of minority voters but also when redistricting plans would not improve those voters' position as much as theoretically possible. Under the DoJ's policy preclearance under Section 5 was denied if redistricting plans failed to satisfy the standard of Section 2 of the act, which applies nationwide and does not require proof that minority voters would be in a worse position but rather that they are not in as strong a position to elect minorities as possible. However, Justice O'Connor held that that policy made it more difficult for the nine Southern states to obtain preclearance under Section 5 than Congress had intended. That policy, in her words, "increase[d] further the serious federalism costs already implicated by Section 5." Justices Stevens and Souter dissented from what they viewed as the Court's "misery interpretation of Section 5."

Abrams v. Johnson, 117 S.Ct. 1925 (1997)	5:4	In *Miller v. Johnson*, 115 S.Ct. 2475 (1995) (see Vol. 1, Ch. 8), the Court invalidated

Georgia's congressional redistricting plan, which created three majority-black districts out of the state's eleven districts, because race was the predominant factor in the redistricting plan. On remand, the federal district court deferred to the legislature to draw a new plan, but it could not reach agreement. The district court thus drew its own plan, containing only one majority-black district. The 1996 general elections were held under that plan, but voters and the Department of Justice challenged the plan on the ground that it did not adequately take into account the interests of the state's black population. Writing for a bare majority as in *Miller v. Johnson*, Justice Kennedy upheld the lower court's redistricting plan and held that the court had abused neither its remedial powers nor its discretion in deciding that it could not draw two majority-black districts without engaging in racial gerrymandering. In holding that the redistricting did not violate either Section 2 or Section 5 of the Voting Rights Act and did not violate the constitutional guarantee of "one person, one vote" under Article 1, Section 2, Justice Kennedy reaffirmed that race "must not be a predominant factor in drawing the district lines." As in *Miller v. Johnson*, Justices Breyer, Ginsburg, Souter, and Stevens dissented. Writing for the dissenters here, Justice Breyer countered that "[t]he majority holds that the District Court could lawfully create a new districting plan that retained only one [majority-minority] district. But in my view that decision departs dramatically from the Georgia Legislature's preference for two such districts—a preference embodied in the legislature's earlier congressional district plans. A two-district plan is not unconstitutional. And the District Court here, like the District Court in *Upham v. Seamon*, 456 U.S. 37 (1982), 'was not free . . . to disregard the political program of the . . . Legislature.' . . . To create a second majority-minority district is not impractical nor would doing so significantly interfere with other important districting objectives. . . . [Moreover,] this is not a suit in which there are claims of interference with the right to cast a ballot or 'dilution' of the majority's vote. . . . Rather, the legislature's plans, insofar as they were race-conscious, sought only to prevent what the legislature could reasonably have believed to be unlawful vote dilution—i.e., to prevent a violation of Section 2 [of the Voting Rights Act], or perhaps Section 5. . . . Nor can I find any legal principle that might constitute a simple, administrable stopping place—a principle that could serve the same function in this context as does the one-person-one-vote rule in the context of reapportionment. A simple 'color-blind' test—a test that rules out race-consciousness across the board—will not work. Legislators can and should use race consciously to prevent creating districting plans that discriminate against racial minorities, say by 'diluting' their votes." . . .

THE DEVELOPMENT OF LAW

Other Post–*Shaw v. Reno* Rulings on Racial Gerrymandering

Case	Vote	Ruling
Lawyer v. Department of Justice, 117 S.Ct. 2186 (1997)	5:4	Writing for a bare majority, Justice Souter rejected a challenge to the configuration of a

Florida legislative district under the Fourteenth Amendment's equal protection clause and the contention that a federal district court should have found a proposed districting plan unconstitutional before approving a mediated redistricting settlement. Following the 1990 census the state legislature adopted a reapportionment plan, but the Department of Justice declined to give it preclearance approval under the Voting Rights Act on the ground that it failed to create a minority majority in the Tampa district. When the state legislature failed to redraw the district because it was out of session, the Supreme Court of Florida revised the redistricting plan to address the Justice Department's objection. That plan called for an irregularly shaped district with a voting-age population 45.8 percent black and 9.4 percent Hispanic, and comprising portions of four counties. In 1994, six residents of that proposed district challenged its constitutionality in federal district court. A three-judge district court was convened and permitted intervention in the suit by the state legislature, the governor, and a group of black and Hispanic voters. Shortly after the Court decided *Miller v. Johnson*, 115 S.Ct. 2475 (1995) (see Vol. 1, Ch. 8), all the parties agreed to the appointment of a mediator for the dispute. Subsequently, in 1995 a settlement agreement was signed by all the parties except the appellant. The agreement proposed revising the Tampa district by decreasing its length by 58 percent, reducing the black voting-age population from 45.8 to 36.2 percent, and including portions of three counties instead of four. The appellant, however, maintained that the district court was required to hold the original plan unconstitutional before adopting the revised plan. The district court disagreed and in March 1996 approved the settlement, concluding that the constitutional objection to the proposed district was not established. In its view, the district's shape and composition was "demonstrably benign and satisfactorily tidy, especially given the prevailing geography." Dissenting from the majority's affirmance of that decision, Justice Scalia, joined by Justices O'Connor, Kennedy, and Thomas, countered that the lower court's decision represented "an unprecedented intrusion upon state sovereignty."

Meadows v. Moon, 117 S.Ct. 2501 (1997)	9:0	Without comment, the Court affirmed a federal district court's ruling invalidating

Virginia's only majority-black congressional district as an unconstitutional racial gerrymander, perhaps signaling that the Court will no longer review every redistricting case that comes to it. The challenged district ran from Richmond to the Tidewater area in irregular ways that made for a 64 percent black voting population.

C. CAMPAIGNS AND ELECTIONS

In its 1998–1999 term, the Court will consider a First Amendment challenge to Colorado's initiative and referendum petition process in *Buckley v. American Constitutional Law Foundation, Inc.* (No. 97-930). At issue is whether recent amendments to the state's law requiring signature gatherers, or proponents of state constitutional amendments, to (1) be registered voters, (2) wear identification badges when gathering signatures, and (3) disclose the names of all paid signature gatherers violate the First Amendment's guarantees for freedom of speech, press, association and assembly.

THE DEVELOPMENT OF LAW

Other Rulings on Campaigns and Elections

Case	Vote	Ruling
Timmons v. Twin Cities Area New Party 117 S.Ct. 1364 (1997)	6:3	Rejected a First Amendment challenge to Minnesota's law barring the listing on ballots

of candidates supported by one of the major parties, Republican or Democrat, as well as a third party. The New Party argued that the ban on such a "fusion" in listing candidates relegated thirty parties to the margins and violated their First Amendment rights of freedom of speech and association. But only dissenting Justices Stevens, Souter, and O'Connor agreed.

Case	Vote	Ruling
Foster v. Love, 118 S.Ct. 464 (1997)	9:0	Struck down Louisiana's 1975 "open primary" law, under which elections are held in

October and if a candidate for a congressional seat receives a majority vote, the candidate "is elected" and not subject to run on the federal election day of the Tuesday after the first Monday in November, which was established in 1872. Writing for the Court, Justice Souter held that the law infringed on Congress's "power to override state regulations" by establishing uniform rules for federal elections.

Case	Vote	Ruling
Arkansas Educational Television Commission v. Forbes, 118 S.Ct. 1633 (1998)	6:3	Writing for the Court, Justice Kennedy held that a public television station may exclude "marginal" candidates from

its televised debates of major candidates for political office. In refusing to extend the concept of a "public forum" to such debates, he held that the decision to exclude Forbes, an independent candidate, was under the circumstances a reasonable, viewpoint-neutral exercise of journalistic discretion consistent with the First Amendment. Dissenting Justice Stevens, joined by Justices Ginsburg and Souter, countered that the majority failed to hold public television to a higher standard, requiring them to have "pre-established, objective criteria" for determining access to televised debates.

VOLUME TWO

3

ECONOMIC RIGHTS AND AMERICAN CAPITALISM

C. THE "TAKINGS CLAUSE" AND JUST COMPENSATION

The Court granted for the 1998–1999 term a Fifth Amendment "takings clause" challenge in *City of Monterey v. Del Monte Dunes*, 95 F.2d 1322 (9th Cir., 1996) (Docket No. 97-1235). At issue is whether Monterey's refusal to permit Del Monte Dunes to develop 37.6 oceanfront acres constitutes a takings without just compensation.

THE DEVELOPMENT OF LAW

Other Important Rulings on the Takings Clause

Case	Vote	Ruling
Phillips v. Washington Legal Foundation, 118 S.Ct. 1925 (1998)	5:4	In the 1980s, Texas and 48 other states established Interest on Lawyers Trust Account

(IOLTA) programs. Under them, certain funds from clients received by attorneys are held in federally authorized "Negotiable Order of Withdrawal" accounts. The interest income of these accounts is paid to the state and used to finance legal services for low-income people. The conservative Washington Legal Foundation challenged the constitutionality of IOLTA programs on the ground that they violate the Fifth Amendment. In a narrow ruling for a bare majority, Chief Justice Rehnquist held that the interest income does constitute "property" under the Fifth Amendment, but declined to rule on whether IOLTA programs constitute a "takings" and whether "just compensation" is required, because those issues had not been addressed by the lower courts. Justices Souter and Breyer filed dissenting opinions, which were joined by Justices Stevens and Ginsburg. They maintained that the interest income was not "property" and, thus, IOLTA programs are not takings under the Fifth Amendment.

Eastern Enterprises v. Apfel   5:4   Writing for the Court, Justice
118 S.Ct. 2131 (1998)   O'Connor held that the Coal
                                          Industry Retiree Health Bene-
fit Act of 1992, which establishes a mechanism for funding health care benefits
for retirees from the coal industry, as applied to Eastern Enterprises constituted an unconstitutional takings in violation of the Fifth Amendment. Under
the act, Eastern was assigned an obligation to pay between 50 and 100 million dollars in back pension funds to miners, in spite of its sale of coal operations in 1965 and its not participating in negotiations over the industry's
contributions to the benefits program. Justice Kennedy concurred in the
judgment and dissented in part in a separate opinion, while Justices Stevens,
Souter, Ginsburg, and Breyer dissented.

4

THE NATIONALIZATION
OF THE BILL OF RIGHTS

B. THE RISE AND RETREAT OF
THE "DUE PROCESS REVOLUTION"

In a widely watched case, *Kansas v. Hendricks* (excerpted below), the Court upheld Kansas's 1994 law for institutionalizing sexual predators even after they have served their prison time. Writing for a bare majority, Justice Thomas rejected constitutional challenges to the law for violating substantive due process and the bans against double jeopardy and the passage of *ex post facto* laws. While agreeing that Kansas's procedures for civil commitment of sexual predators satisfied due process requirements, the dissenters deemed the law to run afoul of the Constitution's prohibition on the passage of *ex post facto* laws. The Court rejected another substantive due process claim in *County of Sacramento v. Lewis* (excerpted below) and sought to clarify its substantive due process analysis in an opinion delivered by Justice Souter and with which Justice Scalia took strong exception. There, the Court held that police who cause accidents that kill even innocent bystanders during high-speed pursuit of criminal suspects are not liable unless their actions "shock the conscience." In Justice Souter's words, "Only a purpose to cause harm unrelated to the legitimate object of arrest will satisfy the element of arbitrary conduct shocking to the conscience, necessary for a due-process violation."

In its 1998–1999 term the Court will consider the constitutionality of Chicago's anti-loitering law aimed at gang members selling drugs on streets and in public parks. Adopted in 1992, the ordinance allows police to order any group of individuals loitering in a public place to disperse if there is reason to believe that someone in the group is a gang member. "Loiter" is defined as "to remain in any one place with no apparent purpose." A conviction under the ordinance carries a penalty of six months in prison, a $500 fine, or up to 120 hours of community service. In *Chicago v. Morales*, the city is appealing the state supreme court's invalidation of the law on the grounds that it is impermissibly vague and violates the due process of law.

In the words of the Illinois Supreme Court, the ordinance fails to give people notice of exactly what conduct is unlawful and deprives "persons suspected of being in criminal street gangs . . . of the personal liberty of being able to freely walk the streets and associate with friends, regardless of whether they are actually gang members or have committed any crime."

Kansas v. Hendricks
117 S.Ct. 2072 (1997)

In 1994, Kansas enacted the Sexually Violent Predator Act, which establishes procedures for the civil commitment of persons who, due to a "mental abnormality" or a "personality disorder," are likely to engage in "predatory acts of sexual violence." Under the law, an offender may be institutionalized, even after serving a prison sentence, if the state convinces a judge or jury "beyond a reasonable doubt" that the prisoner suffers from a mental abnormality that is likely to compel him to molest again. The law also requires the state annually to review the case and justify to a judge the decision to continue the offender's involuntary institutionalization. While serving a ten-year prison sentence for child molestation and shortly before his scheduled release, Leroy Hendricks, who has a forty-year record of sexually molesting children, was the first to be committed under Kansas's law and he immediately challenged its constitutionality. The Supreme Court of Kansas struck down the statute on the grounds that it violated "substantive" due process. That decision was appealed by the state and the Supreme Court granted *certiorari*, as well as a cross-petition filed by Hendricks claiming that the law violated constitutional guarantees according due process and barring double jeopardy and the passage of *ex post facto* laws.

The Court's decision was five to four and its opinion delivered by Justice Thomas. Justice Kennedy filed a concurring opinion. Justice Breyer filed a dissenting opinion, joined by Justices Stevens, Souter, and Ginsburg.

Justice THOMAS delivered the opinion of the Court.

Kansas argues that the Act's definition of "mental abnormality" satisfies "substantive" due process requirements. We agree. Although freedom from physical restraint "has always been at the core of the liberty protected by the Due Process Clause from arbitrary governmental action," *Foucha v. Louisiana*, 504 U.S. 71 (1992), that liberty interest is not absolute. The Court has recognized that an individual's constitutionally protected interest in avoiding physical restraint may be overridden even in the civil context: "The liberty secured by the Constitution of the United States to every person within its jurisdiction does not import an absolute right in each person to be, at all times and in all circumstances, wholly free from restraint. There are manifold restraints to which every person is necessarily subject for the common good. On any other basis organized society could not exist with safety to its members." *Jacobson v. Massachusetts*, 197 U.S. 11 (1905).

Accordingly, States have in certain narrow circumstances provided for the forcible civil detainment of people who are unable to control their behavior and who thereby pose a danger to the public health and safety. We have consistently upheld such involuntary commitment statutes provided the confinement takes place pursuant to proper procedures and evidentiary standards. *Addington v. Texas*, 441 U.S. 418 (1979). It thus cannot be said that the involuntary civil confinement of a limited subclass of dangerous persons is contrary to our understanding of ordered liberty.

The challenged Act unambiguously requires a finding of dangerousness either to one's self or to others as a prerequisite to involuntary confinement. Commitment proceedings can be initiated only when a person "has been convicted of or charged with a sexually violent offense," and "suffers from a mental abnormality or personality disorder which makes the person likely to engage in the predatory acts of sexual violence." The statute thus requires proof of more than a mere predisposition to violence; rather, it requires evidence of past sexually violent behavior and a present mental condition that creates a likelihood of such conduct in the future if the person is not incapacitated. As we have recognized, "previous instances of violent behavior are an important indicator of future violent tendencies." *Heller v. Doe*, 509 U.S. 312 (1993). A finding of dangerousness, standing alone, is ordinarily not a sufficient ground upon which to justify indefinite involuntary commitment. We have sustained civil commitment statutes when they have coupled proof of dangerousness with the proof of some additional factor, such as a "mental illness" or "mental abnormality." These added statutory requirements serve to limit involuntary civil confinement to those who suffer from a volitional impairment rendering them dangerous beyond their control. The Kansas Act is plainly of a kind with these other civil commitment statutes. . . .

Hendricks nonetheless argues that our earlier cases dictate a finding of "mental illness" as a prerequisite for civil commitment, citing *Foucha*, and *Addington*. He then asserts that a "mental abnormality" is not equivalent to a "mental illness" because it is a term coined by the Kansas Legislature, rather than by the psychiatric community. Contrary to Hendricks' assertion, the term "mental illness" is devoid of any talismanic significance. Not only do "psychiatrists disagree widely and frequently on what constitutes mental illness," but the Court itself has used a variety of expressions to describe the mental condition of those properly subject to civil confinement. . . .

We granted Hendricks' cross-petition to determine whether the Act violates the Constitution's double jeopardy prohibition or its ban on *ex post facto* lawmaking. The thrust of Hendricks' argument is that the Act establishes criminal proceedings; hence confinement under it necessarily constitutes punishment. He contends that where, as here, newly enacted "punishment" is predicated upon past conduct for which he has already been convicted and forced to serve a prison sentence, the Constitution's Double Jeopardy and Ex Post Facto Clauses are violated. We are unpersuaded by Hendricks' argument that Kansas has established criminal proceedings. . . .

Although we recognize that a "civil label is not always dispositive," we will reject the legislature's manifest intent only where a party challenging the statute provides "the clearest proof" that "the statutory scheme [is] so punitive either in purpose or effect as to negate [the State's] intention" to deem it "civil." In those limited circumstances, we will consider the statute to have established criminal proceedings for constitutional purposes. Hendricks, however, has failed to satisfy this heavy burden.

As a threshold matter, commitment under the Act does not implicate either of the two primary objectives of criminal punishment: retribution or deterrence. The Act's purpose is not retributive because it does not affix culpability for prior criminal conduct. Instead, such conduct is used solely for evidentiary purposes, either to demonstrate that a "mental abnormality" exists or to support a finding of future dangerousness. . . . Nor can it be said that the legislature intended the Act to function as a deterrent. Those persons committed under the Act are, by definition, suffering from a "mental abnormality" or a "personality disorder" that prevents them from exercising adequate control over their behavior. Such persons are therefore unlikely to be deterred by the threat of confinement. And the conditions surrounding that confinement do not suggest a punitive purpose on the State's part. . . .

Where the State has "disavowed any punitive intent"; limited confinement to a small segment of particularly dangerous individuals; provided strict procedural safeguards; directed that confined persons be segregated from the general prison population and afforded the same status as others who have been civilly committed; recommended treatment if such is possible; and permitted immediate release upon a showing that the individual is no longer dangerous or mentally impaired, we cannot say that it acted with punitive intent. We therefore hold that the Act does not establish criminal proceedings and that involuntary confinement pursuant to the Act is not punitive. Our conclusion that the Act is nonpunitive thus removes an essential prerequisite for both Hendricks' double jeopardy and *ex post facto* claims. . . .

Because we have determined that the Kansas Act is civil in nature, initiation of its commitment proceedings does not constitute a second prosecution. Moreover, as commitment under the Act is not tantamount to "punishment," Hendricks' involuntary detention does not violate the Double Jeopardy Clause, even though that confinement may follow a prison term. . . .

Hendricks' *ex post facto* claim is similarly flawed. The Ex Post Facto Clause, which "'forbids the application of any new punitive measure to a crime already consummated,'" has been interpreted to pertain exclusively to penal statutes. As we have previously determined, the Act does not impose punishment; thus, its application does not raise *ex post facto* concerns. . . .

We hold that the Kansas Sexually Violent Predator Act comports with due process requirements and neither runs afoul of double jeopardy principles nor constitutes an exercise in impermissible ex post facto lawmaking. Accordingly, the judgment of the Kansas Supreme Court is reversed.

Justice BREYER, with whom Justices STEVENS and SOUTER join, (and with whom Justice GINSBURG joins in part) dissenting.

I agree with the majority that the Kansas Act's "definition of 'mental abnormality'" satisfies the "substantive" requirements of the Due Process Clause.

Kansas, however, concedes that Hendricks' condition is treatable; yet the Act did not provide Hendricks (or others like him) with any treatment until after his release date from prison and only inadequate treatment thereafter. These, and certain other, special features of the Act convince me that it was not simply an effort to commit Hendricks civilly, but rather an effort to inflict further punishment upon him. The Ex Post Facto Clause therefore prohibits the Act's application to Hendricks, who committed his crimes prior to its enactment. . . .

Kansas' 1994 Act violates the Federal Constitution's prohibition of "any . . . *ex post facto* Law" if it "inflicts" upon Hendricks "a greater punishment" than did the law "annexed to" his "crimes" when he "committed" those crimes in 1984. The majority agrees that the Clause "'forbids the application of any new punitive measure to a crime already consummated.'" But it finds the Act is not "punitive." With respect to that basic question, I disagree with the majority. . . .

I have found 17 States with laws that seek to protect the public from mentally abnormal, sexually dangerous individuals through civil commitment or other mandatory treatment programs. Ten of those statutes, unlike the Kansas statute, begin treatment of an offender soon after he has been apprehended and charged with a serious sex offense. Only seven, like Kansas, delay "civil" commitment (and treatment) until the offender has served his criminal sentence. Of these seven, however, six (unlike Kansas) require consideration of less restrictive alternatives. Only one State other than Kansas, namely Iowa, both delays civil commitment (and consequent treatment) and does not explicitly consider less restrictive alternatives. But the law of that State applies prospectively only, thereby avoiding *ex post facto* problems. Thus the practical experience of other States, as revealed by their statutes, confirms what the Kansas Supreme Court's finding, the timing of the civil commitment proceeding, and the failure to consider less restrictive alternatives, themselves suggest, namely, that for Ex Post Facto Clause purposes, the purpose of the Kansas Act (as applied to previously convicted offenders) has a punitive, rather than a purely civil, purpose. . . .

To find a violation of that Clause here, however, is not to hold that the Clause prevents Kansas, or other States, from enacting dangerous sexual offender statutes. A statute that operates prospectively, for example, does not offend the Ex Post Facto Clause. Neither does it offend the Ex Post Facto Clause for a State to sentence offenders to the fully authorized sentence, to seek consecutive, rather than concurrent, sentences, or to invoke recidivism statutes to lengthen imprisonment. Moreover, a statute that operates retroactively, like Kansas' statute, nonetheless does not offend the Clause if the confinement that it imposes is not punishment—if, that is to say, the legislature does not simply add a later criminal punishment to an earlier one. . . .

County of Sacramento v. Lewis
118 S.Ct. 1708 (1998)

On May 22, 1990, James Smith, a Sacramento County sheriff's deputy, along with another officer, Murray Stapp, responded to a call to break up a fight. Upon returning to his patrol car, Stapp saw a motorcycle approaching at high speed. It was operated by Brian Willard and carried Philip Lewis as a passenger. Neither had anything to do with the fight that prompted the call to the police. Stapp turned on his rotating lights, yelled to the boys to stop, and pulled his patrol car closer to Smith's, attempting to pen him in. Instead, Willard slowly maneuvered the cycle between the two police cars and sped off. Smith immediately began pursuit at high speed. They wove in and out of oncoming traffic, reaching speeds up to 100 miles per hour. The chase ended after the motorcycle tipped. By the time Smith slammed on his brakes, Willard was out of the way, but Lewis was not. The patrol car skidded into him at 40 miles an hour, propelling him some 70 feet down the road. Lewis was pronounced dead at the scene.

Lewis's parents sued the Sacramento County Sheriff's Department and Deputy Smith, alleging a deprivation of Philip Lewis's Fourteenth Amendment substantive due process right to life. The district court granted summary judgment for Smith, reasoning that even if he violated the Constitution, he was entitled to qualified immunity. The Court of Appeals for the Ninth Circuit reversed and the city appealed to the Supreme Court, which granted review and reversed the appellate court.

The Court's decision was unanimous and opinion delivered by Justice Souter. Concurring opinions were filed by Chief Justice Rehnquist and Justices Breyer, Kennedy, Scalia, and Stevens.

Justice SOUTER delivered the opinion of the Court.

The issue in this case is whether a police officer violates the Fourteenth Amendment's guarantee of substantive due process by causing death through deliberate or reckless indifference to life in a high-speed automobile chase aimed at apprehending a suspected offender. We answer no, and hold that in such circumstances only a purpose to cause harm unrelated to the legitimate object of arrest will satisfy the element of arbitrary conduct shocking to the conscience, necessary for a due process violation. . . .

Our prior cases have held the provision that "no State shall . . . deprive any person of life, liberty, or property, without due process of law," U.S. Const., Amdt. 14, Sec. 1, to "guarantee more than fair process," *Washington v. Glucksberg*, [117 S.Ct. 2258] (1997), and to cover a substantive sphere as well, "barring certain government actions regardless of the fairness of the procedures used to implement them," *Daniels v. Williams*, 474 U.S. 327 (1986). . . .

Since the time of our early explanations of due process, we have understood the core of the concept to be protection against arbitrary action . . . [*Hurtado v. California*, 110 U.S. 516 (1884)].

We have emphasized time and again that "the touchstone of due process is protection of the individual against arbitrary action of government," *Wolff v. McDonnell*, 418 U.S. 539 (1974), whether the fault lies in a denial of fundamental procedural fairness, or in the exercise of power without any reasonable justification in the service of a legitimate governmental objective. While due process protection in the substantive sense limits what the government may do in both its legislative, see, e.g., *Griswold v. Connecticut*, 391 U.S. 145 (1965), and its executive capacities, see, e.g., *Rochin v. California*, 342 U.S. 165 (1952), criteria to identify what is fatally arbitrary differ depending on whether it is legislation or a specific act of a governmental officer that is at issue.

Our cases dealing with abusive executive action have repeatedly emphasized that only the most egregious official conduct can be said to be "arbitrary in the constitutional sense," *Collins v. Harker Heights*, 503 U.S. [112 (1992)], thereby recognizing the point made in different circumstances by Chief Justice MARSHALL, "'that it is a constitution we are expounding,'" *McCulloch v. Maryland*, [17 U.S.] 316 (1819). . . .

To this end, for half a century now we have spoken of the cognizable level of executive abuse of power as that which shocks the conscience. We first put the test this way in *Rochin v. California*, where we found the forced pumping of a suspect's stomach enough to offend due process as conduct "that shocks the conscience" and violates the "decencies of civilized conduct." In the intervening years we have repeatedly adhered to *Rochin*'s benchmark. . . .

It should not be surprising that the constitutional concept of conscience-shocking duplicates no traditional category of common-law fault, but rather points clearly away from liability, or clearly toward it, only at the ends of the tort law's spectrum of culpability. Thus, we have made it clear that the due process guarantee does not entail a body of constitutional law imposing liability whenever someone cloaked with state authority causes harm. . . .

Whether the point of the conscience-shocking is reached when injuries are produced with culpability falling within the middle range, following from something more than negligence but "less than intentional conduct, such as recklessness or 'gross negligence'" is a matter for closer calls. . . .

Rules of due process are not, however, subject to mechanical application in unfamiliar territory. Deliberate indifference that shocks in one environment may not be so patently egregious in another, and our concern with preserving the constitutional proportions of substantive due process demands an exact analysis of circumstances before any abuse of power is condemned as conscience-shocking. What we have said of due process in the procedural sense is just as true here:

"The phrase [due process of law] formulates a concept less rigid and more fluid than those envisaged in other specific and particular provisions of the Bill of Rights. Its application is less a matter of rule. Asserted denial is to be tested by an appraisal of the totality of facts in a given case. That which may, in one setting, constitute a denial of fundamental fairness, shocking to the universal sense of justice, may, in other circumstances, and in the light of other considerations, fall short of such denial." *Betts v. Brady*, 316 U.S. 455 (1942).

Thus, attention to the markedly different circumstances of normal pretrial custody and high-speed law enforcement chases shows why the deliberate indifference that shocks in the one case is less egregious in the other (even assuming that it makes sense to speak of indifference as deliberate in the case of sudden pursuit). As the very term "deliberate indifference" implies, the standard is sensibly employed only when actual deliberation is practical, and in the custodial situation of a prison, forethought about an inmate's welfare is not only feasible but obligatory under a regime that incapacitates a prisoner to exercise ordinary responsibility for his own welfare. . . .

But just as the description of the custodial prison situation shows how deliberate indifference can rise to a constitutionally shocking level, so too does it suggest why indifference may well not be enough for liability in the different circumstances of a case like this one. We have, indeed, found that deliberate indifference does not suffice for constitutional liability (albeit under the Eighth Amendment) even in prison circumstances when a prisoner's claim arises not from normal custody but from response to a violent disturbance. . . .

Like prison officials facing a riot, the police on an occasion calling for fast action have obligations that tend to tug against each other. Their duty is to restore and maintain lawful order, while not exacerbating disorder more than necessary to do their jobs. They are supposed to act decisively and to show restraint at the same moment, and their decisions have to be made "in haste, under pressure, and frequently without the luxury of a second chance." A police officer deciding whether to give chase must balance on one hand the need to stop a suspect and show that flight from the law is no way to freedom, and, on the other, the high-speed threat to everyone within stopping range, be they suspects, their passengers, other drivers, or bystanders.

To recognize a substantive due process violation in these circumstances when only mid-level fault has been shown would be to forget that liability for deliberate indifference to inmate welfare rests upon the luxury enjoyed by prison officials of having time to make unhurried judgments, upon the chance for repeated reflection, largely uncomplicated by the pulls of competing obligations. . . . Just as a purpose to cause harm is needed for Eighth Amendment liability in a riot case, so it ought to be needed for Due Process liability in a pursuit case. Accordingly, we hold that high-speed chases with no intent to harm suspects physically or to worsen their legal plight do not give rise to liability under the Fourteenth Amendment, redressible by an action under Section 1983. . . .

The judgment below is accordingly reversed.

Justice KENNEDY, with whom Justice O'CONNOR joins, concurring.

I join the opinion of the Court, and write this explanation of the objective character of our substantive due process analysis. . . .

The Court decides this case by applying the "shocks the conscience" test first recognized in *Rochin v. California* and reiterated in subsequent decisions. The phrase has the unfortunate connotation of a standard laden with subjective assessments. In that respect, it must be viewed with considerable skepticism. As our opinion in *Collins v. Harker Heights* illustrates, however, the test can be used to mark the beginning point in asking whether or not the objective character of certain conduct is consistent with our traditions, precedents, and historical understanding of the Constitution and its meaning. As Justice SCALIA is correct to point out, we so interpreted the test in *Glucksberg*. In the instant case, the authorities cited by Justice SCALIA are persuasive, indicating that we would contradict our traditions were we to sustain the claims of the respondents.

That said, it must be added that history and tradition are the starting point, but not in all cases the ending point of the substantive due process inquiry. There is room as well for an objective assessment of the necessities of law enforcement, in which the police must be given substantial latitude and discretion, acknowledging, of course, the primacy of the interest in life which the State, by the Fourteenth Amendment, is bound to respect. I agree with the Court's assessment of the State's interests in this regard. Absent intent to injure, the police, in circumstances such as these, may conduct a dangerous chase of a suspect who disobeys a lawful command to stop when they determine it is appropriate to do so. There is a real danger in announcing a rule, or suggesting a principle, that in some cases a suspect is free to ignore a lawful police command to stop. No matter how narrow its formulation, any suggestion that suspects may ignore a lawful command to stop and then sue for damages sustained in an ensuing chase might cause suspects to flee more often, increasing accidents of the kind which occurred here. . . .

Justice SCALIA, with whom Justice THOMAS joins, concurring in the judgment.

Today's opinion gives the lie to those cynics who claim that changes in this Court's jurisprudence are attributable to changes in the Court's membership. It proves that the changes are attributable to nothing but the passage of time (not much time, at that), plus application of the ancient maxim, "That was then, this is now."

Just last Term, in *Washington v. Glucksberg*, the Court specifically rejected the method of substantive-due-process analysis employed by Justice SOUTER in his concurrence in that case, which is the very same method employed by Justice SOUTER in his opinion for the Court today. . . .

Today, so to speak, the stone that the builders had rejected has become the foundation stone of our substantive-due-process jurisprudence. The atavistic methodology that Justice SOUTER announces for the Court is the very same methodology that the Court called atavistic when it was proffered by Justice SOUTER in *Glucksberg*. In fact, if anything, today's opinion is even more of a throwback to highly subjective substantive-due-process methodologies than the concurrence in *Glucksberg* was. Whereas the latter said merely that substantive due process prevents "arbitrary impositions" and "purposeless restraints" (without any objective criterion as to what is arbitrary or purposeless), today's opinion resuscitates the *ne plus ultra*, the Napoleon Brandy, the Mahatma Gandhi, the Celophane of subjectivity, th' ol' "shocks-the-conscience" test. According to today's opinion, this is the measure of arbitrariness when what is at issue is executive rather than legislative action. *Glucksberg*, of course, rejected "shocks-the-conscience," just as it rejected the less subjective "arbitrary action" test. A 1992 executive-action case, *Collins v. Harker Heights*, which had paid lip service to "shocks-the-conscience," was cited in *Glucksberg* for the proposition that "our Nation's history, legal traditions, and practices . . . provide the crucial 'guideposts for responsible decisionmaking.'" In fact, even before *Glucksberg* we had characterized the last "shocks-the-conscience" claim to come before us as "nothing more than [a] bald assertion," and had rejected it on the objective ground that the petitioner "failed to proffer any historical, textual, or controlling precedential support for [his alleged due process right], and we decline to fashion a new due process right out of thin air." *Carlisle v. United States*, 517 U.S. 416 (1996).

Adhering to our decision in *Glucksberg*, rather than ask whether the police conduct here at issue shocks my unelected conscience, I would ask whether our Nation has traditionally protected the right respondents assert. The first step of our analysis, of course, must be a "careful description" of the right asserted. Here the complaint alleges that the police officer deprived Lewis "of his Fourteenth Amendment right to life, liberty and property without due process of law when he operated his vehicle with recklessness, gross negligence and conscious disregard for his safety." I agree with the Court's conclusion that this asserts a substantive right to be free from "deliberate or reckless indifference to life in a high-speed automobile chase aimed at apprehending a suspected offender."

Respondents provide no textual or historical support for this alleged due process right, and, as in *Carlisle*, I would "decline to fashion a new due process right out of thin air." Nor have respondents identified any precedential support. . . .

I would reverse the judgment of the Ninth Circuit, not on the ground that petitioners have failed to shock my still, soft voice within, but on the ground that respondents offer no textual or historical support for their alleged due process right. Accordingly, I concur in the judgment of the Court.

THE DEVELOPMENT OF LAW

Rulings on Substantive and Procedural Due Process

Case	Vote	Ruling
Young v. Harper, 117 S.Ct. 1148 (1997)	9:0	Writing for the Court, Justice Thomas held that the summary reinstitutionalization of

a state prisoner who had been released under a preparole program, aimed at reducing prison overcrowding, deprived him of liberty without the due process of law under the Fourteenth Amendment and that the prisoner was entitled to the procedural protections for parole hearings set forth in *Morrissey v. Brewer*, 408 U.S. 471 (1972).

Case	Vote	Ruling
Kansas v. Hendricks, 117 S.Ct. 2072 (1997)	5:4	Upheld Kansas's law providing for the involuntary civil commitment of sexual preda-

tors, even after they have served their prison sentences, over due process objections. Agreeing with that part of the Court's analysis, Justices Breyer, Ginsburg, Souter, and Stevens dissented on other grounds.

Case	Vote	Ruling
County of Sacramento v. Lewis 118 S.Ct. 1708 (1998)	9:0	Held that police who cause accidents that kill even innocent bystanders during high-

speed pursuit of criminal suspects are not liable unless their actions "shock the conscience." As Justice Souter explained: "Only a purpose to cause harm unrelated to the legitimate object of arrest will satisfy the element of arbitrary conduct shocking to the conscience, necessary for a due-process violation."

5

FREEDOM OF EXPRESSION
AND ASSOCIATION

B. OBSCENITY, PORNOGRAPHY,
AND OFFENSIVE SPEECH

Although in its 1996–1997 term in *Reno v. American Civil Liberties Union* (1997) (excerpted in this chapter in Section F), the Court by a seven to two vote struck down the Communications Decency Act of 1996, which sought to criminalize sending on the Internet "obscene or indecent" messages to recipients under the age of 18, in its 1997–1998 term the Court by a vote of eight to one upheld a 1990 "public decency" amendment to the National Foundation for the Arts and Humanities Act in *National Endowment for the Arts v. Finley* (excerpted below).

National Endowment for the Arts v. Finley
118 S.Ct. 2168 (1998)

Following the public controversies in 1989 over the National Endowment for the Art's (NEA) funding of a retrospective of Robert Mapplethorpe's work and for an exhibit of Andres Serrano's "Piss Christ," among other projects, in 1990 Congress amended the NEA's governing statute, specifically adding a provision (Section 954(d)(1)) requiring the NEA to ensure that "artistic excellence and artistic merit are the criteria by which [grant] applications are judged, taking into consideration general standards of decency and respect for the diverse beliefs and values of the American public."

Four months prior to the enactment of that amendment, the applications for funding of Karen Finley and several other artists were denied by the NEA. At the time, there were newspaper reports that the then NEA director had been advised by friends to veto Finley's and other artists' grants in order to "ease President Bush's deepening troubles with conservatives on his suspect cultural agenda." After being notified that their applications were denied, Finley and three other artists filed a lawsuit, claiming that the NEA violated their First Amendment rights by denying their applications on impermissible political grounds. After Congress passed the 1990 "general standards of decency" provision, the National Association for Artists' Organizations joined Finley and the other plaintiffs in an amended complaint. They challenged the constitutionality of the new provision on the First Amendment ground that it was impermissibly vague and imposed content-based restrictions on protected speech. A federal district court agreed and the Court of Appeals for the Ninth Circuit affirmed. The NEA appealed that decision and the Supreme Court granted review and reversed the appellate court.

The Court's decision was eight to one and its opinion announced by Justice O'Connor. Justice Scalia filed a concurring opinion, joined by Justice Thomas. Justice Souter filed a dissenting opinion.

Justice O'CONNOR delivered the opinion of the Court.

Respondents raise a facial constitutional challenge to Section 954(d)(1), and consequently they confront "a heavy burden" in advancing their claim. Facial invalidation "is, manifestly, strong medicine" that "has been employed by the Court sparingly and only as a last resort." *Broadrick v. Oklahoma*, 413 U.S. 601 (1973). To prevail, respondents must demonstrate a substantial risk that application of the provision will lead to the suppression of speech.

Respondents argue that the provision is a paradigmatic example of viewpoint discrimination because it rejects any artistic speech that either fails to respect mainstream values or offends standards of decency. The premise of respondents' claim is that Section 954(d)(1) constrains the agency's ability to fund certain categories of artistic expression. The NEA, however, reads the provision as merely hortatory, and contends that it stops well short of an absolute restriction. . . . We do not decide whether the NEA's view—that the formulation of diverse advisory panels is sufficient to comply with Congress' command—is in fact a reasonable reading of the statute. It is clear, however, that the text of Section 954(d)(1) imposes no categorical requirement. The advisory language stands in sharp contrast to congressional efforts to prohibit the funding of certain classes of speech. When Congress has in fact intended to affirmatively constrain the NEA's grant-making authority, it has done so in no uncertain terms. See Section 954(d)(2) ("Obscenity is without artistic merit, is not protected speech, and shall not be funded"). . . .

That Section 954(d)(1) admonishes the NEA merely to take "decency and respect" into consideration, and that the legislation was aimed at reforming procedures rather than precluding speech, undercut respondents' argument that the provision inevitably will be utilized as a tool for invidious viewpoint discrimination. In cases where we have struck down legislation as facially unconstitutional, the dangers were both more evident and more substantial. [See] *R.A.V. v. St. Paul*, 505 U.S. 377 (1992). . . .

In contrast, the "decency and respect" criteria do not silence speakers by expressly "threatening censorship of ideas." Thus, we do not perceive a realistic danger that Section 954(d)(1) will compromise First Amendment values. . . .

Respondent's reliance on our decision in *Rosenberger v. Rector and Visitors of Univ. of Va.*, 515 U.S. 819 (1995), is therefore misplaced. In *Rosenberger*, a public university declined to authorize disbursements from its Student Activities Fund to finance the printing of a Christian student newspaper. We held that by subsidizing the Student Activities Fund, the University had created a limited public forum, from which it impermissibly excluded all publications with religious editorial viewpoints. Although the scarcity of NEA funding does not distinguish this case from *Rosenberger*, the competitive process according to which the grants are allocated does. In the context of arts funding, in contrast to many other subsidies, the Government does not indiscriminately "encourage a diversity of views from private speakers." The NEA's mandate is to make aesthetic judgments, and the inherently content-based "excellence" threshold for NEA support sets it apart from the subsidy at issue in *Rosenberger*—which was available to all student organizations that were "'related to the educational purpose of the University,'" and from comparably objective decisions on allocating public benefits, such as access to a school auditorium or a municipal theater, see *Lamb's Chapel v. Center Moriches Union Free School Dist.*, 508 U.S. 384 (1993); or the second-class mailing privileges available to "'all newspapers and other periodical publications,'" see *Hannegan v. Esquire, Inc.*, 327 U.S. 146 (1946). . . .

Finally, although the First Amendment certainly has application in the subsidy context, we note that the Government may allocate competitive funding according to criteria that would be impermissible were direct regulation of speech or a criminal penalty at stake. So long as legislation does not infringe on other constitutionally protected rights, Congress has wide latitude to set spending priorities. In the 1990 Amendments that incorporated Section 954(d)(1), Congress modified the declaration of purpose in the NEA's enabling act to provide that arts funding should "contribute to public support and confidence in the use of taxpayer funds," and that "public funds . . . must ultimately serve public purposes the Congress defines." And as we held in *Rust* [*v. Sullivan*, 500 U.S. 173 (1991)], Congress may "selectively fund a program to encourage certain activities it believes to be in the public interest, without at the same time funding an alternative program which seeks to deal with the problem in another way." In doing so, "the Government has not discriminated on the basis of viewpoint; it has merely chosen to fund one activity to the exclusion of the other." There is a basic difference between direct state interference with a protected activity and state encouragement of an alternative activity consonant with legislative policy." . . .

In the context of selective subsidies, it is not always feasible for Congress to legislate with clarity. Indeed, if this statute is unconstitutionally vague, then so too are all government programs awarding scholarships and grants on the basis of subjective criteria such as "excellence."

Section 954(d)(1) merely adds some imprecise considerations to an already subjective selection process. It does not, on its face, impermissibly infringe on First or Fifth Amendment rights. Accordingly, the judgment of the Court of Appeals is reversed and the case is remanded for further proceedings consistent with this opinion.

Justice SCALIA, with whom Justice THOMAS joins, concurring in the judgment.

"The operation was a success, but the patient died." What such a procedure is to medicine, the Court's opinion in this case is to law. It sustains the constitutionality of Section 954(d)(1) by gutting it. The most avid congressional opponents of the provision could not have asked for more. I write separately because, unlike the Court, I think that Section 954(d)(1) must be evaluated as written, rather than as distorted by the agency it was meant to control. By its terms, it establishes content- and viewpoint-based criteria upon which grant applications are to be evaluated. And that is perfectly constitutional.

THE STATUTE MEANS WHAT IT SAYS

The phrase "taking into consideration general standards of decency and respect for the diverse beliefs and values of the American public" is what my grammar-school teacher would have condemned as a dangling modifier: There is no noun to which the participle is attached (unless one jumps out of paragraph (1) to press "Chairperson" into service). Even so, it is clear enough that the phrase is meant to apply to those who do the judging. The application reviewers must take into account "general standards of decency" and "respect for the diverse beliefs and values of the American public" when evaluating artistic excellence and merit. One can regard this as either suggesting that decency and respect are elements of what Congress regards as artistic excellence and merit, or as suggesting that decency and respect are factors to be taken into account in addition to artistic excellence and merit. But either way, it is entirely, 100 percent clear that decency and respect are to be taken into account in evaluating applications.

This is so apparent that I am at a loss to understand what the Court has in mind (other than the gutting of the statute) when it speculates that the statute is merely "advisory." General standards of decency and respect for Americans' beliefs and values must (for the statute says that the Chairperson "shall ensure" this result) be taken into account (see, e.g., *American Heritage Dictionary* 402 (3d ed. 1992): "consider . . . to take into account; bear in mind") in evaluating all applications. This does not mean that those factors must always be dispositive, but it does mean that they must always be considered. The method of compliance proposed by the National Endowment for the Arts (NEA)—selecting diverse review panels of artists and nonartists that reflect a wide range of geographic and cultural perspectives—is so obviously inadequate that it insults the intelligence. . . .

The statute requires the decency and respect factors to be considered in evaluating all applications—not, for example, just those applications relating to educational programs, or intended for a particular audience. Just as it would violate the statute to apply the artistic excellence and merit requirements to only select categories of applications, it would violate the statute to apply the decency and respect factors less than universally. A reviewer may, of course, give varying weight to the factors depending on the context, and in some categories of cases (such as the Court's example of funding for symphony orchestras) the factors may rarely if ever affect the outcome; but Section 954(d)(1) requires the factors to be considered in every case. . . .

This unquestionably constitutes viewpoint discrimination. That conclusion is not altered by the fact that the statute does not "compel" the denial of funding, any more than a provision imposing a five-point handicap on all black applicants for civil service jobs is saved from being race discrimination by the fact that it does not compel the rejection of black applicants. If viewpoint discrimination in this context is unconstitutional (a point I shall address anon), the law is invalid unless there are some situations in which the decency and respect factors do not constitute viewpoint discrimination. And there is none. . . . And finally, the conclusion of viewpoint discrimination is not affected by the fact that what constitutes "decency" or "the diverse beliefs and values of the American people" is difficult to pin down—any more than a civil-service preference in favor of those who display "Republican-party values" would be rendered nondiscriminatory by the fact that there is plenty of room for argument as to what Republican-party values might be. . . .

WHAT THE STATUTE SAYS IS CONSTITUTIONAL

Section 954(d)(1) is no more discriminatory, and no less constitutional, than virtually every other piece of funding legislation enacted by Congress. "The Government can, without violating the Constitution, selectively fund a program to encourage certain activities it believes to be in the public interest, without at the same time funding an alternative program . . . ." *Rust v. Sullivan*, 500 U.S. 173 (1991). As we noted in *Rust*, when Congress chose to establish the National Endowment for Democracy it was not constitutionally required to fund programs encouraging competing philosophies of government—an example of funding discrimination that cuts much closer than this one to the core of political speech which is the primary concern of the First Amendment. It takes a particularly high degree of chutzpah for the NEA to contradict this proposition, since the agency itself discriminates—and is required by law to discriminate—in favor of artistic (as opposed to scientific, or political, or theological) expression. . . . Surely the NEA itself is nothing less than an institutionalized discrimination against that point of view. Nonetheless it is constitutional, as is the congressional determination to favor decency and respect for beliefs and values over the opposite. Because such favoritism does not "abridge" anyone's freedom of speech.

Respondents, relying on *Rosenberger v. Rector and Visitors of Univ. of Va.*, 515 U.S. 819 (1995), argue that viewpoint-based discrimination is impermissible unless the government is the speaker or the government is "disbursing public funds to private entities to convey a governmental message." It is impossible to imagine why that should be so; one would think that directly involving the government itself in the viewpoint discrimination (if it is unconstitutional) would make the situation even worse. Respondents are mistaken. It is the very business of government to favor and disfavor points of view on (in modern times, at least) innumerable subjects—which is the main reason we have decided to elect those who run the government, rather than save money by making their posts hereditary. And it makes not a bit of difference, insofar as either common sense or the Constitution is concerned, whether these officials further their (and, in a democracy, our) favored point of view by achieving it directly (having government-employed artists paint pictures, for example, or government-employed doctors perform abortions); or by advocating it officially (establishing an Office of Art

Appreciation, for example, or an Office of Voluntary Population Control); or by giving money to others who achieve or advocate it (funding private art classes, for example, or Planned Parenthood). None of this has anything to do with abridging anyone's speech. *Rosenberger*, as the Court explains, found the viewpoint discrimination unconstitutional, not because funding of "private" speech was involved, but because the government had established a limited public forum— to which the NEA's granting of highly selective (if not highly discriminating) awards bears no resemblance.

The nub of the difference between me and the Court is that I regard the distinction between "abridging" speech and funding it as a fundamental divide, on this side of which the First Amendment is inapplicable. The Court, by contrast, seems to believe that the First Amendment, despite its words, has some ineffable effect upon funding, imposing constraints of an indeterminate nature which it announces (without troubling to enunciate any particular test) are not violated by the statute here—or, more accurately, are not violated by the quite different, emasculated statute that it imagines. "The Government," it says, "may allocate competitive funding according to criteria that would be impermissible were direct regulation of speech or a criminal penalty at stake." The government, I think, may allocate both competitive and noncompetitive funding *ad libitum*, insofar as the First Amendment is concerned. . . .

Justice SOUTER, dissenting.

The Court's conclusions that the proviso is not viewpoint based, that it is not a regulation, and that the NEA may permissibly engage in viewpoint-based discrimination, are all patently mistaken. Nor may the question raised be answered in the Government's favor on the assumption that some constitutional applications of the statute are enough to satisfy the demand of facial constitutionality, leaving claims of the proviso's obvious invalidity to be dealt with later in response to challenges of specific applications of the discriminatory standards. This assumption is irreconcilable with our longstanding and sensible doctrine of facial overbreadth, applicable to claims brought under the First Amendment's speech clause. I respectfully dissent.

"If there is a bedrock principle underlying the First Amendment, it is that the government may not prohibit the expression of an idea simply because society finds the idea itself offensive or disagreeable." *Texas v. Johnson*, 491 U.S. 397 (1989). "Above all else, the First Amendment means that government has no power to restrict expression because of its message [or] its ideas," *Police Dept. of Chicago v. Mosley*, 408 U.S. 92 (1972), which is to say that "the principle of viewpoint neutrality . . . underlies the First Amendment," *Bose Corp. v. Consumers Union of United States, Inc.*, 466 U.S. 485 (1984). Because this principle applies not only to affirmative suppression of speech, but also to disqualification for government favors, Congress is generally not permitted to pivot discrimination against otherwise protected speech on the offensiveness or unacceptability of the views it expresses. See, e.g., *Rosenberger v. Rector and Visitors of Univ. of Va.*, 515 U.S. 819 (1995) (public university's student activities funds may not be disbursed on viewpoint-based terms); *Lamb's Chapel v. Center Moriches Union Free School Dist.*, 508 U.S. 384 (1993) (after-hours access to public school property may not be withheld on the basis of viewpoint); *Leathers v. Medlock*, 499 U.S. 439 (1991) ("Differential taxation of First Amendment speakers is constitutionally suspect when it threatens to suppress the expression of particular ideas or viewpoints"); *Pacific Gas & Elec. Co. v. Public Util. Comm'n of Cal.*, 475 U.S. 1 (1986) (government-mandated access to public utility's billing envelopes must not be viewpoint based); *Members of City Council of Los Angeles v. Taxpayers for Vincent*, 466 U.S. 789 (1984) ("The First Amendment forbids the government to regulate speech in ways that favor some viewpoints or ideas at the expense of others").

It goes without saying that artistic expression lies within this First Amendment protection. The constitutional protection of artistic works turns not on the political significance that may be attributable to such productions, though they may indeed comment on the political, but simply on their expressive character, which falls within a spectrum of protected "speech" extending outward from the core of overtly political declarations. Put differently, art is entitled to full protection because our "cultural life," just like our native politics, "rests upon [the] ideal" of governmental viewpoint neutrality. *Turner Broadcasting System, Inc. v. FCC*, 512 U.S. 622 (1994).

When called upon to vindicate this ideal, we characteristically begin by asking "whether the government has adopted a regulation of speech because of disagreement with the message it conveys. The government's purpose is the controlling consideration." *Ward v. Rock Against Racism*, [491 U.S. 781 (1989)]. The answer in this case is damning. One need do nothing more than read the text of the statute to conclude that Congress's purpose in imposing the decency and respect criteria was to prevent the funding of art that conveys an offensive message; the decency and respect provision on its face is quintessentially viewpoint based, and quotations from the Congressional Record merely confirm the obvious legislative purpose. In the words of a cosponsor of the bill that enacted the proviso, "works which deeply offend the sensibilities of significant portions of the public ought not to be supported with public funds." Another supporter of the bill observed that "the Endowment's support for artists like Robert Mapplethorpe and Andres Serrano has offended and angered many citizens," behooving "Congress . . . to listen to these complaints about the NEA and make sure that exhibits like [these] are not funded again."

In the face of such clear legislative purpose, so plainly expressed, the Court has its work cut out for it in seeking a constitutional reading of the statute.

The Court says, first, that because the phrase "general standards of decency and respect for the diverse beliefs and values of the American public" is imprecise and capable of multiple interpretations, "the considerations that the provision introduces, by their nature, do not engender the kind of directed viewpoint discrimination that would prompt this Court to invalidate a statute on its face." Unquestioned case law, however, is clearly to the contrary. . . .

Just as self-evidently, a statute disfavoring speech that fails to respect America's "diverse beliefs and values" is the very model of viewpoint discrimination; it penalizes any view disrespectful to any belief or value espoused by someone in the American populace. Boiled down to its practical essence, the limitation obviously means that art that disrespects the ideology, opinions, or convictions of a significant segment of the American public is to be disfavored, whereas art that reinforces those values is not. After all, the whole point of the proviso was to make sure that works like Serrano's ostensibly blasphemous portrayal of Jesus would not be funded, while a reverent treatment, conventionally respectful of Christian sensibilities, would not run afoul of the law. Nothing could be more viewpoint based than that. Cf. *Rosenberger.* . . .

Another alternative for avoiding unconstitutionality that the Court appears to regard with some favor is the Government's argument that the NEA may comply with Section 954(d) merely by populating the advisory panels that analyze grant applications with members of diverse backgrounds. Would that it were so easy; this asserted implementation of the law fails even to "reflect a plausible construction of the plain language of the statute." *Rust v. Sullivan.* . . .

A third try at avoiding constitutional problems is the Court's disclaimer of any constitutional issue here because "section 954(d)(1) adds 'considerations' to the grant-making process; it does not preclude awards to projects that might be deemed 'indecent' or 'disrespectful,' nor place conditions on grants, or even specify that those factors must be given any particular weight in reviewing an application." Since "Section 954(d)(1) admonishes the NEA merely to take 'decency and respect' into consideration," not to make funding decisions specifically on those grounds, the Court sees no constitutional difficulty.

That is not a fair reading. Just as the statute cannot be read as anything but viewpoint based, or as requiring nothing more than diverse review panels, it cannot be read as tolerating awards to spread indecency or disrespect, so long as the review panel, the National Counsel on the Arts, and the Chairperson have given some thought to the offending qualities and decided to underwrite them anyway. That, after all, is presumably just what prompted the congressional outrage in the first place, and there was nothing naive about the Representative who said he voted for the bill because it does "not tolerate wasting Federal funds for sexually explicit photographs [or] sacrilegious works." . . .

A second basic strand in the Court's treatment of today's question, and the heart of Justice SCALIA's, in effect assumes that whether or not the statute mandates viewpoint discrimination, there is no constitutional issue here because government art subsidies fall within a zone of activity free from First Amendment restraints. The Government calls attention to the roles of government-as-speaker and government-as-buyer, in which the government is of course entitled to engage in viewpoint discrimination: if the Food and Drug Administration launches an advertising campaign on the subject of smoking, it may condemn the habit without also having to show a cowboy taking a puff on the opposite page; and if the Secretary of Defense wishes to buy a portrait to decorate the Pentagon, he is free to prefer George Washington over George the Third.

The Government freely admits, however, that it neither speaks through the expression subsidized by the NEA, nor buys anything for itself with its NEA grants. . . . Accordingly, the Government would have us liberate government-as-patron from First Amendment strictures not by placing it squarely within the categories of government-as-buyer or government-as-speaker, but by recognizing a new category by analogy to those accepted ones. The analogy is, however, a very poor fit, and this patronage falls embarrassingly on the wrong side of the line between government-as-buyer and government-as-regulator-of-private-speech.

The division is reflected quite clearly in our precedents. Drawing on the notion of government-as-speaker, we held in *Rust v. Sullivan* that the Government was entitled to appropriate public funds for the promotion of particular choices among alternatives offered by health and social service providers (e.g., family planning with, and without, resort to abortion). When the government promotes a particular governmental program, "it is entitled to define the limits of that program," and to dictate the viewpoint expressed by speakers who are paid to participate in it. But we added the important qualifying language that "this is not to suggest that funding by the Government, even when coupled with the freedom of the fund recipients to speak outside the scope of the Government-funded project, is invariably sufficient to justify Government control over the content of expression." Indeed, outside of the contexts of government-as-buyer and government-as-speaker, we have held time and time again that Congress may not "discriminate invidiously in its subsidies in such a way as to aim at the suppression of . . . ideas." *Regan v. Taxation with Representation of Wash.*, 461 U.S. 540 (1983); *Hannegan v. Esquire, Inc.*, 327 U.S. 146 (1946) (the Postmaster General may not deny subsidies to certain periodicals on the ground that they are "morally improper and not for the public welfare and the public good").

Our most thorough statement of these principles is found in the recent case of *Rosenberger v. Rector and Visitors of Univ. of Va.*, which held that the University of Virginia could not discriminate on viewpoint in underwriting the speech of student-run publications. We recognized that the government may act on the basis of viewpoint "when the State is the speaker" or when the state "disburses public funds to private entities to convey a governmental message." But we explained that the government may not act on viewpoint when it "does not itself speak or subsidize transmittal of a message it favors but instead expends funds to encourage a diversity of views from private speakers." When the government acts as patron, subsidizing the expression of others, it may not prefer one lawfully stated view over another.

Rosenberger controls here. The NEA, like the student activities fund in *Rosenberger*, is a subsidy scheme created to encourage expression of a diversity of views from private speakers. Congress brought the NEA into being to help all Americans "achieve a better understanding of the past, a better analysis of the present, and a better view of the future." Section 951(3). The NEA's purpose is to "support new ideas" and "to help create and sustain . . . a climate encouraging freedom of thought, imagination, and inquiry." Given this congressional choice to sustain freedom of expression, *Rosenberger* teaches that the First Amendment forbids decisions based on viewpoint popularity. So long as Congress chooses to subsidize expressive endeavors at large, it has no business requiring the NEA to turn down funding applications of artists and exhibitors who devote their "freedom of thought, imagination, and inquiry" to defying our tastes, our beliefs, or our values. It may not use the NEA's purse to "suppress . . . dangerous ideas." *Regan v. Taxation with Representation of Wash.* . . .

Since the decency and respect proviso of Section 954(d)(1) is substantially overbroad and carries with it a significant power to chill artistic production and display, it should be struck down on its face. . . .

D. COMMERCIAL SPEECH

THE DEVELOPMENT OF LAW

Other Important Rulings on Commercial Speech
and the First Amendment

Case	Vote	Ruling
Glickman v. Wileman Brothers & Elliott, Inc., 117 S.Ct. 2130 (1997)	5:4	Upheld regulations pursuant to the Agricultural Marketing Agreement Act of 1937 requiring fruit producers to financially contribute toward generic advertising for fruit in certain markets.

Wileman Brothers & Elliott, Inc., challenged the constitutionality of that regulation as compelled speech in violation of the First Amendment's protection for commercial speech. In rejecting that claim, Justice Stevens distinguished *Abood v. Detroit Board of Education*, 431 U.S. 209 (1977), which held that public employees may be required to contribute to a public union's dues in support of activities related to collective bargaining, but not to support political activities unrelated to collective bargaining. Here, writing for the majority Justice Stevens observed that "requiring respondents to pay the assessments cannot be said to engender any crisis of conscience. None of the advertising in this record promotes any particular message other than encouraging consumers to buy California tree fruit. Neither the fact that respondents may prefer to foster that message independently in order to promote and distinguish their own products, nor the fact that they think more or less money should be spent fostering it, makes this case comparable to those in which an objection rested on political or ideological disagreement with the content of the message. The mere fact that objectors believe their money is not being well spent does not mean [that] they have a First Amendment complaint." *Ellis v. Railway Clerks*, 466 U.S. 435 (1984). Justice Souter filed a dissenting opinion, which was joined by Chief Justice Rehnquist and Justices Scalia and Thomas. Justice Thomas also filed a dissenting opinion.

F. REGULATING THE BROADCAST
AND CABLE MEDIA

Ending a five-year legal battle over the constitutionality of the Cable Television Consumer Protection and Competition Act of 1992, a bare majority of the Court upheld the law's requirement that cable companies "must carry" the signals of local broadcast stations. Attorneys for the cable industry had argued that the regulations effectively dictated what kinds of programs are carried and wrongly favored local broadcasters. As a result of the must-carry regulations, some cable systems dropped C-SPAN in favor of local broadcasters, and 3.5 million viewers have lost all or part of C-SPAN's network. In *Turner Broadcasting System, Inc. v. Federal Communications Commission*, 512 U.S. 622 (1994) (*Turner Broadcasting I*) (see Vol. 2, Ch. 5), the Court held for the first time that the First Amendment extends protection to the cable industry and requires heightened judicial review of regulations and restrictions on the industry. On that issue the justices were unanimous. But Justice Kennedy commanded only four other votes—those of Chief Justice Rehnquist and Justices Stevens, Blackmun, and Souter—on the central issue of the constitutionality of the must-carry provisions. On that issue a bare majority declined to strike down the regulations and remanded the case back to the lower court for reconsideration of the basis for the regulations. When a federal district court again upheld the must-carry requirements, Turner Broadcasting again appealed to the Supreme Court, in *Turner Broadcasting System, Inc. v. Federal Communications Commission*, 117 S.Ct. 1174 (1997) (*Turner Broadcasting II*).

Writing for a bare majority in *Turner Broadcasting II*, Justice Kennedy upheld the must-carry provisions. He was again joined by the chief justice and Justices Stevens and Souter, as well as by Justice Breyer, who replaced Justice Blackmun on the bench. With respect to the First Amendment challenge to the must-carry provisions, Justice Kennedy held that the provision was "content neutral" and therefore had to pass only an intermediate level of First Amendment scrutiny, namely, whether the provisions advanced an "important governmental interest" without burdening speech more than necessary. Turning to the economic theory advanced in *Turner Broadcasting I* as a justification for the must-carry provisions, Justice Kennedy held that it was reasonable for Congress to conclude that local broadcast stations needed special protection and that the Court should defer to Congress on the matter. In his words, "Congress has an independent interest in preserving a multiplicity of broadcasters to ensure that all households have access to information and entertainment on an equal footing with those who subscribe to cable."

The dissenters, however, took issue with the majority's standard of review and with its economic analysis. Joined by Justices Scalia, Thomas, and Ginsburg, Justice O'Connor accused the majority of "trivializ[ing] the First Amendment issue at stake" and rejected its deference to Congress's "highly dubious economic theory" for the regulations. As in *Turner Broadcasting I*, the dissenters contended that the Court should apply the strictest First Amendment scrutiny. But in *Turner Broadcasting II* the dissenters also countered that the must-carry provisions failed even the Court's lower intermediate test because the law rested in their view on bad economics, unproven assumptions, and inadequate attention to technological developments. The notion that the financial viability of the broadcast industry was at stake and threatened by cable monopolies was dismissed by Justice O'Connor as "entirely mythical." In addition, she observed that the "growing use of direct-broadcast satellite television also tends to undercut the notion that cable operators have an inevitable monopoly over video services entering cable households." Finally, Justice O'Connor rejected the majority's deference to Congress as "wholesale deference to judgments about rapidly changing technologies that are based on unquestionably outdated information."

In a broad endorsement of free speech on the Internet, the Court struck down provisions making it a crime to send or display "indecent" materials online in ways available to children in the Communications Decency Act of 1996. Although Chief Justice Rehnquist and Justice O'Connor dissented from part of the Court's ruling in *Reno v. American Civil Liberties Union* (excerpted below), the Court was unanimous in extending First Amendment principles to cyberspace and holding that the Internet is a unique medium unlike broadcast and cable communication.

Reno v. American Civil Liberties Union
117 S.Ct. 2329 (1997)

When enacting the Communications Decency Act of 1996 (CDA), Congress sought to protect minors from harmful material on the Internet. The law, among other things, in Section 223(a) criminalized the "knowing" transmission of "obscene or indecent" messages to any recipient under 18 years of age. Section 223(d) prohibited the "knowing" sending or displaying to a person under 18 of any message "that, in context, depicts or describes, in terms patently offensive as measured by contemporary community standards, sexual or excretory activities or organs." Affirmative defenses were provided for those who take "good faith, . . . effective . . . actions" to restrict access by minors to the prohibited communications (Section 223(e)(5)(A)), and those who restrict such access by requiring certain designated forms of age proof, such as a verified credit card or an adult identification number (Section 223(e)(5)(B)).

Following the law's enactment, the American Civil Liberties Union and a number of businesses and interest groups filed suit challenging the constitutionality of Sections 223(a)(1) and 223(d). Subsequently, a federal district court entered a preliminary injunction against enforcement of both challenged provisions and the government appealed to the Supreme Court.

The Court's decision was seven to two and its opinion delivered by Justice Stevens. Justice O'Connor filed an opinion concurring in the judgment in part and dissenting in part, which Chief Justice Rehnquist joined.

Justice STEVENS delivered the opinion of the Court.

At issue is the constitutionality of two statutory provisions enacted to protect minors from "indecent" and "patently offensive" communications on the Internet. Notwithstanding the legitimacy and importance of the congressional goal of protecting children from harmful materials, we agree with the three-judge District Court that the statute abridges "the freedom of speech" protected by the First Amendment.

The Internet is an international network of interconnected computers. It is the outgrowth of what began in 1969 as a military program called "ARPANET," which was designed to enable computers operated by the military, defense contractors, and universities conducting defense-related research to communicate with one another by redundant channels even if some portions of the network were damaged in a war. While the ARPANET no longer exists, it provided an example for the development of a number of civilian networks that, eventually linking with each other, now enable tens of millions of people to communicate with one another and to access vast amounts of information from around the world. The Internet is "a unique and wholly new medium of worldwide human communication." . . .

Sexually explicit material on the Internet includes text, pictures, and chat and "extends from the modestly titillating to the hardest-core." These files are created, named, and posted in the same manner as material that is not sexually explicit, and may be accessed either deliberately or unintentionally during the course of an imprecise search. "Once a provider posts its content on the Internet, it cannot prevent that content from entering any community." Some of the communications over the Internet that originate in foreign countries are also sexually explicit.

Though such material is widely available, users seldom encounter such content accidentally. "A document's title or a description of the document will usually appear before the document itself . . . and in many cases the user will receive detailed information about a site's content before he or she need take the step to access the document. Almost all sexually explicit images are preceded by warnings as to the content." For that reason, the "odds are slim" that a user would enter a sexually explicit site by accident. Unlike communications received by radio or television, "the receipt of information on the Internet requires a series of affirmative steps more deliberate and directed than merely turning a dial. A child requires some sophistication and some ability to read to retrieve material and thereby to use the Internet unattended."

Systems have been developed to help parents control the material that may be available on a home computer with Internet access. A system may either limit a computer's access to an approved list of sources that have been identified as containing no adult material, it may block designated inappropriate sites, or it may attempt to block messages containing identifiable objectionable features. "Although parental control software currently can screen for certain suggestive words or for known sexually explicit sites, it cannot now screen for sexually explicit images." Nevertheless, the evidence indicates that "a reasonably effective method by which parents can prevent their children from accessing sexually explicit and other material which parents may believe is inappropriate for their children will soon be available."

The problem of age verification differs for different uses of the Internet. The District Court categorically determined that there "is no effective way to determine the identity or the age of a user who is accessing material through e-mail, mail explorers, newsgroups or chat rooms." The Government offered no evidence that there was a reliable way to screen recipients and participants in such fora for age. Moreover, even if it were technologically feasible to block minors' access to newsgroups and chat rooms containing discussions of art, politics or other subjects that potentially elicit "indecent" or "patently offensive" contributions, it would not be possible to block their access to that material and "still allow them access to the remaining content, even if the overwhelming majority of that content was not indecent."

Technology exists by which an operator of a Web site may condition access on the verification of requested information such as a credit card number or an adult password. Credit card verification is only feasible, however, either in connection with a commercial transaction in which the card is used, or by payment to a verification agency. Using credit card possession as a surrogate for proof of age would impose costs on non-commercial Web sites that would require many of them to shut down. For that reason, at the time of the trial, credit card verification was "effectively unavailable to a substantial number of Internet content providers." Moreover, the imposition of such a requirement "would completely bar adults who do not have a credit card and lack the resources to obtain one from accessing any blocked material." . . .

In arguing for reversal, the Government contends that the CDA is plainly constitutional under three of our prior decisions: (1) *Ginsberg v. New York*, 390 U.S. 629 (1968); (2) *FCC v. Pacifica Foundation*, 438 U.S. 726 (1978); and (3) *Renton v. Playtime Theatres, Inc.*, 475 U.S. 41 (1986). A close look at these cases, however, raises—rather than relieves—doubts concerning the constitutionality of the CDA.

In *Ginsberg*, we upheld the constitutionality of a New York statute that prohibited selling to minors under 17 years of age material that was considered obscene as to them even if not obscene as to adults. We rejected the defendant's broad submission that "the scope of the constitutional freedom of expression secured to a citizen to read or see material concerned with sex cannot be made to depend on whether the citizen is an adult or a minor." In four important respects, the statute upheld in *Ginsberg* was narrower than the CDA. First, we noted in *Ginsberg* that "the prohibition against sales to minors does not bar parents who so desire from purchasing the magazines for their children." Under the CDA, by contrast, neither the parents' consent—nor even their participation—in the communication would avoid the application of the statute. Second, the New York statute applied only to commercial transactions, whereas the CDA contains no such limitation. Third, the New York statute cabined its definition of material that is harmful to minors with the requirement that it be "utterly without redeeming social importance for minors." The CDA fails to provide us with any definition of the term "indecent" as used in Section 223(a)(1) and, importantly, omits any requirement that the "patently offensive" material covered by Section 223(d) lack serious literary, artistic, political, or scientific value. Fourth, the New York statute defined a minor as a person under the age of 17, whereas the CDA, in applying to all those under 18 years, includes an additional year of those nearest majority.

In *Pacifica*, we upheld a declaratory order of the Federal Communications Commission, holding that the broadcast of a recording of a 12-minute monologue entitled "Filthy Words" that had previously been delivered to a live audience "could have been the subject of administrative sanctions." The Commission had found that the repetitive use of certain words referring to excretory or sexual activities or organs "in an afternoon broadcast when children are in the audience was patently offensive" and concluded that the monologue was indecent "as broadcast." The respondent did not quarrel with the finding that the afternoon broadcast was patently offensive, but contended that it was not "indecent" within the meaning of the relevant statutes because it contained no prurient appeal. After rejecting respondent's statutory arguments, we confronted its two constitutional arguments: (1) that the Commission's construction of its authority to ban indecent speech was so broad that its order had to be set aside even if the broadcast at issue was unprotected; and (2) that since the recording was not obscene, the First Amendment forbade any abridgment of the right to broadcast it on the radio.

In the portion of the lead opinion not joined by Justices POWELL and BLACKMUN, the plurality stated that the First Amendment does not prohibit all governmental regulation that depends on the content of speech. Accordingly, the availability of constitutional protection for a vulgar and offensive monologue that was not obscene depended on the context of the broadcast. Relying on the premise that "of all forms of communication" broadcasting had received the most limited First Amendment protection, the Court concluded that the ease with which children may obtain access to broadcasts, "coupled with the concerns recognized in *Ginsberg*," justified special treatment of indecent broadcasting.

As with the New York statute at issue in *Ginsberg*, there are significant differences between the order upheld in *Pacifica* and the CDA. First, the order in *Pacifica*, issued by an agency that had been regulating radio stations for decades, targeted a specific broadcast that represented a rather dramatic departure from traditional program content in order to designate when—rather than whether—it would be permissible to air such a program in that particular medium. The CDA's broad categorical prohibitions are not limited to particular times and are not dependent on any evaluation by an agency familiar with the unique characteristics of the Internet. Second, unlike the CDA, the Commission's declaratory order was not punitive; we expressly refused to decide whether the indecent broadcast "would justify a criminal prosecution." Finally, the Commission's order applied to a medium which as a matter of history had "received the most limited First Amendment protection" in large part because warnings could not adequately protect the listener from unexpected program content. The Internet, however, has no comparable history.

In *Renton*, we upheld a zoning ordinance that kept adult movie theatres out of residential neighborhoods. The ordinance was aimed, not at the content of the films shown in the theaters, but rather at the "secondary effects"—such as crime and deteriorating property values—that these theaters fostered: "'It is the secondary effect which these zoning ordinances attempt to avoid, not the dissemination of "offensive" speech.'" According to the Government, the CDA is constitutional because it constitutes a sort of "cyberzoning" on the Internet. But the CDA applies broadly to the entire universe of cyberspace. And the purpose of the CDA is to protect children from the primary effects of "indecent" and "patently offensive" speech, rather than any "secondary" effect of such speech. Thus, the CDA is a content-based blanket restriction on speech, and, as such, cannot be "properly analyzed as a form of time, place, and manner regulation."

These precedents, then, surely do not require us to uphold the CDA and are fully consistent with the application of the most stringent review of its provisions.

In *Southern Promotions, Ltd. v. Conrad*, 420 U.S. 546 (1975), we observed that "each medium of expression . . . may present its own problems." Thus, some of our cases have recognized special justifications for regulation of the broadcast media that are not applicable to other speakers, see *Red Lion Broadcasting Co.*

v. FCC, 395 U.S. 367 (1969); *FCC v. Pacifica Foundation*, 438 U.S. 726 (1978). In these cases, the Court relied on the history of extensive government regulation of the broadcast medium; the scarcity of available frequencies at its inception; and its "invasive" nature.

Those factors are not present in cyberspace. Neither before nor after the enactment of the CDA have the vast democratic fora of the Internet been subject to the type of government supervision and regulation that has attended the broadcast industry. Moreover, the Internet is not as "invasive" as radio or television. The District Court specifically found that "communications over the Internet do not 'invade' an individual's home or appear on one's computer screen unbidden. Users seldom encounter content 'by accident.'" It also found that "almost all sexually explicit images are preceded by warnings as to the content," and cited testimony that "'odds are slim' that a user would come across a sexually explicit sight by accident." . . .

Regardless of whether the CDA is so vague that it violates the Fifth Amendment, the many ambiguities concerning the scope of its coverage render it problematic for purposes of the First Amendment. For instance, each of the two parts of the CDA uses a different linguistic form. The first uses the word "indecent," while the second speaks of material that "in context, depicts or describes, in terms patently offensive as measured by contemporary community standards, sexual or excretory activities or organs." Given the absence of a definition of either term, this difference in language will provoke uncertainty among speakers about how the two standards relate to each other and just what they mean. Could a speaker confidently assume that a serious discussion about birth control practices, homosexuality, the First Amendment issues raised by the Appendix to our *Pacifica* opinion, or the consequences of prison rape would not violate the CDA? This uncertainty undermines the likelihood that the CDA has been carefully tailored to the congressional goal of protecting minors from potentially harmful materials.

The vagueness of the CDA is a matter of special concern for two reasons. First, the CDA is a content-based regulation of speech. The vagueness of such a regulation raises special First Amendment concerns because of its obvious chilling effect on free speech. Second, the CDA is a criminal statute. In addition to the opprobrium and stigma of a criminal conviction, the CDA threatens violators with penalties including up to two years in prison for each act of violation. The severity of criminal sanctions may well cause speakers to remain silent rather than communicate even arguably unlawful words, ideas, and images. . . .

We are persuaded that the CDA lacks the precision that the First Amendment requires when a statute regulates the content of speech. In order to deny minors access to potentially harmful speech, the CDA effectively suppresses a large amount of speech that adults have a constitutional right to receive and to address to one another. That burden on adult speech is unacceptable if less restrictive alternatives would be at least as effective in achieving the legitimate purpose that the statute was enacted to serve.

In evaluating the free speech rights of adults, we have made it perfectly clear that "sexual expression which is indecent but not obscene is protected by the First Amendment." *Sable [Communications v. Federal Communications Commission*, 492 U.S. 115 (1989)]. Indeed, *Pacifica* itself admonished that "the fact that society may find speech offensive is not a sufficient reason for suppressing it."

It is true that we have repeatedly recognized the governmental interest in protecting children from harmful materials. But that interest does not justify an unnecessarily broad suppression of speech addressed to adults. As we have explained, the Government may not "reduce the adult population . . . to . . . only what is fit for children." "Regardless of the strength of the government's interest" in protecting children, "the level of discourse reaching a mailbox simply cannot be limited to that which would be suitable for a sandbox." *Bolger v. Youngs Drug Products Corp.*, 463 U.S. 60 (1983).

In arguing that the CDA does not so diminish adult communication, the Government relies on the incorrect factual premise that prohibiting a transmission whenever it is known that one of its recipients is a minor would not interfere with adult-to-adult communication. The findings of the District Court make clear that this premise is untenable. Given the size of the potential audience for most messages, in the absence of a viable age verification process, the sender must be charged with knowing that one or more minors will likely view it. Knowledge that, for instance, one or more members of a 100-person chat group will be minor—and therefore that it would be a crime to send the group an indecent message—would surely burden communication among adults. . . .

For the purposes of our decision, we need neither accept nor reject the Government's submission that the First Amendment does not forbid a blanket prohibition on all "indecent" and "patently offensive" messages communicated to a 17-year-old—no matter how much value the message may contain and regardless of parental approval. It is at least clear that the strength of the Government's interest in protecting minors is not equally strong throughout the coverage of this broad statute. Under the CDA, a parent allowing her 17-year-old to use the family computer to obtain information on the Internet that she, in her parental judgment, deems appropriate could face a lengthy prison term. Similarly, a parent who sent his 17-year-old college freshman [child] information on birth control via e-mail could be incarcerated even though neither he, his child, nor anyone in their home community, found the material "indecent" or "patently offensive," if the college town's community thought otherwise.

The breadth of this content-based restriction of speech imposes an especially heavy burden on the Government to explain why a less restrictive provision would not be as effective as the CDA. It has not done so. The arguments in this Court have referred to possible alternatives such as requiring that indecent material be "tagged" in a way that facilitates parental control of material coming into their homes, making exceptions for messages with artistic or educational value, providing some tolerance for parental choice, and regulating some portions of the Internet—such as commercial Web sites—differently than others, such as chat rooms. Particularly in the light of the absence of any detailed findings by the Congress, or even hearings addressing the special problems of the CDA, we are persuaded that the CDA is not narrowly tailored if that requirement has any meaning at all. . . .

In this Court, though not in the District Court, the Government asserts that—in addition to its interest in protecting children—its "equally significant" interest in fostering the growth of the Internet provides an independent basis for upholding the constitutionality of the CDA. The Government apparently assumes that the unregulated availability of "indecent" and "patently offensive" material on the Internet is driving countless citizens away from the medium because of the risk of exposing themselves or their children to harmful material.

We find this argument singularly unpersuasive. The dramatic expansion of this new marketplace of ideas contradicts the factual basis of this contention. The record demonstrates that the growth of the Internet has been and continues to be phenomenal. As a matter of constitutional tradition, in the absence of evidence to the contrary, we presume that governmental regulation of the content of speech is more likely to interfere with the free exchange of ideas than to encourage it. The interest in encouraging freedom of expression in a democratic society outweighs any theoretical but unproven benefit of censorship.

For the foregoing reasons, the judgment of the district court is affirmed.

Justice O'CONNOR, with whom the CHIEF JUSTICE joins, concurring in the judgment in part and dissenting in part.

I write separately to explain why I view the Communications Decency Act of 1996 (CDA) as little more than an attempt by Congress to create "adult zones" on the Internet. Our precedent indicates that the creation of such zones can be constitutionally sound. Despite the soundness of its purpose, however, portions of the CDA are unconstitutional because they stray from the blueprint our prior cases have developed for constructing a "zoning law" that passes constitutional muster. . . .

The Court in *Ginsberg* concluded that the New York law created a constitutionally adequate adult zone simply because, on its face, it denied access only to minors. The Court did not question—and therefore necessarily assumed—that an adult zone, once created, would succeed in preserving adults' access while denying minors' access to the regulated speech. Before today, there was no reason to question this assumption, for the Court has previously only considered laws that operated in the physical world, a world with two characteristics that make it possible to create "adult zones": geography and identity. A minor can see an adult dance show only if he enters an establishment that provides such entertainment. And should he attempt to do so, the minor will not be able to conceal completely his identity (or, consequently, his age). Thus, the twin characteristics of geography and identity enable the establishment's proprietor to prevent children from entering the establishment, but to let adults inside.

The electronic world is fundamentally different. Because it is no more than the interconnection of electronic pathways, cyberspace allows speakers and listeners to mask their identities. Cyberspace undeniably reflects some form of geography; chat rooms and Web sites, for example, exist at fixed "locations" on the Internet. Since users can transmit and receive messages on the Internet without revealing anything about their identities or ages, however, it is not currently possible to exclude persons from accessing certain messages on the basis of their identity.

Cyberspace differs from the physical world in another basic way: Cyberspace is malleable. Thus, it is possible to construct barriers in cyberspace and use them to screen for identity, making cyberspace more like the physical world and, consequently, more amenable to zoning laws. This transformation of cyberspace is already underway. Internet speakers (users who post material on the Internet) have begun to zone cyberspace itself through the use of "gateway" technology. Such technology requires Internet users to enter information about themselves—perhaps an adult identification number or a credit card number—before they can access certain areas of cyberspace much like a bouncer checks a person's driver's license before admitting him to a nightclub. Internet users who access information have not attempted to zone cyberspace itself, but have tried to limit their own power to access information in cyberspace, much as a parent controls what her children watch on television by installing a lock box. This user-based zoning is accomplished through the use of screening software (such as Cyber Patrol or SurfWatch) or browsers with screening capabilities, both of which search addresses and text for keywords that are associated with "adult" sites and, if the user wishes, blocks access to such sites. The Platform for Internet Content Selection (PICS) project is designed to facilitate user-based zoning by encouraging Internet speakers to rate the content of their speech using codes recognized by all screening programs. . . .

Although the prospects for the eventual zoning of the Internet appear promising, I agree with the Court that we must evaluate the constitutionality of the CDA as it applies to the Internet as it exists today. Given the present state of cyberspace, I agree with the Court that the "display" provision cannot pass muster. Until gateway technology is available throughout cyberspace, and it is not in 1997, a speaker cannot be reasonably assured that the speech he displays will reach only adults because it is impossible to confine speech to an "adult zone." Thus, the only way for a speaker to avoid liability under the CDA is to refrain completely from using indecent speech. But this forced silence impinges on the First Amendment right of adults to make and obtain this speech and, for all intents and purposes, "reduces the adult population [on the Internet] to reading only what is fit for children." *Butler* [*v. Michigan*, 352 U.S. 380 (1957)]. As a result, the "display" provision cannot withstand scrutiny.

The "indecency transmission" and "specific person" provisions present a closer issue, for they are not unconstitutional in all of their applications. As discussed above, the "indecency transmission" provision makes it a crime to transmit knowingly an indecent message to a person the sender knows is under 18 years of age. The "specific person" provision proscribes the same conduct, although it does not as explicitly require the sender to know that the intended recipient of his indecent message is a minor. Appellant urges the Court to construe the provision to impose such a knowledge requirement and I would do so.

So construed, both provisions are constitutional as applied to a conversation involving only an adult and one or more minors—e.g., when an adult speaker sends an e-mail knowing the addressee is a minor, or when an adult and minor converse by themselves or with other minors in a chat room. In this context, these provisions are no different from the law we sustained in *Ginsberg*. Restricting what the adult may say to the minors in no way restricts the adult's ability to communicate with other adults. He is not prevented from speaking indecently to other adults in a chat room (because there are no other adults participating in the conversation) and he remains free to send indecent e-mails to other adults. The relevant universe contains only one adult, and the adult in that universe has the power to refrain from using indecent speech and consequently to keep all such speech within the room in an "adult" zone.

The analogy to *Ginsberg* breaks down, however, when more than one adult is a party to the conversation. If a minor enters a chat room otherwise occupied by adults, the CDA effectively requires the adults in the room to stop using indecent speech. If they did not, they could be prosecuted under the "indecency transmission" and "specific person" provisions for any indecent statements they make to the group, since they would be transmitting an indecent message to specific persons, one of whom is a minor. The CDA is therefore akin to a law that makes it a crime for a bookstore owner to sell pornographic magazines to anyone once a minor enters his store. Even assuming such a law might be constitutional in the physical world as a reasonable alternative to excluding minors completely from the store, the absence of any means of excluding minors from chat rooms in cyberspace restricts the rights of adults to engage in indecent speech in those rooms. The "indecency transmission" and "specific person" provisions share this defect.

But these two provisions do not infringe on adults' speech in all situations. I do not find that the provisions are overbroad in the sense that they restrict minors' access to a substantial amount of speech that minors have the right to read and view. Accordingly, the CDA can be applied constitutionally in some situations. . . .

[T]he constitutionality of the CDA as a zoning law hinges on the extent to which it substantially interferes with the First Amendment rights of adults. Because the rights of adults are infringed only by the "display" provision and by the "indecency transmission" and "specific person" provisions as applied to communications involving more than one adult, I would invalidate the CDA only to that extent. Insofar as the "indecency transmission" and "specific person" provisions prohibit the use of indecent speech in communications between an adult and one or more minors, however, they can and should be sustained. The Court reaches a contrary conclusion, and from that holding that I respectfully dissent.

H. SYMBOLIC SPEECH AND SPEECH-PLUS-CONDUCT

The First Amendment's protection for anti-abortion protesters has been a major source of litigation and controversy in the 1990s. In *Madsen v. Women's Health Center*, 115 S.Ct. 2338 (1995) (see Vol. 2, Ch. 5), the Rehnquist Court upheld a thirty-six-foot buffer zone around an abortion clinic, but rejected as unconstitutional a three-hundred-foot no-approach zone around the clinic. Approximately one-third of the 900 abortion clinics in the country are protected by court-ordered buffer zones. In *Schenck v. Pro-Choice Network of Western New York*, 117 S.Ct. 855 (1997), the Court revisited the matter and the application of *Madsen* to limitations on the activities of anti-abortion protesters. Here, by a six-to-three vote the Court upheld a lower court's creation of a "fifteen-foot fixed buffer zone" around doorways and parking lot entrances, but also permitting two anti-abortion counselors to enter the zone at any one time. By an eight-to-one vote, the Court struck down "floating buffer zones" around anyone entering or leaving abortion clinics as a violation of the First Amendment.

THE DEVELOPMENT OF LAW

Places That Have Been Held Not to Be Public Forums

Arkansas Educational Television Commission v. Forbes, 118 S.Ct. 1633 (1998)

Public televisions may exclude "marginal" candidates from televised debates of major candidates for political office. In refusing to extend the concept of a "public forum" to such debates, Justice Kennedy ruled that the televised debate was a "nonpublic forum" and that the decision to exclude Forbes, an independent candidate, was under the circumstances a reasonable, viewpoint-neutral exercise of journalistic discretion consistent with the First Amendment. Justices Stevens, Ginsburg, and Souter dissented.

6

FREEDOM FROM AND
OF RELIGION

A. THE (DIS)ESTABLISHMENT OF RELIGION

In the early 1990s the Rehnquist Court handed down a number of rulings on the (dis)establishment clause and a number of justices called for overturning the three-prong test, set forth in *Lemon v. Kurtzman*, 403 U.S. 603 (1971) (see Vol. 2, Ch. 6), for determining whether states and localities run afoul of the First Amendment. In *Lee v. Weisman*, 505 U.S. 577 (1992) (see Vol. 2, Ch. 6), however, a bare majority declined to overturn *Lemon* and held unconstitutional a faculty-organized invocation and benediction at a junior high school graduation ceremony. That ruling renewed the controversy over the Court's earlier decisions forbidding the opening of classes with prayers and readings from the Bible. In response, at graduation ceremonies around the country a number of students voluntarily recited prayers. In 1994, Mississippi also enacted a law authorizing student-led prayers at all school events. But when that law was challenged, a federal district court and the Court of Appeals for the Fifth Circuit held that the law was unconstitutional because it fostered state involvement in school prayer, since teachers would help decide where and when the prayers would take place; the district court, though, ruled that voluntary student-led prayers at graduation were permissible. When the appellate court's decision was appealed, in *Moore v. Ingrebretsen*, 117 S.Ct. 388 (1996), the Court declined to revisit the controversy and denied review.

The Court also declined to abandon the *Lemon* test in *Agostini v. Felton* (excerpted below). However, a bare majority overruled two earlier decisions, *Aguilar v. Felton*, 473 U.S. 402 (1985), and its companion case, *School District of Grand Rapids v. Ball*, 473 U.S. 373 (1985), in an opinion delivered by Justice O'Connor, who has criticized *Lemon* but relied on it in *Agostini*. In dissent, Justice Souter sharply criticized the majority's analysis and reversal of those precedents, while Justice Ginsburg challenged the propriety of the majority's activism in reaching out to overturn those decisions; Justices Breyer and Stevens joined each of their dissents.

Agostini v. Felton
117 S.Ct. 1997 (1997)

In *Aguilar v. Felton*, 473 U.S. 402 (1985), the Burger Court held that New York City's program, pursuant to Title I of the Elementary and Secondary Education Act of 1965, of sending public school teachers into parochial schools to provide remedial education to disadvantaged children constituted an excessive entanglement of government with religion in violation of the First Amendment's Establishment Clause. On remand, the district court entered a permanent injunction reflecting that ruling. As a result, instead of sending teachers onto parochial school grounds, teachers and mobile classrooms were sent to the schools, parked on the streets, and children were brought to the vans for remedial instruction. A decade later, the Board of Education of the City of New York and a group of parents of parochial school children filed motions in the district court seeking relief from the injunction's operation under Federal Rule of Civil Procedure 60(b)(5). They emphasized the significant costs, approximately $6 million a year, of complying with *Aguilar*. They also contended that *Aguilar* was no longer good law because, in *Board of Education of Kiryas Joel Village School District v. Grumet*, 512 U.S. 687 (1994) (see Vol. 2, Ch. 6), five justices on the Rehnquist Court indicated that *Aguilar* should be reconsidered. The district court denied the motion, declaring that *Aguilar*'s demise has "not yet occurred," and an appellate court agreed. Subsequently, the Supreme Court granted a petition for *certiorari* and the Clinton administration filed a friend-of-the-court brief, contending that "hundreds of millions of dollars . . . which otherwise could have been used for instructional services have been spent on administrative costs made necessary only because of the need to comply" with the Court's 1985 ruling.

The Court's decision was five to four and its opinion announced by Justice O'Connor. Justices Souter and Ginsburg filed dissenting opinions, which were joined by Justices Stevens and Breyer.

Justice O'CONNOR delivered the opinion of the Court.

Petitioners maintain that *Aguilar v. Felton*, 473 U.S. 402 (1985), cannot be squared with our intervening Establishment Clause jurisprudence and ask that we explicitly recognize what our more recent cases already dictate: *Aguilar* is no longer good law. We agree with petitioners that *Aguilar* is not consistent with our subsequent Establishment Clause decisions and further conclude that, on the facts presented here, petitioners are entitled under Federal Rule of Civil Procedure 60(b)(5) to relief from the operation of the District Court's prospective injunction. . . .

In *Rufo v. Inmates of Suffolk County Jail*, 502 U.S. 367 (1992), we held that it is appropriate to grant a Rule 60(b)(5) motion when the party seeking relief from an injunction or consent decree can show "a significant change either in factual conditions or in law." A court may recognize subsequent changes in either statutory or decisional law. A court errs when it refuses to modify an injunction or consent decree in light of such changes.

Petitioners point to three changes in the factual and legal landscape that they believe justify their claim for relief under Rule 60(b)(5). They first contend that the exorbitant costs of complying with the District Court's injunction constitute a significant factual development warranting modification of the injunction. Petitioners also argue that there have been two significant legal developments since *Aguilar* was decided: a majority of Justices have expressed their views that *Aguilar* should be reconsidered or overruled; and *Aguilar* has in any event been undermined by subsequent Establishment Clause decisions, including *Witters v. Washington Dept. of Servs. for Blind*, 474 U.S. 481 (1986), *Zobrest v. Catalina Foothills School Dist.*, 509 U.S. 1 (1993), and *Rosenberger v. Rector and Visitors of Univ. of Va.*, [515 U.S. 819] (1995).

Respondents counter that, because the costs of providing Title I services off-site were known at the time *Aguilar* was decided, and because the relevant case law has not changed, the District Court did not err in denying petitioners' motions. Obviously, if neither the law supporting our original decision in this litigation nor the facts have changed, there would be no need to decide the propriety of a Rule 60(b)(5) motion. Accordingly, we turn to the threshold issue whether the factual or legal landscape has changed since we decided *Aguilar*.

We agree with respondents that petitioners have failed to establish the significant change in factual conditions required by *Rufo*. . . . We also agree with respondents that the statements made by five Justices [Chief Justice REHNQUIST and Justices O'CONNOR, KENNEDY, SCALIA, and THOMAS] in *Kiryas Joel* do not, in themselves, furnish a basis for concluding that our Establishment Clause jurisprudence has changed. . . .

In light of these conclusions, petitioners' ability to satisfy the prerequisites of Rule 60(b)(5) hinges on whether our later Establishment Clause cases have so undermined *Aguilar* that it is no longer good law. We now turn to that inquiry.

In order to evaluate whether *Aguilar* has been eroded by our subsequent Establishment Clause cases, it is necessary to understand the rationale upon which *Aguilar*, as well as its companion case, *School Dist. of Grand Rapids v. Ball*, 473 U.S. 373 (1985), rested.

In *Ball*, the Court evaluated two programs implemented by the School District of Grand Rapids, Michigan. The district's Shared Time program, the one most analogous to Title I, provided remedial and "enrichment" classes, at public expense, to students attending nonpublic schools. The classes were taught during regular school hours by publicly employed teachers, using materials purchased with public funds, on the premises of nonpublic schools.

The Court conducted its analysis by applying the three-part test set forth in *Lemon v. Kurtzman*, 403 U.S. 602 (1971): "First, the statute must have a secular legislative purpose; second, its principal or primary effect must be one that neither advances nor inhibits religion; finally, the statute must not foster an excessive government entanglement with religion." The Court acknowledged that the Shared Time program served a purely secular purpose, thereby satisfying the first part of the so-called *Lemon* test. Nevertheless, it ultimately concluded that the program had the impermissible effect of advancing religion.

The Court found that the program violated the Establishment Clause's prohibition against "government-financed or government-sponsored indoctrination into the beliefs of a particular religious faith" in at least three ways. . . .

Distilled to essentials, the Court's conclusion that the Shared Time program in *Ball* had the impermissible effect of advancing religion rested on three assumptions: (i) any public employee who works on the premises of a religious school is presumed to inculcate religion in her work; (ii) the presence of public employees on private school premises creates a symbolic union between church and state; and (iii) any and all public aid that directly aids the educational function of religious schools impermissibly finances religious indoctrination, even if the aid reaches such schools as a consequence of private decisionmaking. Additionally, in *Aguilar* there was a fourth assumption: that New York City's Title I program necessitated an excessive government entanglement with religion because public employees who teach on the premises of religious schools must be closely monitored to ensure that they do not inculcate religion.

Our more recent cases have undermined the assumptions upon which *Ball* and *Aguilar* relied. To be sure, the general principles we use to evaluate whether government aid violates the Establishment Clause have not changed since *Aguilar* was decided. For example, we continue to ask whether the government acted with the purpose of advancing or inhibiting religion, and the nature of that inquiry has remained largely unchanged. Likewise, we continue to explore whether the aid has the "effect" of advancing or inhibiting religion. What has changed since we decided *Ball* and *Aguilar* is our understanding of the criteria used to assess whether aid to religion has an impermissible effect.

As we have repeatedly recognized, government inculcation of religious beliefs has the impermissible effect of advancing religion. Our cases subsequent to *Aguilar* have, however, modified in two significant respects the approach we use to assess indoctrination. First, we have abandoned the presumption erected in *Meek* [*v. Pittenger*, 421 U.S. 349 (1975)] and *Ball* that the placement of public employees on parochial school grounds inevitably results in the impermissible effect of state-sponsored indoctrination or constitutes a symbolic union between government and religion. In *Zobrest v. Catalina Foothills School Dist.*, 509 U.S. 1 (1993), we examined whether the IDEA [Individuals with Disabilities Education Act] was constitutional as applied to a deaf student who sought to bring his state-employed sign-language interpreter with him to his Roman Catholic high school. We held that this was permissible, expressly disavowing the notion that "the Establishment Clause [laid] down [an] absolute bar to the placing of a public employee in a sectarian school." . . . *Zobrest* therefore expressly rejected the notion—relied on in *Ball* and *Aguilar*—that, solely because of her presence on private school property, a public employee will be presumed to inculcate religion in the students. *Zobrest* also implicitly repudiated another assumption on which *Ball* and *Aguilar* turned: that the presence of a public employee on private school property creates an impermissible "symbolic link" between government and religion.

Justice SOUTER contends that *Zobrest* did not undermine the "presumption of inculcation" erected in *Ball* and *Aguilar*, and that our conclusion to the contrary rests on a "mistaken reading" of *Zobrest*. . . . In *Zobrest*, however, we did not expressly or implicitly rely upon the basis Justice SOUTER now advances for distinguishing *Ball* and *Aguilar*. . . . The signer in *Zobrest* had the same opportunity to inculcate religion in the performance of her duties as do Title I employees, and there is no genuine basis upon which to confine *Zobrest*'s underlying rationale—that public employees will not be presumed to inculcate religion—to sign-language interpreters. Indeed, even the *Zobrest* dissenters acknowledged the shift *Zobrest* effected in our Establishment Clause law when they criticized the majority for "straying . . . from the course set by nearly five decades of Establishment Clause jurisprudence." (BLACKMUN, J., dissenting). Thus, it was *Zobrest*—and not this case—that created "fresh law."

Second, we have departed from the rule relied on in *Ball* that all government aid that directly aids the educational function of religious schools is invalid. In *Witters v. Washington Dept. of Servs. for Blind*, 474 U.S. 481 (1986), we held that the Establishment Clause did not bar a State from issuing a vocational tuition grant to a blind person who wished to use the grant to attend a Christian college and become a pastor, missionary, or youth director. Even though the grant recipient clearly would use the money to obtain religious education, we observed that the tuition grants were "'made available generally without regard to the sectarian–nonsectarian, or public–nonpublic nature of the institution benefited.'" . . .

Zobrest and *Witters* make clear that, under current law, the Shared Time program in *Ball* and New York City's Title I program in *Aguilar* will not, as a matter of law, be deemed to have the effect of advancing religion through indoctrination. Indeed, each of the premises upon which we relied in *Ball* to reach a contrary conclusion is no longer valid. First, there is no reason to presume that, simply because she enters a parochial school classroom, a full-time public employee such as a Title I teacher will depart from her assigned duties and instructions and embark on religious indoctrination, any more than there was a reason in *Zobrest* to think an interpreter would inculcate religion by altering her translation of classroom lectures. Certainly, no evidence has ever shown that any New York City Title I instructor teaching on parochial school premises attempted to inculcate religion in students. Thus, both our precedent and our experience require us to reject respondents' remarkable argument that we must presume Title I instructors to be "uncontrollable and sometimes very unprofessional."

As discussed above, *Zobrest* also repudiates *Ball*'s assumption that the presence of Title I teachers in parochial school classrooms will, without more, create the impression of a "symbolic union" between church and state. Justice SOUTER maintains that *Zobrest* is not dispositive on this point because *Aguilar*'s implicit conclusion that New York City's Title I program created a "symbolic union" rested on more than the presence of Title I employees on parochial school grounds. . . . We do not see any perceptible (let alone dispositive) difference in the degree of symbolic union between a student receiving remedial instruction in a classroom on his sectarian school's campus and one receiving instruction in a van parked just at the school's curbside.

Nor under current law can we conclude that a program placing full-time public employees on parochial campuses to provide Title I instruction would impermissibly finance religious indoctrination. In all relevant respects, the provision of instructional services under Title I is indistinguishable from the provision of sign-language interpreters under the IDEA. Both programs make aid available only to eligible recipients. That aid is provided to students at whatever school they choose to attend. . . .

We are also not persuaded that Title I services supplant the remedial instruction and guidance counseling already provided in New York City's sectarian schools. Although Justice SOUTER maintains that the sectarian schools provide such services and that those schools reduce those services once their students begin to receive Title I instruction, his claims rest on speculation about the impossibility of drawing any line between supplemental and general education, and not on any evidence in the record that the Board is in fact violating Title I regulations by providing services that supplant those offered in the sectarian schools.

What is most fatal to the argument that New York City's Title I program directly subsidizes religion is that it applies with equal force when those services are provided off campus, and *Aguilar* implied that providing the services off campus is entirely consistent with the Establishment Clause. . . . Justice SOUTER does not explain why a sectarian school would not have the same incentive to "make patently significant cut-backs" in its curriculum no matter where Title I services are offered, since the school would ostensibly be excused from having to provide the Title I–type services itself. Because the incentive is the same either way, we find no logical basis upon which to conclude that Title I services are an impermissible subsidy of religion when offered on campus, but not when offered off campus. Accordingly, contrary to our conclusion in *Aguilar*, placing full-time employees on parochial school campuses does not as a matter of law have the impermissible effect of advancing religion through indoctrination. . . .

We turn now to *Aguilar*'s conclusion that New York City's Title I program resulted in an excessive entanglement between church and state. Whether a government aid program results in such an entanglement has consistently been an aspect of our Establishment Clause analysis. We have considered entanglement both in the course of assessing whether an aid program has an impermissible effect of advancing religion, *Walz v. Tax Comm'n of City of New York*, 397 U.S. 664 (1970), and as a factor separate and apart from "effect," *Lemon v. Kurtzman*. Regardless of how we have characterized the issue, however, the factors we use to assess whether an entanglement is "excessive" are similar to the factors we use to examine "effect." . . . Indeed, in *Lemon* itself, the entanglement that the Court found "independently" to necessitate the program's invalidation also was found to have the effect of inhibiting religion. Thus, it is simplest to recognize why entanglement is significant and treat it—as we did in *Walz*—as an aspect of the inquiry into a statute's effect.

Not all entanglements, of course, have the effect of advancing or inhibiting religion. Interaction between church and state is inevitable, and we have always tolerated some level of involvement between the two. Entanglement must be "excessive" before it runs afoul of the Establishment Clause.

The pre-*Aguilar* Title I program does not result in an "excessive" entanglement that advances or inhibits religion. As discussed previously, the Court's finding of "excessive" entanglement in *Aguilar* rested on three grounds: (i) the program would require "pervasive monitoring by public authorities" to ensure that Title I employees did not inculcate religion; (ii) the program required "administrative cooperation" between the Board and parochial schools; and (iii) the program might increase the dangers of "political divisiveness." Under our current understanding of the Establishment Clause, the last two considerations are insufficient by themselves to create an "excessive" entanglement. They are present no matter where Title I services are offered, and no court has held that Title I services cannot be offered off campus. Further, the assumption underlying the first consideration has been undermined. In *Aguilar*, the Court presumed that full-time public employees on parochial school grounds would be tempted to inculcate religion, despite the ethical standards they were required to uphold. Because of this risk pervasive monitoring would be required. But after *Zobrest* we no longer presume that public employees will inculcate religion simply because they happen to be in a sectarian environment. Since we have abandoned the assumption that properly instructed public employees will fail to discharge their duties faithfully, we must also discard the assumption that pervasive monitoring of Title I teachers is required. There is no suggestion in the record before us that unannounced monthly visits of public supervisors are insufficient to prevent or to detect inculcation of religion by public employees. Moreover, we have not found excessive entanglement in cases in which States imposed far more onerous burdens on religious institutions than the monitoring system at issue here.

To summarize, New York City's Title I program does not run afoul of any of three primary criteria we currently use to evaluate whether government aid has the effect of advancing religion: it does not result in governmental indoctrination; define its recipients by reference to religion; or create an excessive entanglement. We therefore hold that a federally funded program providing supplemental, remedial instruction to disadvantaged children on a neutral basis is not invalid under the Establishment Clause when such instruction is given on the premises of sectarian schools by government employees pursuant to a program containing safeguards such as those present here. The same considerations that justify this holding require us to conclude that this carefully constrained program also cannot reasonably be viewed as an endorsement of religion. Accordingly, we must acknowledge that *Aguilar*, as well as the portion of *Ball* addressing Grand Rapids' Shared Time program, are no longer good law.

The doctrine of *stare decisis* does not preclude us from recognizing the change in our law and overruling *Aguilar* and those portions of *Ball* inconsistent with our more recent decisions. As we have often noted, "*stare decisis* is not an inexorable command," *Payne v. Tennessee*, 501 U.S. 808 (1991), but instead reflects a policy judgment that "in most matters it is more important that the applicable rule of law be settled than that it be settled right," *Burnet v. Coronado Oil & Gas Co.*, 285 U.S. 393 (1932) (BRANDEIS, J., dissenting). . . . As discussed above, our Establishment Clause jurisprudence has changed significantly since we decided *Ball* and *Aguilar*, so our decision to overturn those cases rests on far more than "a present doctrinal disposition to come out differently from the Court of [1985]." We therefore overrule *Ball* and *Aguilar* to the extent those decisions are inconsistent with our current understanding of the Establishment Clause. We do not acknowledge, and we do not hold, that other courts should conclude our more recent cases have, by implication, overruled an earlier precedent. We reaffirm that "if a precedent of this Court has direct application in a case, yet appears to rest on reasons rejected in some other line of decisions, the Court of Appeals should follow the case which directly controls, leaving to this Court the prerogative of overruling its own decisions." Adherence to this teaching by the District Court and Court of Appeals in this case does not insulate a legal principle on which they relied from our review to determine its continued vitality. . . .

For these reasons, we reverse the judgment of the Court of Appeals and remand to the District Court with instructions to vacate its September 26, 1985, order.

It is so ordered.

Justice SOUTER, with whom Justice STEVENS and Justice GINSBURG join, and with whom Justice BREYER joins as to Part II, dissenting.

I

I believe *Aguilar* was a correct and sensible decision, and my only reservation about its opinion is that the emphasis on the excessive entanglement produced by monitoring religious instructional content obscured those facts that independently called for the application of two central tenets of Establishment Clause jurisprudence. The State is forbidden to subsidize religion directly and is just as surely forbidden to act in any way that could reasonably be viewed as religious endorsement.

As is explained elsewhere, the flat ban on subsidization antedates the Bill of Rights and has been an unwavering rule in Establishment Clause cases, qualified only by the conclusion two Terms ago that state exactions from college students are not the sort of public revenues subject to the ban. See *Rosenberger v. Rector and Visitors of Univ. of Va.*, [515 U.S. 819] (1995) (SOUTER, J., dissenting); and (O'CONNOR, J., concurring). The rule expresses the hard lesson learned over and over again in the American past and in the experiences of the countries from which we have come, that religions supported by governments are compromised just as surely as the religious freedom of dissenters is burdened when the government supports religion. . . .

These principles were violated by the programs at issue in *Aguilar* and *Ball*. . . . [E]ach provided classes on the premises of the religious schools, covering a wide range of subjects including some at the core of primary and secondary education, like reading and mathematics; while their services were termed "supplemental," the programs and their instructors necessarily assumed responsibility for teaching subjects that the religious schools would otherwise have been obligated to provide. . . .

What, therefore, was significant in *Aguilar* and *Ball* about the placement of state-paid teachers into the physical and social settings of the religious schools was not only the consequent temptation of some of those teachers to reflect the schools' religious missions in the rhetoric of their instruction, with a resulting need for monitoring and the certainty of entanglement. What was so remarkable was that the schemes in issue assumed a teaching responsibility indistinguishable from the responsibility of the schools themselves. The obligation of primary and secondary schools to teach reading necessarily extends to teaching those who are having a hard time at it, and the same is true of math. Calling some classes remedial does not distinguish their subjects from the schools' basic subjects, however inadequately the schools may have been addressing them.

What was true of the Title I scheme as struck down in *Aguilar* will be just as true when New York reverts to the old practices with the Court's approval after today. There is simply no line that can be drawn between the instruction paid for at taxpayers' expense and the instruction in any subject that is not identified as formally religious. While it would be an obvious sham, say, to channel cash to religious schools to be credited only against the expense of "secular" instruction, the line between "supplemental" and general education is likewise impossible to draw. If a State may constitutionally enter the schools to teach in the manner in question, it must in constitutional principle be free to assume, or assume payment for, the entire cost of instruction provided in any ostensibly secular subject in any religious school. This Court explicitly recognized this in *Ball*, and although in *Aguilar* the Court concentrated on entanglement it noted the similarity to *Ball*, and Judge Friendly's opinion for the Second Circuit made it expressly clear that there was no stopping place in principle once the public teacher entered the religious schools to teach their secular subjects.

In sum, if a line is to be drawn short of barring all state aid to religious schools for teaching standard subjects, the *Aguilar–Ball* line was a sensible one capable of principled adherence. It is no less sound, and no less necessary, today.

II

The Court today ignores this doctrine and claims that recent cases rejected the elemental assumptions underlying *Aguilar* and much of *Ball*. But the Court errs. Its holding that *Aguilar* and the portion of *Ball* addressing the Shared Time program are "no longer good law" rests on mistaken reading.

In *Zobrest* the Court did indeed recognize that the Establishment Clause lays down no absolute bar to placing public employees in a sectarian school, but the rejection of such a *per se* rule was hinged expressly on the nature of the employee's job, sign-language interpretation (or signing) and the circumscribed role of the signer. . . .

The Court, however, ignores the careful distinction drawn in *Zobrest* and insists that a full-time public employee such as a Title I teacher is just like the signer, asserting that "there is no reason to presume that, simply because she enters a parochial school classroom, . . . [this] teacher will depart from her assigned duties and instructions and embark on religious indoctrination. . . ." Whatever may be the merits of this position (and I find it short on merit), it does not enjoy the authority of *Zobrest*. The Court may disagree with *Ball*'s assertion that a publicly employed teacher working in a sectarian school is apt to reinforce the pervasive inculcation of religious beliefs, but its disagreement is fresh law. . . .

It is accordingly puzzling to find the Court insisting that the aid scheme administered under Title I and considered in *Aguilar* was comparable to the programs in *Witters* and *Zobrest*. Instead of aiding isolated individuals within a school system, New York City's Title I program before *Aguilar* served about 22,000 private school students, all but 52 of whom attended religious schools. Instead of serving individual blind or deaf students, as such, Title I as administered in New York City before *Aguilar* (and as now to be revived) funded instruction in core subjects (remedial reading, reading skills, remedial mathematics, English as a second language) and provided guidance services. Instead of providing a service the school would not otherwise furnish, the Title I services necessarily relieved a religious school of "an expense that it otherwise would have assumed," *Zobrest*, and freed its funds for other, and sectarian uses.

Finally, instead of aid that comes to the religious school indirectly in the sense that its distribution results from private decisionmaking, a public educational agency distributes Title I aid in the form of programs and services directly to the religious schools. In *Zobrest* and *Witters*, it was fair to say that individual students were themselves applicants for individual benefits on a scale that could not amount to a systemic supplement. But under Title I, a local educational agency (which in New York City is the Board of Education) may receive federal funding by proposing programs approved to serve individual students who meet the criteria of need, which it then uses to provide such programs at the religious schools; students eligible for such programs may not apply directly for Title I funds. The aid, accordingly, is not even formally aid to the individual students (and even formally individual aid must be seen as aid to a school system when so many individuals receive it that it becomes a significant feature of the system).

In sum, nothing since *Ball* and *Aguilar* and before this case has eroded the distinction between "direct and substantial" and "indirect and incidental." That principled line is being breached only here and now. . . .

Justice GINSBURG, with whom Justice STEVENS, Justice SOUTER, and Justice BREYER join, dissenting.

The Court today finds a way to rehear a legal question decided in respondents' favor in this very case some 12 years ago. Subsequent decisions, the majority says, have undermined *Aguilar* and justify our immediate reconsideration. This Court's Rules do not countenance the rehearing here granted. For good reason, a proper application of those rules and the Federal Rules of Civil Procedure would lead us to defer reconsideration of *Aguilar* until we are presented with the issue in another case. . . .

The majority acknowledges that there has been no significant change in factual conditions. The majority also recognizes that *Aguilar* had not been overruled, but remained the governing Establishment Clause law, until this very day. Because *Aguilar* had not been overruled at the time the District Court acted, the law the District Court was bound to respect had not changed. The District Court therefore did not abuse its discretion in denying petitioners' Rule 60(b) motion. . . .

Unlike the majority, I find just cause to await the arrival . . . of another case in which our review appropriately may be sought, before deciding whether *Aguilar* should remain the law of the land. That cause lies in the maintenance of integrity in the interpretation of procedural rules, preservation of the responsive, non-agenda-setting character of this Court, and avoidance of invitations to reconsider old cases based on "speculations on chances from changes in [the Court's membership]."

B. FREE EXERCISE OF RELIGION

In a highly controversial ruling, the Court struck down the Religious Freedom Restoration Act of 1993 (RFRA) (see Vol. 2, Ch. 6). Congress enacted that law following the Supreme Court's ruling in *Employment Division, Department of Human Resources of Oregon v. Smith*, 494 U.S. 872 (1990) (in Vol. 2, Ch.6) and established as a matter of federal statutory law the pre–*Smith* test for balancing claims to religious freedom against governmental interests in otherwise generally applicable laws. But in *City of Boerne v.*

Flores (excerpted below) the Court struck down the RFRA for exceeding Congress's authority under Section 5 of the Fourteenth Amendment. Writing for the Court, Justice Kennedy held that Congress's power under Section 5 is remedial but does not authorize Congress to expand the scope of constitutional rights. Justices O'Connor, Souter, and Breyer dissented from the majority's continued support for the analysis and ruling in *Smith* on the First Amendment's guarantee for the free exercise of religion.

City of Boerne v. Flores
117 S.Ct. 2157 (1997)

Situated on a hill in the city of Boerne, Texas, is St. Peter Catholic Church, built in 1923 and replicating the mission style of the region's earlier history. The church seats about 230 worshippers, but in the 1990s became too small to accommodate the growing number of parishioners. Accordingly, the archbishop of San Antonio gave permission to the parish to enlarge the building. Shortly afterwards, however, the Boerne City Council passed an ordinance authorizing the city's Historic Landmark Commission to prepare a preservation plan with proposed historic landmarks and districts. Under the ordinance, the Commission must preapprove construction affecting historic landmarks or buildings in a historic district. When the archbishop applied for a building permit so construction could proceed, city authorities, relying on the ordinance and the designation of the church as a historic landmark, denied the application. The archbishop in turn challenged that decision in federal district court, claiming that the city violated the church's religious freedom as guaranteed by the Religious Freedom Restoration Act of 1993 (RFRA) (see Vol. 2, Ch. 6). Congress enacted that law following the Supreme Court's ruling in *Employment Division, Department of Human Resources of Oregon v. Smith,* 494 U.S. 872 (1990) (in Vol. 2, Ch. 6) and established as a matter of federal statutory law the pre–*Smith* test for balancing claims to religious freedom against governmental interests in otherwise generally applicable laws, like Boerne's zoning ordinance. And in defending the decision to deny the church a building permit, attorneys for the city countered that Congress had exceeded its enforcement powers under Section 5 of the Fourteenth Amendment in enacting the RFRA. The district court held the RFRA unconstitutional as a violation of the separation of powers. When the Court of Appeals for the Fifth Circuit reversed, the city of Boerne appealed to the Supreme Court, which granted *certiorari.*

The Court's decision was six to three and its opinion delivered by Justice Kennedy. Justices Stevens and Scalia filed concurring opinions. Justice O'Connor filed a dissenting opinion, which Justices Souter and Breyer joined in part. In a brief dissent omitted here, Justice Souter reiterated his doubts, expressed in *Church of Lukumi Babalu Aye, Inc. v. Hialeah*, 508 U.S. 520 (1993) (in Vol. 2, Ch. 6), about the precedential value of *Smith*, and indicated that the Court here should have either reconsidered the soundness of the *Smith* rule or dismissed this case as improvidently granted. In another brief dissent, Justice Breyer expressed agreement with Justice O'Connor's dissent except for her views of Congress's enforcement power under Section 5 of the Fourteenth Amendment, an issue which he would not have reached in this case.

Justice KENNEDY delivered the opinion of the Court, in which CHIEF JUSTICE REHNQUIST and Justices STEVENS, THOMAS, and GINSBURG joined, and in all but Part III-A-1 of which Justice SCALIA joined.

A decision by local zoning authorities to deny a church a building permit was challenged under the Religious Freedom Restoration Act of 1993 (RFRA). The case calls into question the authority of Congress to enact RFRA. We conclude the statute exceeds Congress' power. . . .

II

Congress enacted RFRA in direct response to the Court's decision in *Employment Div., Dept. of Human Resources of Ore. v. Smith*, 494 U.S. 872 (1990). There we considered a Free Exercise Clause claim brought by members of the Native American Church who were denied unemployment benefits when they lost their jobs because they had used peyote. In evaluating the claim, we declined to apply the balancing test set forth in *Sherbert v. Verner*, 374 U.S. 398 (1963), under which we would have asked whether Oregon's prohibition substantially burdened a religious practice and, if it did, whether the burden was justified by a compelling government interest. . . . The application of the *Sherbert* test, the *Smith* decision explained, would have produced an anomaly in the law, a constitutional right to ignore neutral laws of general applicability. The anomaly would have been accentuated, the Court reasoned, by the difficulty of determining whether a particular practice was central to an individual's religion. We explained, moreover, that it "is not within the judicial ken to question the centrality of particular beliefs or practices to a faith, or the validity of particular litigants' interpretations of those creeds." . . .

Four Members of the Court disagreed. They argued the law placed a substantial burden on the Native American Church members so that it could be upheld only if the law served a compelling state interest and was narrowly tailored to achieve that end. Justice O'CONNOR concluded Oregon had satisfied the test, while Justice BLACKMUN, joined by Justice BRENNAN and Justice MARSHALL, could see no compelling interest justifying the law's application to the members.

These points of constitutional interpretation were debated by Members of Congress in hearings and floor debates. Many criticized the Court's reasoning, and this disagreement resulted in the passage of RFRA. Congress announced:

"(1) The framers of the Constitution, recognizing free exercise of religion as an unalienable right, secured its protection in the First Amendment to the Constitution;

"(2) laws 'neutral' toward religion may burden religious exercise as surely as laws intended to interfere with religious exercise;

"(3) governments should not substantially burden religious exercise without compelling justification;

"(4) in *Employment Division v. Smith*, 494 U.S. 872 (1990), the Supreme Court virtually eliminated the requirement that the government justify burdens on religious exercise imposed by laws neutral toward religion; and

"(5) the compelling interest test as set forth in prior Federal court rulings is a workable test for striking sensible balances between religious liberty and competing prior governmental interests."

The Act's stated purposes are:

"(1) to restore the compelling interest test as set forth in *Sherbert v. Verner*, 374 U.S. 398 (1963) and *Wisconsin v. Yoder*, 406 U.S. 205 (1972) and to guarantee its application in all cases where free exercise of religion is substantially burdened; and

"(2) to provide a claim or defense to persons whose religious exercise is substantially burdened by government."

RFRA prohibits "government" from "substantially burdening" a person's exercise of religion even if the burden results from a rule of general applicability unless the government can demonstrate the burden "(1) is in furtherance of a compelling governmental interest; and (2) is the least restrictive means of furthering that compelling governmental interest." The Act's mandate applies to any "branch, department, agency, instrumentality, and official (or other person acting under color of law) of the United States," as well as to any "State, or . . . subdivision of a State." . . .

III (A)

Under our Constitution, the Federal Government is one of enumerated powers. *McCulloch v. Maryland*, [17 U.S.] 316 (1819). The judicial authority to determine the constitutionality of laws, in cases and controversies, is based on the premise that the "powers of the legislature are defined and limited; and that those limits may not be mistaken, or forgotten, the constitution is written." *Marbury v. Madison*, 1 Cranch 137 (1803).

Congress relied on its Fourteenth Amendment enforcement power in enacting the most far reaching and substantial of RFRA's provisions, those which impose its requirements on the States. . . .

The parties disagree over whether RFRA is a proper exercise of Congress' Section 5 power "to enforce" by "appropriate legislation" the constitutional guarantee that no State shall deprive any person of "life, liberty, or property, without due process of law" nor deny any person "equal protection of the laws." . . .

All must acknowledge that Section 5 is "a positive grant of legislative power" to Congress, *Katzenbach v. Morgan*, 384 U.S. 641 (1966). In *Ex parte Virginia*, 100 U.S. 339 (1880), we explained the scope of Congress' Section 5 power in the following broad terms: "Whatever legislation is appropriate, that is, adapted to carry out the objects the amendments have in view, whatever tends to enforce submission to the prohibitions they contain, and to secure to all persons the enjoyment of perfect equality of civil rights and the equal protection of the laws against State denial or invasion, if not prohibited, is brought within the domain of congressional power." Legislation which deters or remedies constitutional violations can fall within the sweep of Congress' enforcement power even if in the process it prohibits conduct which is not itself unconstitutional and intrudes into "legislative spheres of autonomy previously reserved to the States." *Fitzpatrick v. Bitzer*, 427 U.S. 445 (1976). For example, the Court upheld a suspension of literacy tests and similar voting requirements under Congress' parallel power to enforce the provisions of the Fifteenth Amendment, see U.S. Const., Amdt. 15, Sec. 2, as a measure to combat racial discrimination in voting, *South Carolina v. Katzenbach*, 383 U.S. 301 (1966), despite the facial constitutionality of the tests under *Lassiter v. Northampton County Bd. of Elections*, 360 U.S. 45 (1959). We have also concluded that other measures protecting voting rights are within Congress' power to enforce the Fourteenth and Fifteenth Amendments, despite the burdens those measures placed on the States. . . .

It is also true, however, that "as broad as the congressional enforcement power is, it is not unlimited." *Oregon v. Mitchell*, 400 U.S. 112 (1970). In assessing the breadth of Section 5's enforcement power, we begin with its text. Congress has been given the power "to enforce" the "provisions of this article." We agree with respondent, of course, that Congress can enact legislation under Section 5 enforcing the constitutional right to the free exercise of religion. The "provisions of this article," to which Section 5 refers, include the Due Process Clause of the Fourteenth Amendment. Congress' power to enforce the Free Exercise Clause follows from our holding in *Cantwell v. Connecticut*, 310 U.S. 296 (1940), that the "fundamental concept of liberty embodied in [the Fourteenth Amendment's due process clause] embraces the liberties guaranteed by the First Amendment."

Congress' power under Section 5, however, extends only to "enforcing" the provisions of the Fourteenth Amendment. The Court has described this power as "remedial," *South Carolina v. Katzenbach*. The design of the Amendment and the text of Section 5 are inconsistent with the suggestion that Congress has the power to decree the substance of the Fourteenth Amendment's restrictions on the States. Legislation which alters the meaning of the Free Exercise Clause cannot be said to be enforcing the Clause. Congress does not enforce a constitutional right by changing what the right is. It has been given the power "to enforce," not the power to determine what constitutes a constitutional violation. Were it not so, what Congress would be enforcing would no longer be, in any meaningful sense, the "provisions of [the Fourteenth Amendment]."

While the line between measures that remedy or prevent unconstitutional actions and measures that make a substantive change in the governing law is not easy to discern, and Congress must have wide latitude in determining where it lies, the distinction exists and must be observed. There must be a congruence and proportionality between the injury to be prevented or remedied and the means adopted to that end. Lacking such a connection, legislation may become substantive in operation and effect. History and our case law support drawing the distinction, one apparent from the text of the Amendment.

1

The Fourteenth Amendment's history confirms the remedial, rather than sub-stantive, nature of the Enforcement Clause. The Joint Committee on Reconstruc-tion of the 39th Congress began drafting what would become the Fourteenth Amendment in January 1866. The objections to the Committee's first draft of the Amendment, and the rejection of the draft, have a direct bearing on the central issue of defining Congress' enforcement power. In February, Republican Repre-sentative John Bingham of Ohio reported the following draft amendment to the House of Representatives on behalf of the Joint Committee: "The Congress shall have power to make all laws which shall be necessary and proper to secure to the citizens of each State all privileges and immunities of citizens in the several States, and to all persons in the several States equal protection in the rights of life, liberty, and property."

The proposal encountered immediate opposition, which continued through three days of debate. Members of Congress from across the political spectrum criticized the Amendment, and the criticisms had a common theme: The pro-posed Amendment gave Congress too much legislative power at the expense of the existing constitutional structure. Democrats and conservative Republicans argued that the proposed Amendment would give Congress a power to intrude into traditional areas of state responsibility, a power inconsistent with the federal design central to the Constitution. Typifying these views, Republican Representative Robert Hale of New York labeled the Amendment "an utter departure from every principle ever dreamed of by the men who framed our Con-stitution," and warned that under it "all State legislation, in its codes of civil and criminal jurisprudence and procedures . . . may be overridden, may be repealed or abolished, and the law of Congress established instead." . . .

As a result of these objections having been expressed from so many different quarters, the House voted to table the proposal until April. The Amendment in its early form was not again considered. Instead, the Joint Committee began drafting a new article of Amendment, which it reported to Congress on April 30, 1866.

Section 1 of the new draft Amendment imposed self-executing limits on the States. Section 5 prescribed that "the Congress shall have power to enforce, by appropriate legislation, the provisions of this article." The revised Amendment proposal did not raise the concerns expressed earlier regarding broad congres-sional power to prescribe uniform national laws with respect to life, liberty, and property. After revisions not relevant here, the new measure passed both Houses and was ratified in July 1868 as the Fourteenth Amendment. . . .

The design of the Fourteenth Amendment has proved significant also in main-taining the traditional separation of powers between Congress and the Judiciary. The first eight Amendments to the Constitution set forth self-executing prohibi-tions on governmental action, and this Court has had primary authority to inter-pret those prohibitions. The Bingham draft, some thought, departed from that tradition by vesting in Congress primary power to interpret and elaborate on the meaning of the new Amendment through legislation. Under it, "Congress, and not the courts, was to judge whether or not any of the privileges or immunities were not secured to citizens in the several States." While this separation of powers aspect did not occasion the widespread resistance which was caused by the proposal's threat to the federal balance, it nonetheless attracted the attention of various Members. As enacted, the Fourteenth Amendment confers substantive rights against the States which, like the provisions of the Bill of Rights, are self-executing. The power to interpret the Constitution in a case or controversy remains in the Judiciary.

2

The remedial and preventive nature of Congress' enforcement power, and the limitation inherent in the power, were confirmed in our earliest cases on the Fourteenth Amendment. In the *Civil Rights Cases*, 109 U.S. 3 (1883), the Court invalidated sections of the Civil Rights Act of 1875 which prescribed criminal penalties for denying to any person "the full enjoyment of" public accommodations and conveyances, on the grounds that it exceeded Congress' power by seeking to regulate private conduct. The Enforcement Clause, the Court said, did not authorize Congress to pass "general legislation upon the rights of the citizen, but corrective legislation; that is, such as may be necessary and proper for counteracting such laws as the States may adopt or enforce, and which, by the amendment, they are prohibited from making or enforcing . . . ." Although the specific holdings of these early cases might have been superseded or modified, see, e.g., *Heart of Atlanta Motel, Inc. v. United States*, 379 U.S. 241 (1964), their treatment of Congress' Section 5 power as corrective or preventive, not definitional, has not been questioned.

3

Any suggestion that Congress has a substantive, non-remedial power under the Fourteenth Amendment is not supported by our case law. In *Oregon v. Mitchell*, a majority of the Court concluded Congress had exceeded its enforcement powers by enacting legislation lowering the minimum age of voters from 21 to 18 in state and local elections. The five Members of the Court who reached this conclusion explained that the legislation intruded into an area reserved by the Constitution to the States. . . .

If Congress could define its own powers by altering the Fourteenth Amendment's meaning, no longer would the Constitution be "superior paramount law, unchangeable by ordinary means." It would be "on a level with ordinary legislative acts, and, like other acts, . . . alterable when the legislature shall please to alter it." *Marbury v. Madison*. Under this approach, it is difficult to conceive of a principle that would limit congressional power. Shifting legislative majorities could change the Constitution and effectively circumvent the difficult and detailed amendment process contained in Article V.

We now turn to consider whether RFRA can be considered enforcement legislation under Section 5 of the Fourteenth Amendment.

III (B)

If Congress can prohibit laws with discriminatory effects in order to prevent racial discrimination in violation of the Equal Protection Clause, see *Fullilove v. Klutznick*, 448 U.S. 448 (1980), then it can do the same, respondent argues, to promote religious liberty.

While preventive rules are sometimes appropriate remedial measures, there must be a congruence between the means used and the ends to be achieved. The appropriateness of remedial measures must be considered in light of the evil presented. Strong measures appropriate to address one harm may be an unwarranted response to another, lesser one. . . .

Regardless of the state of the legislative record, RFRA cannot be considered remedial, preventive legislation, if those terms are to have any meaning. RFRA is so out of proportion to a supposed remedial or preventive object that it cannot be understood as responsive to, or designed to prevent, unconstitutional behavior. It appears, instead, to attempt a substantive change in constitutional protections. Preventive measures prohibiting certain types of laws may be appropriate when there is reason to believe that many of the laws affected by the congressional enactment have a significant likelihood of being unconstitutional. Remedial legislation under Section 5 "should be adapted to the mischief and wrong which the [Fourteenth] Amendment was intended to provide against." *Civil Rights Cases.*

RFRA is not so confined. Sweeping coverage ensures its intrusion at every level of government, displacing laws and prohibiting official actions of almost every description and regardless of subject matter. RFRA's restrictions apply to every agency and official of the Federal, State, and local Governments. RFRA has no termination date or termination mechanism. Any law is subject to challenge at any time by any individual who alleges a substantial burden on his or her free exercise of religion.

The reach and scope of RFRA distinguish it from other measures passed under Congress' enforcement power, even in the area of voting rights. In *South Carolina v. Katzenbach*, the challenged provisions were confined to those regions of the country where voting discrimination had been most flagrant and affected a discrete class of state laws, i.e., state voting laws. Furthermore, to ensure that the reach of the Voting Rights Act was limited to those cases in which constitutional violations were most likely (in order to reduce the possibility of overbreadth), the coverage under the Act would terminate "at the behest of States and political subdivisions in which the danger of substantial voting discrimination has not materialized during the preceding five years." This is not to say, of course, that Section 5 legislation requires termination dates, geographic restrictions or egregious predicates. Where, however, a congressional enactment pervasively prohibits constitutional state action in an effort to remedy or to prevent unconstitutional state action, limitations of this kind tend to ensure Congress' means are proportionate to ends legitimate under Section 5.

The stringent test RFRA demands of state laws reflects a lack of proportionality or congruence between the means adopted and the legitimate end to be achieved. If an objector can show a substantial burden on his free exercise, the

State must demonstrate a compelling governmental interest and show that the law is the least restrictive means of furthering its interest. Claims that a law substantially burdens someone's exercise of religion will often be difficult to contest. Laws valid under *Smith* would fall under RFRA without regard to whether they had the object of stifling or punishing free exercise. We make these observations not to reargue the position of the majority in *Smith* but to illustrate the substantive alteration of its holding attempted by RFRA. . . .

The substantial costs RFRA exacts, both in practical terms of imposing a heavy litigation burden on the States and in terms of curtailing their traditional general regulatory power, far exceed any pattern or practice of unconstitutional conduct under the Free Exercise Clause as interpreted in *Smith*. Simply put, RFRA is not designed to identify and counteract state laws likely to be unconstitutional because of their treatment of religion. In most cases, the state laws to which RFRA applies are not ones which will have been motivated by religious bigotry. If a state law disproportionately burdened a particular class of religious observers, this circumstance might be evidence of an impermissible legislative motive. RFRA's substantial burden test, however, is not even a discriminatory effects or disparate impact test. It is a reality of the modern regulatory state that numerous state laws, such as the zoning regulations at issue here, impose a substantial burden on a large class of individuals. When the exercise of religion has been burdened in an incidental way by a law of general application, it does not follow that the persons affected have been burdened any more than other citizens, let alone burdened because of their religious beliefs. In addition, the Act imposes in every case a least restrictive means requirement—a requirement that was not used in the pre-*Smith* jurisprudence RFRA purported to codify—which also indicates that the legislation is broader than is appropriate if the goal is to prevent and remedy constitutional violations. . . .

Broad as the power of Congress is under the Enforcement Clause of the Fourteenth Amendment, RFRA contradicts vital principles necessary to maintain separation of powers and the federal balance. The judgment of the Court of Appeals sustaining the Act's constitutionality is reversed.

Justice STEVENS, concurring.

In my opinion, the Religious Freedom Restoration Act of 1993 (RFRA) is a "law respecting an establishment of religion" that violates the First Amendment to the Constitution.

If the historic landmark on the hill in Boerne happened to be a museum or an art gallery owned by an atheist, it would not be eligible for an exemption from the city ordinances that forbid an enlargement of the structure. Because the landmark is owned by the Catholic Church, it is claimed that RFRA gives its owner a federal statutory entitlement to an exemption from a generally applicable, neutral civil law. Whether the Church would actually prevail under the statute or not, the statute has provided the Church with a legal weapon that no atheist or agnostic can obtain. This governmental preference for religion, as opposed to irreligion, is forbidden by the First Amendment. *Wallace v. Jaffree*, 472 U.S. 38 (1985).

Justice SCALIA, with whom Justice STEVENS joins, concurring in part.

I write to respond briefly to the claim of Justice O'CONNOR's dissent (hereinafter "the dissent") that historical materials support a result contrary to the one reached in *Employment Div., Dept. of Human Resources of Ore. v. Smith*, 494 U.S. 872 (1990). The material that the dissent claims is at odds with *Smith* either has little to say about the issue or is in fact more consistent with *Smith* than with the dissent's interpretation of the Free Exercise Clause. . . .

The dissent first claims that *Smith*'s interpretation of the Free Exercise Clause departs from the understanding reflected in various statutory and constitutional protections of religion enacted by Colonies, States, and Territories in the period leading up to the ratification of the Bill of Rights. But the protections afforded by those enactments are in fact more consistent with *Smith*'s interpretation of free exercise than with the dissent's understanding of it. [T]he early "free exercise" enactments cited by the dissent protect only against action that is taken "for" or "in respect of" religion; or action taken "on account of" religion; or "discriminatory" action; or, finally (and unhelpfully for purposes of interpreting "free exercise" in the Federal Constitution), action that interferes with the "free exercise" of religion. It is eminently arguable that application of neutral, generally applicable laws of the sort the dissent refers to—such as zoning laws— would not constitute action taken "for," "in respect of," or "on account of" one's religion, or "discriminatory" action.

Assuming, however, that the affirmative protection of religion accorded by the early "free exercise" enactments sweeps as broadly as the dissent's theory would require, those enactments do not support the dissent's view, since they contain "provisos" that significantly qualify the affirmative protection they grant. According to the dissent, the "provisos" support its view because they would have been "superfluous" if "the Court was correct in *Smith* that generally applicable laws are enforceable regardless of religious conscience." I disagree. In fact, the most plausible reading of the "free exercise" enactments (if their affirmative provisions are read broadly, as the dissent's view requires) is a virtual restatement of *Smith*: Religious exercise shall be permitted so long as it does not violate general laws governing conduct. The "provisos" in the enactments negate a license to act in a manner "unfaithfull to the Lord Proprietary" (Maryland Act Concerning Religion of 1649), or "behave" in other than a "peaceable and quiet" manner (Rhode Island Charter of 1663), or "disturb the public peace" (New Hampshire Constitution), or interfere with the "peace [and] safety of the State" (New York, Maryland, and Georgia Constitutions), or "demean" oneself in other than a "peaceable and orderly manner" (Northwest Ordinance of 1787). At the time these provisos were enacted, keeping "peace" and "order" seems to have meant, precisely, obeying the laws. "Every breach of law is against the peace." Even as late as 1828, when Noah Webster published his *American Dictionary of the English Language*, he gave as one of the meanings of "peace": "8. Public tranquility; that quiet, order and security which is guaranteed by the laws; as, to keep the peace; to break the peace." This limitation upon the scope of religious exercise would have been in accord with the background political philosophy of the age (associated most prominently with John Locke), which regarded freedom as the right "to do only what was not lawfully prohibited." And while, under this interpretation, these early "free exercise" enactments support the Court's judgment in *Smith*, I see no sensible interpretation that could cause them to support what I understand to be the position of Justice O'CONNOR, or any of *Smith*'s other critics. No one in that camp, to my knowledge, contends that their favored "compelling state interest" test conforms to any possible interpretation of "breach of peace and order"—i.e., that only violence or force, or any other category of action (more limited than "violation of law") which can possibly be conveyed by the phrase "peace and order," justifies state prohibition of religiously motivated conduct.

Apart from the early "free exercise" enactments of Colonies, States, and Territories, the dissent calls attention to those bodies', and the Continental Congress's, legislative accommodation of religious practices prior to ratification of the Bill of Rights. This accommodation—which took place both before and after enactment of the state constitutional protections of religious liberty—suggests (according to the dissent) that "the drafters and ratifiers of the First Amendment . . . assumed courts would apply the Free Exercise Clause similarly." But that legislatures sometimes (though not always) found it "appropriate" to accommodate religious practices does not establish that accommodation was understood to be constitutionally mandated by the Free Exercise Clause. As we explained in *Smith*, "To say that a nondiscriminatory religious-practice exemption is permitted, or even that it is desirable, is not to say that it is constitutionally required."

The dissent's final source of claimed historical support consists of statements of certain of the Framers in the context of debates about proposed legislative enactments or debates over general principles (not in connection with the drafting of State or Federal Constitutions). Those statements are subject to the same objection as was the evidence about legislative accommodation: There is no reason to think they were meant to describe what was constitutionally required (and judicially enforceable), as opposed to what was thought to be legislatively or even morally desirable. . . .

Justice O'CONNOR, with whom Justice BREYER joins except as to a portion of Part I, dissenting.

I dissent from the Court's disposition of this case. I agree with the Court that the issue before us is whether the Religious Freedom Restoration Act (RFRA) is a proper exercise of Congress' power to enforce Section 5 of the Fourteenth Amendment. But as a yardstick for measuring the constitutionality of RFRA, the Court uses its holding in *Employment Div., Dept. of Human Resources of Ore. v. Smith*, 494 U.S. 872 (1990), the decision that prompted Congress to enact RFRA as a means of more rigorously enforcing the Free Exercise Clause. I remain of the view that *Smith* was wrongly decided, and I would use this case to reexamine the Court's holding there. Therefore, I would direct the parties to brief the question whether *Smith* represents the correct understanding of the Free Exercise Clause and set the case for reargument. If the Court were to correct the misinterpretation of the Free Exercise Clause set forth in *Smith*, it would simultaneously put our First Amendment jurisprudence back on course and allay the legitimate concerns of a majority in Congress who believed that *Smith* improperly restricted religious liberty. We would then be in a position to review RFRA in light of a proper interpretation of the Free Exercise Clause.

II

I shall not restate what has been said in other opinions, which have demonstrated that *Smith* is gravely at odds with our earlier free exercise precedents. See *Church of Lukumi Babalu Aye, Inc. v. Hialeah*, 508 U.S. 520 (1993) (SOUTER, J., concurring); *Smith* (O'CONNOR, J., concurring). Rather, I examine here the early American tradition of religious free exercise to gain insight into the original understanding of the Free Exercise Clause—an inquiry the Court in *Smith* did not undertake. We have previously recognized the importance of interpreting the Religion Clauses in light of their history.

The historical evidence casts doubt on the Court's current interpretation of the Free Exercise Clause. The record instead reveals that its drafters and ratifiers more likely viewed the Free Exercise Clause as a guarantee that government may not unnecessarily hinder believers from freely practicing their religion, a position consistent with our pre–*Smith* jurisprudence. . . .

The term "free exercise" appeared in an American legal document as early as 1648, when Lord Baltimore extracted from the new Protestant governor of Maryland and his councilors a promise not to disturb Christians, particularly Roman Catholics, in the "free exercise" of their religion. Soon after, in 1649, the Maryland Assembly enacted the first free exercise clause by passing the Act Concerning Religion: "Noe person . . . professing to beleive in Jesus Christ, shall from henceforth bee any waies troubled, Molested or discountenanced for or in respect of his or her religion nor in the free exercise thereof . . . nor any way [be] compelled to the beleife or exercise of any other Religion against his or her consent, soe as they be not unfaithfull to the Lord Proprietary, or molest or conspire against the civill Government." Rhode Island's Charter of 1663 used the analogous term "liberty of conscience." It protected residents from being "in any ways molested, punished, disquieted, or called into question, for any differences in opinion, in matters of religion, and do not actually disturb the civil peace of our said colony." The Charter further provided that residents may "freely, and fully have and enjoy his and their own judgments, and conscience in matters of religious concernments . . . ; they behaving themselves peaceably and quietly and not using this liberty to licentiousness and profaneness; nor to the civil injury, or outward disturbance of others." Various agreements between prospective settlers and the proprietors of Carolina, New York, and New Jersey similarly guaranteed religious freedom, using language that paralleled that of the Rhode Island Charter of 1663.

These documents suggest that, early in our country's history, several colonies acknowledged that freedom to pursue one's chosen religious beliefs was an essential liberty. . . .

The principles expounded in these early charters re-emerged over a century later in state constitutions that were adopted in the flurry of constitution-drafting that followed the American Revolution. By 1789, every State but Connecticut had incorporated some version of a free exercise clause into its constitution.

These state provisions, which were typically longer and more detailed than the federal Free Exercise Clause, are perhaps the best evidence of the original understanding of the Constitution's protection of religious liberty. After all, it is reasonable to think that the States that ratified the First Amendment assumed that the meaning of the federal free exercise provision corresponded to that of their existing state clauses. The precise language of these state precursors to the Free Exercise Clause varied, but most guaranteed free exercise of religion or liberty of conscience, limited by particular, defined state interests. . . .

The practice of the colonies and early States bears out the conclusion that, at the time the Bill of Rights was ratified, it was accepted that government should, when possible, accommodate religious practice. . . . Nevertheless, tension between religious conscience and generally applicable laws, though rare, was not unknown in pre-Constitutional America. Most commonly, such conflicts arose from oath requirements, military conscription, and religious assessments. The ways in which these conflicts were resolved suggest that Americans in the colonies and early States thought that, if an individual's religious scruples prevented him from complying with a generally applicable law, the government should, if possible, excuse the person from the law's coverage. For example, Quakers and certain other Protestant sects refused on Biblical grounds to subscribe to oaths or "swear" allegiance to civil authority. Without accommodation, their beliefs would have prevented them from participating in civic activities involving oaths, including testifying in court. Colonial governments created alternatives to the oath requirement for these individuals. In early decisions, for example, the Carolina proprietors applied the religious liberty provision of the Carolina Charter of 1665 to permit Quakers to enter pledges in a book. Similarly, in 1691, New York enacted a law allowing Quakers to testify by affirmation, and in 1734, it permitted Quakers to qualify to vote by affirmation. By 1789, virtually all of the States had enacted oath exemptions. . . .

III

The Religion Clauses of the Constitution represent a profound commitment to religious liberty. Our Nation's Founders conceived of a Republic receptive to voluntary religious expression, not of a secular society in which religious expression is tolerated only when it does not conflict with a generally applicable law. As the historical sources discussed above show, the Free Exercise Clause is properly understood as an affirmative guarantee of the right to participate in religious activities without impermissible governmental interference, even where a believer's conduct is in tension with a law of general application. Certainly, it is in no way anomalous to accord heightened protection to a right identified in the text of the First Amendment.

Although it may provide a bright line, the rule the Court declared in *Smith* does not faithfully serve the purpose of the Constitution. Accordingly, I believe that it is essential for the Court to reconsider its holding in *Smith*—and to do so in this very case. I would therefore direct the parties to brief this issue and set the case for reargument.

7

THE FOURTH AMENDMENT GUARANTEE AGAINST UNREASONABLE SEARCHES AND SEIZURES

A. REQUIREMENTS FOR A WARRANT AND REASONABLE SEARCHES AND SEIZURES

A number of rulings on the Fourth Amendment were handed down during the 1996–1997 term. Among them was a challenge to a state supreme court ruling creating a blanket exception for drug cases to the Fourth Amendment requirement that police knock and announce their entry when serving search and arrest warrants. Following the Court's decision in *Wilson v. Arkansas*, 115 S.Ct. 1914 (1995), which held that police must generally announce their presence and entry, the supreme court of Wisconsin ruled that a permissible blanket exception to the knock-and-announce requirement could be made for all felony drug investigations. On appeal, the Court unanimously reversed that decision in an opinion by Justice Stevens in *Richards v. Wisconsin*, 117 S.Ct. 1416 (1997). Although rejecting a blanket exception for drug-related cases to the knock-and-announce requirement, Justice Stevens nonetheless held that exceptions may be made, depending on the circumstances, if police have a "reasonable suspicion" that announcing their entry would result in the destruction of drugs or otherwise inhibit their investigation. In its 1997–1998 term, the Court then unanimously held that police with a search warrant do not need extra justification to enter a home without knocking first, even if the entry results in property damage. Writing for the Court in *United States v. Ramirez*, 118 S.Ct. 992 (1998), Chief Justice Rehnquist noted that prior rulings had not addressed the question of "whether the lawfulness of a no-knock entry depends on whether property is damaged," but concluded that "it does not," while acknowledging that "excessive or unnecessary destruction of property in the course of a search may violate the Fourth Amendment, even though the entry itself is lawful and the fruits of the search are not subject to suppression."

Another decision dealt with a challenge to a rule fashioned by the supreme court of Ohio requiring police, after making a routine traffic stop and ticketing the driver, to state "At this time you legally are free to go," before engaging in further questioning of the driver. That court's ruling, however, was ambiguous as to whether it rested on independent state grounds or the Fourth Amendment and federal law. The ruling was in turn appealed by the state attorney general to the Supreme Court, which reversed and held that police are not required to give such warnings, in *Ohio v. Robinette* (1996) (excerpted below).

The Rehnquist Court also extended a prior ruling, in *Pennsylvania v. Mimms*, 434 U.S. 106 (1977), holding that police may after stopping drivers for routine traffic violations order them out of the car, to include ordering passengers out of stopped cars as well. In *Maryland v. Wilson* (excerpted below), Justices Stevens and Kennedy dissented.

Finally, during its 1998–1999 term the Court will hear two search and seizure cases. *Knowles v. Iowa*, 569 N.W. 2d (S.Ct. of Iowa, 1997) (Docket No. 97-7597), challenges the constitutionality of Iowa's statute permitting the search of a vehicle whenever a traffic violation has occurred that provides the basis for arrest, on the ground that the basis for arrest suffices to establish probable cause to search under the Fourth Amendment. The justices will also consider the scope of police searches of areas in plain view in *Minnesota v. Carter* (Docket No. 97-1147).

Ohio v. Robinette
117 S.Ct. 417 (1996)

Just north of Dayton, Ohio, on Interstate 70, Robert D. Robinette was clocked driving at 69 miles per hour and pulled over by Roger Newsome, a county sheriff. After examining Robinette's driver's license and running a computer check, Newsome asked Robinette to get out of his car and stand in front of a television camera. At this point, Newsome returned the license and said, "One question before you get gone: Are you carrying any illegal contraband in your car? Any weapons of any kind, drugs, anything like that?" Robinette responded "no," but Newsome then asked if he could search the car and Robinette agreed. In the car, Newsome discovered a small amount of marijuana and, in a film container, a methylenedioxymethamphetamine (MDMA) pill. Robinette was arrested.

At a pretrial hearing, Robinette unsuccessfully sought to suppress the evidence. He subsequently plead "no contest" and was found guilty. On appeal, the Ohio Court of Appeals reversed, ruling that the search resulted from an unlawful detention. The Supreme Court of Ohio affirmed and established a bright-line rule for consensual interrogation under these circumstances: "The right, guaranteed by the federal and Ohio Constitutions, to be secure in one's person and property requires that citizens stopped for traffic offenses be clearly informed by the detaining officer when they are free to go after a valid detention, before an officer attempts to engage in a consensual interrogation. Any attempt at consensual interrogation must be preceded by the phrase 'At this time you legally are free to go' or by words of similar import." The state appealed that ruling and the Supreme Court granted *certiorari*.

The Court's decision was eight to one and opinion announced by Chief Justice Rehnquist. Justice Ginsburg filed a concurring opinion and Justice Stevens filed a dissenting opinion.

CHIEF JUSTICE REHNQUIST delivered the opinion of the Court.

We are here presented with the question whether the Fourth Amendment requires that a lawfully seized defendant must be advised that he is "free to go" before his consent to search will be recognized as voluntary. We hold that it does not. . . .

We have long held that the "touchstone of the Fourth Amendment is reasonableness." *Florida v. Jimeno*, 500 U.S. 248 (1991). Reasonableness, in turn, is measured in objective terms by examining the totality of the circumstances.

In applying this test we have consistently eschewed bright-line rules, instead emphasizing the fact-specific nature of the reasonableness inquiry. Thus, in *Florida v. Royer*, 460 U.S. 491 (1983), we expressly disavowed any "litmus-paper test" or single "sentence or . . . paragraph . . . rule," in recognition of the "endless variations in the facts and circumstances" implicating the Fourth Amendment. . . . And again, in *Florida v. Bostick*, 501 U.S. 429 (1991), when the Florida Supreme Court adopted a *per se* rule that questioning aboard a bus always constitutes a seizure, we reversed, reiterating that the proper inquiry necessitates a consideration of "all the circumstances surrounding the encounter."

We have previously rejected a *per se* rule very similar to that adopted by the Supreme Court of Ohio in determining the validity of a consent to search. In *Schneckloth v. Bustamonte*, 412 U.S. 218 (1973), it was argued that such a consent could not be valid unless the defendant knew that he had a right to refuse the request. We rejected this argument: "While knowledge of the right to refuse consent is one factor to be taken into account, the government need not establish such knowledge as the *sine qua non* of an effective consent." And just as it "would be thoroughly impractical to impose on the normal consent search the detailed requirements of an effective warning," so too would it be unrealistic to require police officers to always inform detainees that they are free to go before a consent to search may be deemed voluntary.

The Fourth Amendment test for a valid consent to search is that the consent be voluntary, and "voluntariness is a question of fact to be determined from all the circumstances." The Supreme Court of Ohio having held otherwise, its judgment is reversed, and the case is remanded for further proceedings not inconsistent with this opinion.

It is so ordered.

Justice GINSBURG, concurring in the judgment.

Today's opinion reversing the decision of the Ohio Supreme Court does not pass judgment on the wisdom of the first-tell-then-ask rule. This Court's opinion simply clarifies that the Ohio Supreme Court's instruction to police officers in Ohio is not, under this Court's controlling jurisprudence, the command of the Federal Constitution. The Ohio Supreme Court invoked both the Federal Constitution and the Ohio Constitution without clearly indicating whether state law, standing alone, independently justified the court's rule. The ambiguity in the Ohio Supreme Court's decision renders this Court's exercise of jurisdiction proper under *Michigan v. Long*, [463 U.S. 1032 (1983)], and this Court's decision on the merits is consistent with the Court's "totality of the circumstances" Fourth Amendment precedents. I therefore concur in the Court's judgment.

I write separately, however, because it seems to me improbable that the Ohio Supreme Court understood its first-tell-then-ask rule to be the Federal Constitution's mandate for the Nation as a whole. "[A] State is free as a matter of its own law to impose greater restrictions on police activity than those this Court holds to be necessary upon federal constitutional standards." *Oregon v. Hass*, 420 U.S. 714 (1975). But ordinarily, when a state high court grounds a rule of criminal procedure in the Federal Constitution, the court thereby signals its view that the Nation's Constitution would require the rule in all 50 States. Given this Court's decisions in consent-to-search cases such as *Schneckloth v. Bustamonte* (1973), and *Florida v. Bostick* (1991), however, I suspect that the Ohio Supreme Court may not have homed in on the implication ordinarily to be drawn from a state court's reliance on the Federal Constitution. In other words, I question whether the Ohio court thought of the strict rule it announced as a rule for the governance of police conduct not only in Miami County, Ohio, but also in Miami, Florida. . . .

It is incumbent on a state court, therefore, when it determines that its State's laws call for protection more complete than the Federal Constitution demands, to be clear about its ultimate reliance on state law. Similarly, a state court announcing a new legal rule arguably derived from both federal and state law can definitively render state law an adequate and independent ground for its decision by a simple declaration to that effect. . . .

On remand, the Ohio Supreme Court may choose to clarify that its instructions to law-enforcement officers in Ohio find adequate and independent support in state law, and that in issuing these instructions, the court endeavored to state dispositively only the law applicable in Ohio. To avoid misunderstanding, the Ohio Supreme Court must itself speak with the clarity it sought to require of its State's police officers.

Justice STEVENS, dissenting.

As I read the state court opinion, the prophylactic rule announced in the second syllabus was intended as a guide to the decision of future cases rather than an explanation of the decision in this case. I would therefore affirm the judgment of the Supreme Court of Ohio because it correctly held that respondent's consent to the search of his vehicle was the product of an unlawful detention. Moreover, it is important to emphasize that nothing in the Federal Constitution—or in this Court's opinion—prevents a State from requiring its law enforcement officers to give detained motorists the advice mandated by the Ohio Court. . . .

[A]s an objective matter it is fair to presume that most drivers who have been stopped for speeding are in a hurry to get to their destinations; such drivers have no interest in prolonging the delay occasioned by the stop just to engage in idle conversation with an officer, much less to allow a potentially lengthy search. I also assume that motorists—even those who are not carrying contraband—have an interest in preserving the privacy of their vehicles and possessions from the prying eyes of a curious stranger. The fact that this particular officer successfully used a similar method of obtaining consent to search roughly 786 times in one year, indicates that motorists generally respond in a manner that is contrary to their self-interest. Repeated decisions by ordinary citizens to surrender that interest cannot satisfactorily be explained on any hypothesis other than an assumption that they believed they had a legal duty to do so.

The Ohio Supreme Court was therefore entirely correct to presume in the first syllabus preceding its opinion that a "continued detention" was at issue here. The Ohio Court of Appeals reached a similar conclusion. In response to the State's contention that Robinette "was free to go" at the time consent was sought, that court held—after reviewing the record—that "a reasonable person in Robinette's position would not believe that the investigative stop had been concluded, and that he or she was free to go, so long as the police officer was continuing to ask investigative questions." As I read the Ohio opinions, these determinations were independent of the bright-line rule criticized by the majority. I see no reason to disturb them. . . .

Maryland v. Wilson
117 S.Ct. 882 (1997)

After stopping a speeding car in which Jerry Wilson was a passenger, a Maryland state trooper ordered Wilson out of the car upon noticing his apparent nervousness. When Wilson exited, a quantity of cocaine fell to the ground. He was arrested and charged with possession of cocaine with intent to distribute. The Baltimore County Circuit Court granted his motion to suppress the evidence on the ground that the trooper's ordering him out of the car constituted an unreasonable seizure under the Fourth Amendment. A state appellate court affirmed, holding that the ruling in *Pennsylvania v. Mimms*, 434 U.S. 106 (1977), that an officer may order the driver of a lawfully stopped car to exit his vehicle, does not apply to passengers. The state appealed that decision and the Supreme Court granted *certiorari*.

The Court's decision was seven to two and opinion announced by Chief Justice Rehnquist. Justices Stevens and Kennedy filed dissenting opinions.

CHIEF JUSTICE REHNQUIST delivered the opinion of the Court.

In this case we consider whether the rule of *Pennsylvania v. Mimms*, 434 U.S. 106 (1977), that a police officer may as a matter of course order the driver of a lawfully stopped car to exit his vehicle, extends to passengers as well. We hold that it does. . . .

In *Mimms*, we . . . concluded that "once a motor vehicle has been lawfully detained for a traffic violation, the police officers may order the driver to get out of the vehicle without violating the Fourth Amendment's proscription of unreasonable seizures." . . .

We must therefore now decide whether the rule of *Mimms* applies to passengers as well as to drivers. On the public interest side of the balance, the same weighty interest in officer safety is present regardless of whether the occupant of the stopped car is a driver or passenger. Regrettably, traffic stops may be dangerous encounters. In 1994 alone, there were 5,762 officer assaults and 11 officers killed during traffic pursuits and stops. In the case of passengers, the danger of the officer's standing in the path of oncoming traffic would not be present except in the case of a passenger in the left rear seat, but the fact that there is more than one occupant of the vehicle increases the possible sources of harm to the officer.

On the personal liberty side of the balance, the case for the passengers is in one sense stronger than that for the driver. There is probable cause to believe that the driver has committed a minor vehicular offense, but there is no such reason to stop or detain the passengers. But as a practical matter, the passengers are already stopped by virtue of the stop of the vehicle. The only change in their circumstances which will result from ordering them out of the car is that they will be outside of, rather than inside of, the stopped car. Outside the car, the passengers will be denied access to any possible weapon that might be concealed in the interior of the passenger compartment. It would seem that the possibility of a violent encounter stems not from the ordinary reaction of a motorist stopped for a speeding violation, but from the fact that evidence of a more serious crime might be uncovered during the stop. And the motivation of a passenger to employ violence to prevent apprehension of such a crime is every bit as great as that of the driver.

We think that our opinion in *Michigan v. Summers*, 452 U.S. 692 (1981), offers guidance by analogy here. There the police had obtained a search warrant for contraband thought to be located in a residence, but when they arrived to execute the warrant they found Summers coming down the front steps. The question in the case depended "upon a determination whether the officers had the authority to require him to re-enter the house and to remain there while they conducted their search." In holding as it did, the Court said: "Although no special danger to the police is suggested by the evidence in this record, the execution of a warrant to search for narcotics is the kind of transaction that may give rise to sudden violence or frantic efforts to conceal or destroy evidence. The risk of harm to both the police and the occupants is minimized if the officers routinely exercise unquestioned command of the situation."

In summary, danger to an officer from a traffic stop is likely to be greater when there are passengers in addition to the driver in the stopped car. While there is not the same basis for ordering the passengers out of the car as there is for ordering the driver out, the additional intrusion on the passenger is minimal. We therefore hold that an officer making a traffic stop may order passengers to get out of the car pending completion of the stop.

The judgment of the Court of Special Appeals of Maryland is reversed, and the case is remanded for proceedings not inconsistent with this opinion.

Justice STEVENS, with whom Justice KENNEDY joins, dissenting.

My concern is not with the ultimate disposition of this particular case, but rather with the literally millions of other cases that will be affected by the rule the Court announces. Though the question is not before us, I am satisfied that— under the rationale of *Terry v. Ohio*, 392 U.S. 1 (1968)—if a police officer conducting a traffic stop has an articulable suspicion of possible danger, the officer may order passengers to exit the vehicle as a defensive tactic without running afoul of the Fourth Amendment. . . . But the Court's ruling . . . applies equally to traffic stops in which there is not even a scintilla of evidence of any potential risk to the police officer. In those cases, I firmly believe that the Fourth Amendment prohibits routine and arbitrary seizures of obviously innocent citizens. . . .

The Court correctly observes that "traffic stops may be dangerous encounters." The magnitude of the danger to police officers is reflected in the statistic that, in 1994 alone, "there were 5,762 officer assaults and 11 officers killed during traffic pursuits and stops." There is, unquestionably, a strong public interest in minimizing the number of such assaults and fatalities. The Court's statistics, however, provide no support for the conclusion that its ruling will have any such effect.

Those statistics do not tell us how many of the incidents involved passengers. Assuming that many of the assaults were committed by passengers, we do not know how many occurred after the passenger got out of the vehicle, how many took place while the passenger remained in the vehicle, or indeed, whether any of them could have been prevented by an order commanding the passengers to exit. There is no indication that the number of assaults was smaller in jurisdictions where officers may order passengers to exit the vehicle without any suspicion than in jurisdictions where they were then prohibited from doing so. Indeed, there is no indication that any of the assaults occurred when there was a complete absence of any articulable basis for concern about the officer's safety—the only condition under which I would hold that the Fourth Amendment prohibits an order commanding passengers to exit a vehicle. . . .

In my view, wholly innocent passengers in a taxi, bus, or private car have a constitutionally protected right to decide whether to remain comfortably seated within the vehicle rather than exposing themselves to the elements and the observation of curious bystanders. The Constitution should not be read to permit law enforcement officers to order innocent passengers about simply because they have the misfortune to be seated in a car whose driver has committed a minor traffic offense.

Unfortunately, the effect of the Court's new rule on the law may turn out to be far more significant than its immediate impact on individual liberty. Throughout most of our history the Fourth Amendment embodied a general rule requiring that official searches and seizures be authorized by a warrant, issued "upon probable cause, supported by Oath or affirmation, and particularly describing the place to be searched, and the persons or things to be seized." During the prohibition era, the exceptions for warrantless searches supported by probable cause started to replace the general rule. In 1968, in the landmark "stop and frisk" case *Terry v. Ohio*, the Court placed its stamp of approval on seizures supported by specific and articulable facts that did not establish probable cause. The Court crafted *Terry* as a narrow exception to the general rule that "the police must, whenever practicable, obtain advance judicial approval of searches and seizures through the warrant procedure." The intended scope of the Court's major departure from prior practice was reflected in its statement that the "demand for specificity in the information upon which police action is predicated is the central teaching of this Court's Fourth Amendment jurisprudence." In the 1970s, the Court twice rejected attempts to justify suspicionless seizures that caused only "modest" intrusions on the liberty of passengers in automobiles. Today, however, the Court takes the unprecedented step of authorizing seizures that are unsupported by any individualized suspicion whatsoever.

I respectfully dissent.

D. OTHER GOVERNMENTAL SEARCHES IN THE ADMINISTRATIVE STATE

After upholding drug and alcohol testing requirements over Fourth Amendment objections in three earlier cases, the Court finally drew line in *Chandler v. Miller* (excerpted below). There, writing for the Court, Justice Ginsburg struck down Georgia's 1990 law requiring candidates for public office to submit to drug testing and to certify that they are drug-free. Only Chief Justice Rehnquist dissented.

Chandler v. Miller
117 S.Ct. 1295 (1997)

In 1990, the Georgia legislature enacted a law requiring "each candidate seeking to qualify for nomination or election to a state office . . . to certify that [she or he] has tested negative for illegal drugs." Section 21-2-140(b). Under the statute, candidates must present a certificate from a state-approved laboratory, in a form approved by the Secretary of State, reporting that the candidate submitted to a urinalysis drug test within thirty days prior to qualifying for nomination or election and that the results were negative. The statute lists as "illegal drugs" marijuana, cocaine, opiates, amphetamines, and phencyclidines.

In 1994, Walker Chandler and other Libertarian Party nominees challenged the constitutionality of the requirement for drug testing. A federal district upheld the law and was affirmed by the Court of Appeals for the Eleventh Circuit. Subsequently, Chandler appealed that decision and the Supreme Court granted review.

The Court's decision was eight to one and announced by Justice Ginsburg. Chief Justice Rehnquist dissented.

Justice GINSBURG delivered the opinion of the Court.

The Fourth Amendment requires government to respect "the right of the people to be secure in their persons . . . against unreasonable searches and seizures."

This restraint on government conduct generally bars officials from undertaking a search or seizure absent individualized suspicion. Searches conducted without grounds for suspicion of particular individuals have been upheld, however, in "certain limited circumstances." See [*National Treasury Employees Union v. Von Raab*], 489 U.S. 656 (1989). These circumstances include brief stops for questioning or observation at a fixed Border Patrol checkpoint, *United States v. Martinez-Fuerte*, 428 U.S. 543 (1976), or at a sobriety checkpoint, *Michigan Dept. of State Police v. Sitz*, 496 U.S. 444 (1990), and administrative inspections in "closely regulated" businesses, *New York v. Burger*, 482 U.S. 691 (1987).

Georgia requires candidates for designated state offices to certify that they have taken a drug test and that the test result was negative. We confront in this case the question whether that requirement ranks among the limited circumstances in which suspicionless searches are warranted. Relying on this Court's precedents sustaining drug-testing programs for student athletes, customs employees, and railway employees, see *Vernonia School Dist. 47J v. Acton*, [115 S.Ct. 2386] (1995) (random drug testing of students who participate in interscholastic sports); *Von Raab* (drug tests for United States Customs Service employees who seek transfer or promotion to certain positions); *Skinner v. Railway Labor Executives Assn.*, 489 U.S. 602 (1989) (drug and alcohol tests for railway employees involved in train accidents and for those who violate particular safety rules), the United States Court of Appeals for the Eleventh Circuit judged Georgia's law constitutional. We reverse that judgment. Georgia's requirement that candidates for state office pass a drug test, we hold, does not fit within the closely guarded category of constitutionally permissible suspicionless searches. . . .

Because "these intrusions [are] searches under the Fourth Amendment," we focus on the question: Are the searches reasonable?

To be reasonable under the Fourth Amendment, a search ordinarily must be based on individualized suspicion of wrongdoing. But particularized exceptions to the main rule are sometimes warranted based on "special needs, beyond the normal need for law enforcement." *Skinner.* When such "special needs"—concerns other than crime detection—are alleged in justification of a Fourth Amendment intrusion, courts must undertake a context-specific inquiry, examining closely the competing private and public interests advanced by the parties. . . .

Respondents' defense of the statute rests primarily on the incompatibility of unlawful drug use with holding high state office. The statute is justified, respondents contend, because the use of illegal drugs draws into question an official's judgment and integrity; jeopardizes the discharge of public functions, including antidrug law enforcement efforts; and undermines public confidence and trust in elected officials. The statute, according to respondents, serves to deter unlawful drug users from becoming candidates and thus stops them from attaining high state office. Notably lacking in respondents' presentation is any indication of a concrete danger demanding departure from the Fourth Amendment's main rule. . . .

What is left, after close review of Georgia's scheme, is the image the State seeks to project. By requiring candidates for public office to submit to drug testing, Georgia displays its commitment to the struggle against drug abuse. The suspicionless tests, according to respondents, signify that candidates, if elected, will be fit to serve their constituents free from the influence of illegal drugs. But Georgia asserts no evidence of a drug problem among the State's elected officials, those officials typically do not perform high-risk, safety-sensitive tasks, and the required certification immediately aids no interdiction effort. The need revealed, in short, is symbolic, not "special," as that term draws meaning from our case law. . . .

For the reasons stated, the judgment of the Court of Appeals for the Eleventh Circuit is Reversed.

CHIEF JUSTICE REHNQUIST, dissenting.

Few would doubt that the use of illegal drugs and abuse of legal drugs is one of the major problems of our society. Cases before this Court involving drug use extend to numerous occupations—railway employees, *Skinner*, border patrol officers, *Von Raab*, high school students, *Vernonia*, and machine operators, *Paperworkers v. Misco, Inc.*, 484 U.S. 29 (1987). It would take a bolder person than I to say that such widespread drug usage could never extend to candidates for public office such as Governor of Georgia. . . .

The test under the Fourth Amendment, as these cases have held, is whether the search required by the Georgia statute is "reasonable." Today's opinion speaks of a "closely guarded" class of permissible suspicionless searches which must be justified by a "special need." But this term, as used in *Skinner* and *Von Raab* and on which the Court now relies, was used in a quite different sense than it is used by the Court today. In *Skinner* and *Von Raab* it was used to describe a basis for a search apart from the regular needs of law enforcement. The "special needs" inquiry as delineated there has not required especially great "importance," unless one considers "the supervision of probationers," or the "operation of a government office," to be especially "important." Under our precedents, if there was a proper governmental purpose other than law enforcement, there was a "special need," and the Fourth Amendment then required the familiar balancing between that interest and the individual's privacy interest.

Under normal Fourth Amendment analysis, the individual's expectation of privacy is an important factor in the equation. But here, the Court perversely relies on the fact that a candidate for office gives up so much privacy—"candidates for public office . . . are subject to relentless scrutiny—by their peers, the public and the press"—as a reason for sustaining a Fourth Amendment claim. The Court says, in effect, that the kind of drug test for candidates required by the Georgia law is unnecessary, because the scrutiny to which they are already subjected by reason of their candidacy will enable people to detect any drug use on their part. But this is a strange holding, indeed. One might just as easily say that the railroad employees in *Skinner*, or the Customs officials in *Von Raab*, would be subjected to the same sort of scrutiny from their fellow employees and their supervisors. But the clear teaching of those cases is that the government is not required to settle for that sort of a vague and uncanalized scrutiny; if in fact preventing persons who use illegal drugs from concealing that fact from the public is a legitimate government interest, these cases indicate that the government may require a drug test. . . .

Nothing in the Fourth Amendment or in any other part of the Constitution prevents a State from enacting a statute whose principal vice is that it may seem misguided or even silly to the members of this Court. I would affirm the judgment of the Court of Appeals.

F. THE EXCLUSIONARY RULE

THE DEVELOPMENT OF LAW

Other Rulings on the Exclusionary Rule

Case	Vote	Ruling
Pennsylvania Board of Probation and Parole v. Scott, 118 U.S. 2014 (1998)	6:3	Held that the federal exclusionary rule does not bar the use at parole revocation hearings of evidence seized in

violation of the Fourth Amendment. As a condition of parole, Keith Scott was to refrain from possessing weapons. When parole officers suspected that he had violated that provision, they illegally entered his home and found firearms, a bow, and arrows. Subsequently, Scott objected to the use of that evidence in a parole revocation hearing, but the hearing examiner rejected his challenge. The state supreme court reversed that decision. In writing for the Court and reversing the state supreme court, Justice Thomas emphasized that "the use of evidence obtained in violation of the Fourth Amendment does not itself violate the Constitution" and that the exclusionary rule is simply "a judicially created means of deterring illegal searches and seizures." And, thus, the application of the exclusionary rule turns on whether "its deterrence benefits outweigh its 'substantial social costs.'" Justices Stevens and Souter filed dissenting opinions, which Justice Breyer joined.

8

THE FIFTH AMENDMENT
GUARANTEE AGAINST
SELF-ACCUSATION

In *United States v. Aloyzas Balsys*, 118 S.Ct. 2218 (1998), the Court ruled that individuals may not claim the Fifth Amendment privilege against self-accusation because they fear possible deportation and prosecution by a foreign nation. Writing for the Court, Justice Souter rejected Mr. Balsys's claim of the privilege when asked to explain his activities in Germany between 1940 and 1945 by the Department of Justice's Office of Special Investigations. The possibility of criminal prosecution by a foreign government, according to Justice Souter, does not constitute a "criminal case" for the purpose of the Fifth Amendment and thus does not entitle a claim to the privilege. Justice Stevens concurred, while Justices Ginsburg and Breyer dissented.

9

THE RIGHTS TO COUNSEL AND OTHER PROCEDURAL GUARANTEES

F. THE RIGHTS TO BE INFORMED OF CHARGES AND TO CONFRONT ACCUSERS

In *Gray v. Maryland*, 118 S.Ct. 1151 (1998), a bare majority held that the Sixth Amendment's guarantee of a defendant's right to confront witnesses against him or her was violated by the introduction into evidence of an edited confession of a co-defendant, without giving the defendant an opportunity to cross-examine the witness. Justice Breyer's opinion was joined by Justices Stevens, O'Connor, Souter, and Ginsburg. Dissenting Justice Scalia, joined by Chief Justice Rehnquist and Justices Kennedy and Thomas, countered that, "The U.S. Constitution guarantees, not a perfect system of criminal justice, . . . but a minimum standard of justice."

G. THE GUARANTEE AGAINST DOUBLE JEOPARDY

In *Kansas v. Hendricks* (excerpted above in Vol. 2, Ch. 4), the Court rejected a double jeopardy and due process challenge to Kansas's 1994 law for institutionalizing sexual predators after they have served their jail sentences.

THE DEVELOPMENT OF LAW

Other Recent Rulings on Double Jeopardy

Case	Vote	Ruling
Hudson v. United States, 118 S.Ct. 488 (1998)	5:4	Held that the double jeopardy clause does not bar federal criminal prosecution of an

individual for banking violations after the individual has been fined by the Comptroller of the Currency for the same violations. Writing for the Court, Chief Justice Rehnquist ruled that the Comptroller's proceedings were civil, not criminal, and therefore the double jeopardy clause does not bar subsequent criminal prosecution. In so holding, the Court rejected as unworkable its previous analysis and ruling in *United States v. Halper,* 490 U.S. 435 (1989), that civil fines may not be placed on top of criminal penalties for the same offense if the sanction is grossly disproportionate, and reaffirmed the rule in *United States v. Ward,* 448 U.S. 242 (1980), that the threshold question is whether a legislature intended a successive punishment to be "civil" or "criminal." Justices Stevens, Scalia, Souter, and Breyer dissented.

Monge v. California, 118 S.Ct. 2246 (1998)	6:3	Writing for the Court, Justice O'Connor ruled that the double jeopardy clause does

not apply to noncapital sentencing proceedings. Under California's "three-strikes" law, a second conviction for a felony can lead to a doubling of a person's sentence if it is shown that the first felony involved great bodily injury or the use of deadly weapon. Rejecting the double jeopardy challenge to California's law, Justice O'Connor distinguished the application of the clause to death penalty sentencing in holding that, in contrast, noncapital sentencing procedures are "a matter of legislative grace" and do not compel the extension of the bar on double jeopardy. Justices Stevens, Scalia, and Souter dissented.

Kansas v. Hendricks
117 S.Ct. 2072 (1997)

(Excerpted above in Vol. 2, Ch. 4.)

10

CRUEL AND UNUSUAL PUNISHMENT

B. CAPITAL PUNISHMENT

THE DEVELOPMENT OF LAW

Other Recent Rulings of the Rehnquist Court
on Capital Punishment

Case	Vote	Ruling
O'Dell v. Netherland, 117 S.Ct. 1969 (1997)	5:4	Held that the ruling in *Simmons v. South Carolina*, 512 U.S. 154 (1994), was a new

rule and therefore not retroactive in order to disturb the petitioner's 1988 death sentence. *Simmons* held that when seeking a death sentence, if the prosecution argues that the defendant poses a future dangerousness, then the defendant should be permitted to inform the sentencing jury that he is ineligible for parole, should he receive life imprisonment. Under *Teague v. Lane*, 489 U.S. 288 (1989), a final state conviction or sentence will not be disturbed unless it can be said that at the time the state court acted unreasonably by not extending the relief later sought in federal court. Here, writing for the majority Justice Thomas held that it would not have been unreasonable for the state court in 1988 to choose not to advise jurors about events that would (or would not) follow their recommendation of a death sentence instead of life imprisonment. Justice Stevens, joined by Justices Breyer, Ginsburg, and Souter, dissented.

Ohio Adult Parole Authority v. Woodard, 118 S.Ct. 1244 (1998)	8:1	Rejected Woodard's claim that he had a constitutional "liberty" interest in clemency.

Writing for the Court, Chief Justice Rehnquist ruled that Woodard, a death-row inmate, did not have a protected liberty interest under the Fourteenth Amendment that justified judicial scrutiny of Ohio's clemency process, and that Ohio's giving inmates the option of voluntary participation in the clemency process did not violate Woodard's Fifth Amendment rights to due process and non-self-incrimination. Although rejecting Woodard's claims, the majority was divided over what due process protections are afforded prisoners in clemency proceedings. On that issue, Justices Souter, Ginsburg, and Breyer joined a separate concurring opinion by Justice O'Connor. Justice Stevens dissented in part.

Calderon v. Thompson, 118 S.Ct. 1489 (1998)	5:4	Writing for the Court, Justice Kennedy sharply rebuked the Court of Appeals for the

Ninth Circuit for abusing its discretion in recalling its earlier mandate denying a death-row inmate any further *habeas corpus* petitions challenging his death sentence. Federal appellate courts may intervene in such a fashion, according to the majority, only when necessary "to avoid a miscarriage of justice," based on a strong showing of the inmate's "actual innocence." Justice Kennedy thereby underscored the majority's growing impatience with delays in carrying out executions. The four dissenters—Justices Souter, Stevens, Ginsburg, and Breyer—countered that the majority's standard was too strict and that appellate courts should be given greater deference and discretion.

Stewart v. Martinez-Villareal, 118 S.Ct. 1618 (1998)	7:2	Writing for the Court, Chief Justice Rehnquist held that, even under the Antiterrorism

and Effective Death Penalty Act of 1996, which forbids more than one *habeas corpus* petition from death-row inmates, Martinez-Villareal could file a petition for a hearing on his claim that he was too mentally ill to be executed. He had earlier raised that claim in 1993, but it was judged premature since no date had been set for his execution. When he raised it a second time in the face of his impending execution, the chief justice held that it should be treated as an extension of his first petition, and not as a second petition. Justices Scalia and Thomas issued strong dissenting opinions.

11

THE RIGHT OF PRIVACY

A. PRIVACY AND REPRODUCTIVE FREEDOM

THE DEVELOPMENT OF LAW

Other Post–*Roe* Rulings on Abortion

Case	Vote	Ruling
Lambert v. Wicklund, 117 S.Ct. 1169 (1997)	6:3	Without hearing oral arguments, the Court reversed the Court of Appeals for the

Ninth Circuit's ruling striking down Montana's 1995 Parental Notice of Abortion Act. In an unsigned opinion, the Court held that that statute's judicial bypass provision, allowing a waiver of a notice requirement if notification of a minor's parent or guardian was not in her best interest, was sufficient to protect the minor's right to an abortion. Justice Stevens, joined by Justices Ginsburg and Breyer, dissented.

Case	Vote	Ruling
Mazurek v. Armstrong, 117 S.Ct. 1865 (1997)	6:3	Without hearing oral arguments, in an unsigned opinion the Court vacated a decision

of the Court of Appeals for the Ninth Circuit that reversed a district court's invalidation of Montana's 1995 law restricting the performance of abortions to licensed physicians. (Forty other states have similar laws.) Sarah Cahill, a licensed physician's assistant, had been performing first-trimester abortions; she was the only non-physician in the state doing so. The Court reaffirmed that such restrictions do not constitute an "undue burden" under *Planned Parenthood of Southeastern Pennsylvania v. Casey*, 505 U.S. 833 (1992) (see Vol. 2, Ch. 11). Justice Stevens, joined by Justices Ginsburg and Breyer, dissented.

B. PRIVACY AND PERSONAL AUTONOMY

Washington v. Glucksberg
117 S.Ct. 2258 (1997)
and
Vacco v. Quill
117 S.Ct. 2293 (1997)

These cases arose from the growing controversy over the so-called "right to die." The Court unanimously reversed two appellate court rulings that had struck down state laws barring physician-assisted suicide. In *Cruzan by Cruzan v. Director, Missouri Department of Health*, 497 U.S. 261 (1990) (see Vol. 2, Ch. 11), the Court held that individuals have a "fundamental liberty" interest under the Fourteenth Amendment in terminating life-support systems. In 1996, two federal appellate courts extended that ruling to forbid states from passing laws barring physicians from prescribing lethal dosages of drugs at the request of their terminally ill patients. At issue was not whether doctors like Jack Kevorkian may help the terminally ill end their lives, but rather whether they may prescribe lethal drugs to terminally ill patients. The Court of Appeals for the Ninth Circuit struck down Washington's law forbidding physician-assisted suicide on the ground that it violated individuals' "right of privacy" and substantive liberty protected by the due process clause of the Fourteenth Amendment. The Court of Appeals for the Second Circuit invalidated New York's law on the basis of the Fourteenth Amendment's equal protection clause upon rejecting the state's distinction between the terminally ill patient's right to terminate life-support systems and his or her claim to a right to physician-assisted suicide.

Both appellate court decisions were unanimously reversed by the Supreme Court. Overturning the Second Circuit's decision in his opinion for the Court in *Vacco v. Quill*, Chief Justice Rehnquist rejected its equal protection analysis, observing:

> The Equal Protection Clause commands that no State "deny to any person within its jurisdiction the equal protection of the laws." This provision creates no substantive rights. Instead, it embodies a general rule that States must treat like cases alike but may treat unlike cases accordingly. If a legislative classification or distinction "neither burdens a fundamental right nor targets a suspect class, we will uphold [it] so long as it bears a rational relation to some legitimate end." *Romer v. Evans*, [116 S.Ct. 1620] (1996). . . .
>
> On their faces, neither New York's ban on assisting suicide nor its statutes permitting patients to refuse medical treatment treat anyone differently than anyone else or draw any distinctions between persons. Everyone, regardless of physical condition, is entitled, if competent, to

refuse unwanted lifesaving medical treatment; no one is permitted to assist a suicide. Generally speaking, laws that apply evenhandedly to all "unquestionably comply" with the Equal Protection Clause.

The Court's unanimous decision in *Washington v. Glucksberg* was delivered by Chief Justice Rehnquist but, as in *Vacco v. Quill*, only Justices O'Connor, Scalia, Kennedy, and Thomas joined his opinion for the Court. Moreover, in each case, four justices—O'Connor, Stevens, Souter, and Breyer—issued concurring opinions rejecting some or all of Chief Justice Rehnquist's analysis and indicating that they might be prepared, depending on the particular circumstances of the case, to recognize a right to physician-assisted suicide, which the chief justice's opinion did not entirely rule out. For now, though, the justices agreed to let the controversy continue to play out in state legislatures and the lower courts.

CHIEF JUSTICE REHNQUIST delivered the opinion of the Court.

The question presented in this case is whether Washington's prohibition against "causing" or "aiding" a suicide offends the Fourteenth Amendment to the United States Constitution. We hold that it does not. . . .

The plaintiffs asserted "the existence of a liberty interest protected by the Fourteenth Amendment which extends to a personal choice by a mentally competent, terminally ill adult to commit physician-assisted suicide." Relying primarily on *Planned Parenthood v. Casey*, 505 U.S. 833 (1992), and *Cruzan v. Director, Missouri Dept. of Health*, 497 U.S. 261 (1990), the District Court agreed and concluded that Washington's assisted-suicide ban is unconstitutional because it "places an undue burden on the exercise of [that] constitutionally protected liberty interest." The District Court also decided that the Washington statute violated the Equal Protection Clause's requirement that "'all persons similarly situated . . . be treated alike.'" Id. (quoting *Cleburne v. Cleburne Living Center, Inc.*, 473 U.S. 432 (1985)).

A panel of the Court of Appeals for the Ninth Circuit reversed, emphasizing that "in the two hundred and five years of our existence no constitutional right to aid in killing oneself has ever been asserted and upheld by a court of final jurisdiction." The Ninth Circuit reheard the case *en banc*, reversed the panel's decision, and affirmed the District Court. . . .

We begin, as we do in all due-process cases, by examining our Nation's history, legal traditions, and practices. In almost every State—indeed, in almost every western democracy—it is a crime to assist a suicide. The States' assisted-suicide bans are not innovations. Rather, they are longstanding expressions of the States' commitment to the protection and preservation of all human life. . . .

Though deeply rooted, the States' assisted-suicide bans have in recent years been reexamined and, generally, reaffirmed. Because of advances in medicine and technology, Americans today are increasingly likely to die in institutions, from chronic illnesses. Public concern and democratic action are therefore sharply focused on how best to protect dignity and independence at the end of life, with the result that there have been many significant changes in state laws and in the attitudes these laws reflect. Many States, for example, now permit "living wills," surrogate health-care decisionmaking, and the withdrawal or refusal of life-sustaining medical treatment. At the same time, however, voters and legislators continue for the most part to reaffirm their States' prohibitions on assisting suicide.

The Washington statute at issue in this case was enacted in 1975 as part of a revision of that State's criminal code. Four years later, Washington passed its Natural Death Act, which specifically stated that the "withholding or withdrawal of life-sustaining treatment . . . shall not, for any purpose, constitute a suicide" and that "nothing in this chapter shall be construed to condone, authorize, or approve mercy killing. . . ." In 1991, Washington voters rejected a ballot initiative which, had it passed, would have permitted a form of physician-assisted suicide. Washington then added a provision to the Natural Death Act expressly excluding physician-assisted suicide.

California voters rejected an assisted-suicide initiative similar to Washington's in 1993. On the other hand, in 1994, voters in Oregon enacted, also through ballot initiative, that State's "Death With Dignity Act," which legalized physician-assisted suicide for competent, terminally ill adults. Since the Oregon vote, many proposals to legalize assisted-suicide have been and continue to be introduced in the States' legislatures, but none has been enacted. . . .

Thus, the States are currently engaged in serious, thoughtful examinations of physician-assisted suicide and other similar issues. For example, New York State's Task Force on Life and the Law—an ongoing, blue-ribbon commission composed of doctors, ethicists, lawyers, religious leaders, and interested laymen— was convened in 1984 and commissioned with "a broad mandate to recommend public policy on issues raised by medical advances." Over the past decade, the Task Force has recommended laws relating to end-of-life decisions, surrogate pregnancy, and organ donation. After studying physician-assisted suicide, however, the Task Force unanimously concluded that "legalizing assisted suicide and euthanasia would pose profound risks to many individuals who are ill and vulnerable. . . . The potential dangers of this dramatic change in public policy would outweigh any benefit that might be achieved." . . .

The Due Process Clause guarantees more than fair process, and the "liberty" it protects includes more than the absence of physical restraint. The Clause also provides heightened protection against government interference with certain fundamental rights and liberty interests. In a long line of cases, we have held that, in addition to the specific freedoms protected by the Bill of Rights, the "liberty" specially protected by the Due Process Clause includes the rights to marry, *Loving v. Virginia*, 388 U.S. 1 (1967); to have children, *Skinner v. Oklahoma ex rel. Williamson*, 316 U.S. 535 (1942); to direct the education and upbringing of one's children, *Meyer v. Nebraska*, 262 U.S. 390 (1923); *Pierce v. Society of Sisters*, 268 U.S. 510 (1925); to marital privacy, *Griswold v. Connecticut*, 391 U.S. 479 (1965); to use contraception, *ibid.*; *Eisenstadt v. Baird*, 405 U.S. 438 (1972); to bodily integrity, *Rochin v. California*, 342 U.S. 165 (1952), and to abortion, *Casey*. We have also assumed, and strongly suggested, that the Due Process Clause protects the traditional right to refuse unwanted lifesaving medical treatment. *Cruzan*.

But we "have always been reluctant to expand the concept of substantive due process because guideposts for responsible decisionmaking in this unchartered area are scarce and open-ended." By extending constitutional protection to an asserted right or liberty interest, we, to a great extent, place the matter outside the arena of public debate and legislative action. We must therefore "exercise the utmost care whenever we are asked to break new ground in this field," lest the liberty protected by the Due Process Clause be subtly transformed into the policy preferences of the members of this Court.

Our established method of substantive-due-process analysis has two primary features: First, we have regularly observed that the Due Process Clause specially protects those fundamental rights and liberties which are, objectively, "deeply rooted in this Nation's history and tradition," *Snyder v. Massachusetts*, 291 U.S. 97 (1934) ("so rooted in the traditions and conscience of our people as to be ranked as fundamental"), and "implicit in the concept of ordered liberty," such that "neither liberty nor justice would exist if they were sacrificed," *Palko v. Connecticut*, 302 U.S. 319 (1937). Second, we have required in substantive-due-process cases a "careful description" of the asserted fundamental liberty interest. [*Reno v.*] *Flores*, [507 U.S. 292 (1993)]; *Cruzan*. Our Nation's history, legal traditions, and practices thus provide the crucial "guideposts for responsible decisionmaking" that direct and restrain our exposition of the Due Process Clause. As we stated recently in *Flores*, the Fourteenth Amendment "forbids the government to infringe . . . 'fundamental' liberty interests at all, no matter what process is provided, unless the infringement is narrowly tailored to serve a compelling state interest."

Justice SOUTER, relying on Justice HARLAN's dissenting opinion in *Poe v. Ullman*, [367 U.S. 497 (1961),] would largely abandon this restrained methodology, and instead ask "whether [Washington's] statute sets up one of those 'arbitrary impositions' or 'purposeless restraints' at odds with the Due Process Clause of the Fourteenth Amendment." In our view, however, the development of this Court's substantive-due-process jurisprudence, described briefly above, has been a process whereby the outlines of the "liberty" specially protected by the Fourteenth Amendment—never fully clarified, to be sure, and perhaps not capable of being fully clarified—have at least been carefully refined by concrete examples involving fundamental rights found to be deeply rooted in our legal tradition. This approach tends to rein in the subjective elements that are necessarily present in due-process judicial review. In addition, by establishing a threshold requirement—that a challenged state action implicate a fundamental right—before requiring more than a reasonable relation to a legitimate state interest to justify the action, it avoids the need for complex balancing of competing interests in every case.

Turning to the claim at issue here, the Court of Appeals stated that "properly analyzed, the first issue to be resolved is whether there is a liberty interest in determining the time and manner of one's death," or, in other words, "is there a right to die?" Similarly, respondents assert a "liberty to choose how to die" and a right to "control of one's final days," and describe the asserted liberty as "the right to choose a humane, dignified death," and "the liberty to shape death." . . . The Washington statute at issue in this case prohibits "aiding another person to attempt suicide," and, thus, the question before us is whether the "liberty" specially protected by the Due Process Clause includes a right to commit suicide which itself includes a right to assistance in doing so.

We now inquire whether this asserted right has any place in our Nation's traditions. Here, as discussed above, we are confronted with a consistent and almost universal tradition that has long rejected the asserted right, and continues explicitly to reject it today, even for terminally ill, mentally competent adults. To hold for respondents, we would have to reverse centuries of legal doctrine and practice, and strike down the considered policy choice of almost every State. . . .

Respondents contend that in *Cruzan* we "acknowledged that competent, dying persons have the right to direct the removal of life-sustaining medical treatment and thus hasten death," and that "the constitutional principle behind recognizing the patient's liberty to direct the withdrawal of artificial life support applies at least as strongly to the choice to hasten impending death by consuming lethal medication."

The right assumed in *Cruzan*, however, was not simply deduced from abstract concepts of personal autonomy. Given the common-law rule that forced medication was a battery, and the long legal tradition protecting the decision to refuse unwanted medical treatment, our assumption was entirely consistent with this Nation's history and constitutional traditions. The decision to commit suicide with the assistance of another may be just as personal and profound as the decision to refuse unwanted medical treatment, but it has never enjoyed similar legal protection. Indeed, the two acts are widely and reasonably regarded as quite distinct. In *Cruzan* itself, we recognized that most States outlawed assisted suicide—and even more do today—and we certainly gave no intimation that the right to refuse unwanted medical treatment could be somehow transmuted into a right to assistance in committing suicide. . . .

The history of the law's treatment of assisted suicide in this country has been and continues to be one of the rejection of nearly all efforts to permit it. That being the case, our decisions lead us to conclude that the asserted "right" to assistance in committing suicide is not a fundamental liberty interest protected by the Due Process Clause. The Constitution also requires, however, that Washington's assisted-suicide ban be rationally related to legitimate government interests. See *Heller v. Doe*, 509 U.S. 312 (1993); *Flores*. This requirement is unquestionably met here. As the court below recognized, Washington's assisted-suicide ban implicates a number of state interests.

First, Washington has an "unqualified interest in the preservation of human life." *Cruzan*. The State's prohibition on assisted suicide, like all homicide laws, both reflects and advances its commitment to this interest. . . .

Relatedly, all admit that suicide is a serious public-health problem, especially among persons in otherwise vulnerable groups. Those who attempt suicide—terminally ill or not—often suffer from depression or other mental disorders. Research indicates, however, that many people who request physician-assisted suicide withdraw that request if their depression and pain are treated. The New York Task Force, however, expressed its concern that, because depression is difficult to diagnose, physicians and medical professionals often fail to respond adequately to seriously ill patients' needs. Thus, legal physician-assisted suicide could make it more difficult for the State to protect depressed or mentally ill persons, or those who are suffering from untreated pain, from suicidal impulses.

The State also has an interest in protecting the integrity and ethics of the medical profession. In contrast to the Court of Appeals' conclusion that "the integrity of the medical profession would [not] be threatened in any way by [physician-assisted suicide]," the American Medical Association, like many other medical and physicians' groups, has concluded that "physician-assisted suicide is fundamentally incompatible with the physician's role as healer."

Next, the State has an interest in protecting vulnerable groups—including the poor, the elderly, and disabled persons—from abuse, neglect, and mistakes. The Court of Appeals dismissed the State's concern that disadvantaged persons might be pressured into physician-assisted suicide as "ludicrous on its face." We have recognized, however, the real risk of subtle coercion and undue influence in end-of-life situations. *Cruzan.* Similarly, the New York Task Force warned that "legalizing physician-assisted suicide would pose profound risks to many individuals who are ill and vulnerable. . . . The risk of harm is greatest for the many individuals in our society whose autonomy and well-being are already compromised by poverty, lack of access to good medical care, advanced age, or membership in a stigmatized social group." If physician-assisted suicide were permitted, many might resort to it to spare their families the substantial financial burden of end-of-life health-care costs.

The State's interest here goes beyond protecting the vulnerable from coercion; it extends to protecting disabled and terminally ill people from prejudice, negative and inaccurate stereotypes, and "societal indifference." The State's assisted-suicide ban reflects and reinforces its policy that the lives of terminally ill, disabled, and elderly people must be no less valued than the lives of the young and healthy, and that a seriously disabled person's suicidal impulses should be interpreted and treated the same way as anyone else's.

Finally, the State may fear that permitting assisted suicide will start it down the path to voluntary and perhaps even involuntary euthanasia. The Court of Appeals struck down Washington's assisted-suicide ban only "as applied to competent, terminally ill adults who wish to hasten their deaths by obtaining medication prescribed by their doctors." Washington insists, however, that the impact of the court's decision will not and cannot be so limited. If suicide is protected as a matter of constitutional right, it is argued, "every man and woman in the United States must enjoy it." The Court of Appeals' decision, and its expansive reasoning, provide ample support for the State's concerns. The court noted, for example, that the "decision of a duly appointed surrogate decision maker is for all legal purposes the decision of the patient himself;" that "in some instances, the patient may be unable to self-administer the drugs and . . . administration by the physician . . . may be the only way the patient may be able to receive them;" and that not only physicians, but also family members and loved ones, will inevitably participate in assisting suicide. Thus, it turns out that what is couched as a limited right to "physician-assisted suicide" is likely, in effect, a much broader license, which could prove extremely difficult to police and contain. Washington's ban on assisting suicide prevents such erosion. . . .

Throughout the Nation, Americans are engaged in an earnest and profound debate about the morality, legality, and practicality of physician-assisted suicide. Our holding permits this debate to continue, as it should in a democratic society. The decision of the *en banc* Court of Appeals is reversed, and the case is remanded for further proceedings consistent with this opinion.

Justice O'CONNOR, concurring.

Death will be different for each of us. For many, the last days will be spent in physical pain and perhaps the despair that accompanies physical deterioration and a loss of control of basic bodily and mental functions. Some will seek medication to alleviate that pain and other symptoms.

The Court frames the issue in this case as whether the Due Process Clause of the Constitution protects a "right to commit suicide which itself includes a right to assistance in doing so," and concludes that our Nation's history, legal traditions, and practices do not support the existence of such a right. I join the Court's opinions because I agree that there is no generalized right to "commit suicide." But respondents urge us to address the narrower question whether a mentally competent person who is experiencing great suffering has a constitutionally cognizable interest in controlling the circumstances of his or her imminent death. I see no need to reach that question in the context of the facial challenges to the New York and Washington laws at issue here. The parties and *amici* agree that in these States a patient who is suffering from a terminal illness and who is experiencing great pain has no legal barriers to obtaining medication, from qualified physicians, to alleviate that suffering, even to the point of causing unconsciousness and hastening death. In this light, even assuming that we would recognize such an interest, I agree that the State's interests in protecting those who are not truly competent or facing imminent death, or those whose decisions to hasten death would not truly be voluntary, are sufficiently weighty to justify a prohibition against physician-assisted suicide.

Every one of us at some point may be affected by our own or a family member's terminal illness. There is no reason to think the democratic process will not strike the proper balance between the interests of terminally ill, mentally competent individuals who would seek to end their suffering and the State's interests in protecting those who might seek to end life mistakenly or under pressure. . . .

In sum, there is no need to address the question whether suffering patients have a constitutionally cognizable interest in obtaining relief from the suffering that they may experience in the last days of their lives. There is no dispute that dying patients in Washington and New York can obtain palliative care, even when doing so would hasten their deaths. The difficulty in defining terminal illness and the risk that a dying patient's request for assistance in ending his or her life might not be truly voluntary justifies the prohibitions on assisted suicide we uphold here.

Justice STEVENS, concurring in the judgments.

The Court ends its opinion with the important observation that our holding today is fully consistent with a continuation of the vigorous debate about the "morality, legality, and practicality of physician-assisted suicide" in a democratic society. I write separately to make it clear that there is also room for further debate about the limits that the Constitution places on the power of the States to punish the practice.

History and tradition provide ample support for refusing to recognize an open-ended constitutional right to commit suicide. Much more than the State's paternalistic interest in protecting the individual from the irrevocable consequences of an ill-advised decision motivated by temporary concerns is at stake. There is truth in John Donne's observation that "No man is an island." The State has an interest in preserving and fostering the benefits that every human being may provide to the community—a community that thrives on the exchange of ideas, expressions of affection, shared memories and humorous incidents as well as on the material contributions that its members create and support. The value to others of a person's life is far too precious to allow the individual to claim a constitutional entitlement to complete autonomy in making a decision to end that life. Thus, I fully agree with the Court that the "liberty" protected by the Due Process Clause does not include a categorical "right to commit suicide which itself includes a right to assistance in doing so."

But just as our conclusion that capital punishment is not always unconstitutional did not preclude later decisions holding that it is sometimes impermissibly cruel, so is it equally clear that a decision upholding a general statutory prohibition of assisted suicide does not mean that every possible application of the statute would be valid. A State, like Washington, that has authorized the death penalty and thereby has concluded that the sanctity of human life does not require that it always be preserved, must acknowledge that there are situations in which an interest in hastening death is legitimate. Indeed, not only is that interest sometimes legitimate, I am also convinced that there are times when it is entitled to constitutional protection.

In *Cruzan v. Director, Mo. Dept. of Health*, 497 U.S. 261 (1990), the Court assumed that the interest in liberty protected by the Fourteenth Amendment encompassed the right of a terminally ill patient to direct the withdrawal of life-sustaining treatment. As the Court correctly observes today, that assumption "was not simply deduced from abstract concepts of personal autonomy." Instead, it was supported by the common-law tradition protecting the individual's general right to refuse unwanted medical treatment. We have recognized, however, that this common-law right to refuse treatment is neither absolute nor always sufficiently weighty to overcome valid countervailing state interests. In most cases, the individual's constitutionally protected interest in his or her own physical autonomy, including the right to refuse unwanted medical treatment, will give way to the State's interest in preserving human life.

Cruzan, however, was not the normal case. Given the irreversible nature of her illness and the progressive character of her suffering, Nancy Cruzan's interest in refusing medical care was incidental to her more basic interest in controlling the manner and timing of her death. In finding that her best interests would be served by cutting off the nourishment that kept her alive, the trial court did more than simply vindicate Cruzan's interest in refusing medical treatment; the court, in essence, authorized affirmative conduct that would hasten her death. When this Court reviewed the case and upheld Missouri's requirement that there be clear and convincing evidence establishing Nancy Cruzan's intent to have life-sustaining nourishment withdrawn, it made two important assumptions: (1) that there was a "liberty interest" in refusing unwanted treatment protected by the Due Process Clause; and (2) that this liberty interest did not "end the inquiry" because it might be outweighed by relevant state interests. I agree with both of those assumptions, but I insist that the source of Nancy Cruzan's right to refuse treatment was not just a common-law rule. Rather, this right is an aspect of a far broader and more basic concept of freedom that is even older than the common law. This freedom embraces, not merely a person's right to refuse a particular kind of unwanted treatment, but also her interest in dignity, and in determining the character of the memories that will survive long after her death. In recognizing that the State's interests did not outweigh Nancy Cruzan's liberty interest in refusing medical treatment, *Cruzan* rested not simply on the common-law right to refuse medical treatment, but—at least implicitly—on the even more fundamental right to make this "deeply personal decision."

Thus, the common-law right to protection from battery, which included the right to refuse medical treatment in most circumstances, did not mark "the outer limits of the substantive sphere of liberty" that supported the Cruzan family's decision to hasten Nancy's death. *Planned Parenthood of Southeastern Pa. v. Casey*, 505 U.S. 833 (1992). Those limits have never been precisely defined. They are generally identified by the importance and character of the decision confronted by the individual. Whatever the outer limits of the concept may be, it definitely includes protection for matters "central to personal dignity and autonomy." *Casey*. The *Cruzan* case demonstrated that some state intrusions on the right to decide how death will be encountered are also intolerable. The now-deceased plaintiffs in this action may in fact have had a liberty interest even stronger than Nancy Cruzan's because, not only were they terminally ill, they were suffering constant and severe pain. Avoiding intolerable pain and the indignity of living one's final days incapacitated and in agony is certainly "at the heart of [the] liberty . . . to define one's own concept of existence, of meaning, of the universe, and of the mystery of human life." *Casey*.

While I agree with the Court that *Cruzan* does not decide the issue presented by these cases, *Cruzan* did give recognition, not just to vague, unbridled notions of autonomy, but to the more specific interest in making decisions about how to confront an imminent death. Although there is no absolute right to physician-assisted suicide, *Cruzan* makes it clear that some individuals who no longer have the option of deciding whether to live or to die because they are already on the threshold of death have a constitutionally protected interest that may outweigh the State's interest in preserving life at all costs. The liberty interest at stake in a case like this differs from, and is stronger than, both the common-law right to refuse medical treatment and the unbridled interest in deciding whether to live or die. It is an interest in deciding how, rather than whether, a critical threshold shall be crossed. . . .

[A]lthough the differences the majority notes in causation and intent between terminating life-support and assisting in suicide support the Court's rejection of the respondents' facial challenge, these distinctions may be inapplicable to particular terminally ill patients and their doctors. Our holding today in *Vacco v. Quill* that the Equal Protection Clause is not violated by New York's classification, just like our holding in *Washington v. Glucksberg* that the Washington statute is not invalid on its face, does not foreclose the possibility that some applications of the New York statute may impose an intolerable intrusion on the patient's freedom.

There remains room for vigorous debate about the outcome of particular cases that are not necessarily resolved by the opinions announced today. How such cases may be decided will depend on their specific facts. In my judgment, however, it is clear that the so-called "unqualified interest in the preservation of human life," *Cruzan*, *Glucksberg*, is not itself sufficient to outweigh the interest in liberty that may justify the only possible means of preserving a dying patient's dignity and alleviating her intolerable suffering.

Justice SOUTER, concurring in the judgment.

Three terminally ill individuals and four physicians who sometimes treat terminally ill patients brought this challenge to the Washington statute making it a crime "knowingly . . . [to] aid another person to attempt suicide," claiming on behalf of both patients and physicians that it would violate substantive due process to enforce the statute against a doctor who acceded to a dying patient's request for a drug to be taken by the patient to commit suicide. The question is whether the statute sets up one of those "arbitrary impositions" or "purposeless restraints" at odds with the Due Process Clause of the Fourteenth Amendment. *Poe v. Ullman*, 367 U.S. 497 (1961) (HARLAN, J., dissenting). I conclude that the statute's application to the doctors has not been shown to be unconstitutional, but I write separately to give my reasons for analyzing the substantive due process claims as I do, and for rejecting this one. . . .

Justice HARLAN's *Poe* dissent just cited, the conclusion of which was adopted in *Griswold v. Connecticut*, 381 U.S. 478 (1965), and the authority of which was acknowledged in *Planned Parenthood of Southeastern Pa. v. Casey*, 505 U.S. 833 (1992), . . . is important for three things that point to our responsibilities today. The first is Justice Harlan's respect for the tradition of substantive due process review itself, and his acknowledgment of the Judiciary's obligation to carry it on. For two centuries American courts, and for much of that time this Court, have thought it necessary to provide some degree of review over the substantive content of legislation under constitutional standards of textual breadth. . . . This enduring tradition of American constitutional practice is, in Justice HARLAN's view, nothing more than what is required by the judicial authority and obligation to construe constitutional text and review legislation for conformity to that text. Like many judges who preceded him and many who followed, he found it impossible to construe the text of due process without recognizing substantive, and not merely procedural, limitations. "Were due process merely a procedural safeguard it would fail to reach those situations where the deprivation of life, liberty or property was accomplished by legislation which by operating in the future could, given even the fairest possible procedure in application to individuals, nevertheless destroy the enjoyment of all three." *Poe.* The text of the Due Process Clause thus imposes nothing less than an obligation to give substantive content to the words "liberty" and "due process of law."

The second of the dissent's lessons is a reminder that the business of such review is not the identification of extratextual absolutes but scrutiny of a legislative resolution (perhaps unconscious) of clashing principles, each quite possibly worthy in and of itself, but each to be weighed within the history of our values as a people. It is a comparison of the relative strengths of opposing claims that informs the judicial task, not a deduction from some first premise. Thus informed, judicial review still has no warrant to substitute one reasonable resolution of the contending positions for another, but authority to supplant the balance already struck between the contenders only when it falls outside the realm of the reasonable. [I deal below] with this second point, and also with the dissent's third, which takes the form of an object lesson in the explicit attention to detail that is no less essential to the intellectual discipline of substantive due process review than an understanding of the basic need to account for the two sides in the controversy and to respect legislation within the zone of reasonableness.

My understanding of unenumerated rights in the wake of the *Poe* dissent and subsequent cases avoids the absolutist failing of many older cases without embracing the opposite pole of equating reasonableness with past practice described at a very specific level. That understanding begins with a concept of "ordered liberty," comprising a continuum of rights to be free from "arbitrary impositions and purposeless restraints." . . . This approach calls for a court to assess the relative "weights" or dignities of the contending interests, and to this extent the judicial method is familiar to the common law. Common law method is subject, however, to two important constraints in the hands of a court engaged in substantive due process review. First, such a court is bound to confine the values that it recognizes to those truly deserving constitutional stature, either to those expressed in constitutional text, or those exemplified by "the traditions from which [the Nation] developed," or revealed by contrast with "the traditions from which it broke." *Poe* (HARLAN, J., dissenting). " 'We may not draw on our merely personal and private notions and disregard the limits . . . derived from considerations that are fused in the whole nature of our judicial process[,] . . . considerations deeply rooted in reason and in the compelling traditions of the legal profession.' " Id. (quoting *Rochin v. California*, 342 U.S. 165 (1952)); see also *Palko v. Connecticut* (looking to " 'principles of justice so rooted in the traditions and conscience of our people as to be ranked as fundamental' ") (quoting *Snyder v. Massachusetts*, 291 U.S. 97 (1934)).

The second constraint, again, simply reflects the fact that constitutional review, not judicial lawmaking, is a court's business here. The weighing or valuing of contending interests in this sphere is only the first step, forming the basis for determining whether the statute in question falls inside or outside the zone of what is reasonable in the way it resolves the conflict between the interests of state and individual. It is no justification for judicial intervention merely to identify a reasonable resolution of contending values that differs from the terms of the legislation under review. It is only when the legislation's justifying principle, critically valued, is so far from being commensurate with the individual interest as to be arbitrarily or pointlessly applied that the statute must give way. Only if this standard points against the statute can the individual claimant be said to have a constitutional right.

The *Poe* dissent thus reminds us of the nature of review for reasonableness or arbitrariness and the limitations entailed by it. But the opinion cautions against the repetition of past error in another way as well, more by its example than by any particular statement of constitutional method: it reminds us that the process of substantive review by reasoned judgment is one of close criticism going to the details of the opposing interests and to their relationships with the historically recognized principles that lend them weight or value. . . .

Respondents base their claim on the traditional right to medical care and counsel, subject to the limiting conditions of informed, responsible choice when death is imminent, conditions that support a strong analogy to rights of care in other situations in which medical counsel and assistance have been available as a matter of course. There can be no stronger claim to a physician's assistance than at the time when death is imminent, a moral judgment implied by the State's own recognition of the legitimacy of medical procedures necessarily hastening the moment of impending death.

In my judgment, the importance of the individual interest here, as within that class of "certain interests" demanding careful scrutiny of the State's contrary claim, cannot be gainsaid. Whether that interest might in some circumstances, or at some time, be seen as "fundamental" to the degree entitled to prevail is not, however, a conclusion that I need draw here, for I am satisfied that the State's interests . . . are sufficiently serious to defeat the present claim that its law is arbitrary or purposeless. . . .

One must bear in mind that the nature of the right claimed, if recognized as one constitutionally required, would differ in no essential way from other constitutional rights guaranteed by enumeration or derived from some more definite textual source than "due process." An unenumerated right should not therefore be recognized, with the effect of displacing the legislative ordering of things, without the assurance that its recognition would prove as durable as the recognition of those other rights differently derived. To recognize a right of lesser promise would simply create a constitutional regime too uncertain to bring with it the expectation of finality that is one of this Court's central obligations in making constitutional decisions. Legislatures, however, are not so constrained. The experimentation that should be out of the question in constitutional adjudication displacing legislative judgments is entirely proper, as well as highly desirable, when the legislative power addresses an emerging issue like assisted suicide. The Court should accordingly stay its hand to allow reasonable legislative consideration. While I do not decide for all time that respondents' claim should not be recognized, I acknowledge the legislative institutional competence as the better one to deal with that claim at this time.

Justice GINSBURG, concurring in the judgments.

I concur in the Court's judgments in these cases substantially for the reasons stated by Justice O'CONNOR in her concurring opinion.

Justice BREYER, concurring in the judgments.

I believe that Justice O'CONNOR's views, which I share, have greater legal significance than the Court's opinion suggests. I join her separate opinion, except insofar as it joins the majority. And I concur in the judgments. I shall briefly explain how I differ from the Court.

I agree with the Court in *Vacco v. Quill*, that the articulated state interests justify the distinction drawn between physician assisted suicide and withdrawal of life support. I also agree with the Court that the critical question in both of the cases before us is whether "the 'liberty' specially protected by the Due Process Clause includes a right" of the sort that the respondents assert. *Washington v. Glucksberg*. I do not agree, however, with the Court's formulation of that claimed "liberty" interest. The Court describes it as a "right to commit suicide with another's assistance." But I would not reject the respondents' claim without considering a different formulation, for which our legal tradition may provide greater support. That formulation would use words roughly like a "right to die with dignity." But irrespective of the exact words used, at its core would lie personal control over the manner of death, professional medical assistance, and the avoidance of unnecessary and severe physical suffering—combined.

As Justice SOUTER points out, Justice HARLAN's dissenting opinion in *Poe v. Ullman* offers some support for such a claim. In that opinion, Justice HARLAN referred to the "liberty" that the Fourteenth Amendment protects as including "a freedom from all substantial arbitrary impositions and purposeless restraints" and also as recognizing that "certain interests require particularly careful scrutiny of the state needs asserted to justify their abridgment." The "certain interests" to which Justice HARLAN referred may well be similar (perhaps identical) to the rights, liberties, or interests that the Court today, as in the past, regards as "fundamental."

Justice HARLAN concluded that marital privacy was such a "special interest." . . . The respondents here essentially ask us to do the same. They argue that one can find a "right to die with dignity" by examining the protection the law has provided for related, but not identical, interests relating to personal dignity, medical treatment, and freedom from state-inflicted pain.

I do not believe, however, that this Court need or now should decide whether or a not such a right is "fundamental." That is because, in my view, the avoidance of severe physical pain (connected with death) would have to comprise an essential part of any successful claim and because, as Justice O'CONNOR points out, the laws before us do not force a dying person to undergo that kind of pain. Rather, the laws of New York and of Washington do not prohibit doctors from providing patients with drugs sufficient to control pain despite the risk that those drugs themselves will kill. And under these circumstances the laws of New York and Washington would overcome any remaining significant interests and would be justified, regardless. . . .

This legal circumstance means that the state laws before us do not infringe directly upon the (assumed) central interest (what I have called the core of the interest in dying with dignity) as, by way of contrast, the state anticontraceptive laws at issue in *Poe* did interfere with the central interest there at stake—by bringing the State's police powers to bear upon the marital bedroom.

Were the legal circumstances different—for example, were state law to prevent the provision of palliative care, including the administration of drugs as needed to avoid pain at the end of life—then the law's impact upon serious and otherwise unavoidable physical pain (accompanying death) would be more directly at issue. And as Justice O'CONNOR suggests, the Court might have to revisit its conclusions in these cases.

12

THE EQUAL PROTECTION
OF THE LAWS

A. RACIAL DISCRIMINATION AND STATE ACTION

In its 1997–1998 term, the Court extended its rulings in *Batson v. Kentucky*, 476 U.S. 79 (1986), and *Powers v. Ohio*, 499 U.S. 400 (1991) (see Vol. 2, Ch. 12), barring prosecutors from using preemptory challenges to strike blacks from juries, to grand juries. Writing for the Court in *Campbell v. Louisiana*, 118 S.Ct. 1419 (1998), Justice Kennedy held that a white defendant, challenging on the basis of the Fourteenth Amendment's due process and equal protection clauses, had standing to allege racial bias in the selection of grand jury forepersons, because between 1976 and 1993 no black person served as grand jury foreman even though more than 20 percent of the registered voters in the Parish were black. Justices Thomas and Scalia concurred and dissented in part.

D. NONRACIAL CLASSIFICATIONS AND THE
EQUAL PROTECTION OF THE LAWS

(1) Gender-Based Discrimination

In *Miller v. Albright* (excerpted below), the justices rejected by a six to three vote an equal rights challenge to a federal statute that automatically grants citizenship to illegitimate children born in a foreign country if the mother is a United States citizen, but sets a higher standard if the father is a citizen and the mother a foreign national. In his opinion for the Court, joined only by Chief Justice Rehnquist, Justice Stevens upheld the statute on the ground that, presumptively, there is a closer connection between a mother and her child than the father and a child. In a concurring opinion joined by Justice Kennedy, Justice O'Connor agreed that the law should be upheld but would not have reached that issue because in her view the petitioner lacked standing. In another concurring opinion, joined by Justice Thomas, Justice Scalia agreed with the result but criticized the Court for not dismissing the suit in the first place, since it could not provide any relief, namely conferral of citizenship, on any basis other than that provided by Congress in the statute. By contrast, in separate dissenting opinions—each joined by Justice Souter—Justices Ginsburg and Breyer contended that the statute's gender-based discrimination was unconstitutional. In particular, Justice Ginsburg chastised the majority for relying on sexual stereotypes and countered that the law plainly "treats mothers one way, fathers another, shaping governmental policy to fit and reinforce the stereotype or historical pattern" of gender discrimination.

In its 1997–1998 term, the Court also decided a number of cases involving the application of federal law to claims of sexual harassment; see "The Development of Law" box below. Notably, in *Oncale v. Sundowner Offshore Services*, 118 S.Ct. 998 (1998), the Court held that the Civil Rights Act of 1964 applies to claims of same-sex harassment, as well as the harassment of employees of a different gender.

Miller v. Albright
118 S.Ct. 1428 (1998)

Ms. Lorelyn Miller was born in the Philippines. Her birth certificate states that she was illegitimate and identifies her mother as a Filipino national. It does not identify her father, Mr. Charlie R. Miller, a U.S. citizen who, at the time of her birth, was a member of the U.S. military stationed in the Philippines. After her twenty-first birthday, Ms. Miller applied to the U.S. State Department for registration as a United States citizen. In 1992, the State Department denied her application on the ground that she failed to meet the requirements of a provision of the Immigration and Naturalization Act. Specifically, it did so because Ms. Miller failed to show that her father had agreed in writing to provide financial support for her until she reached the age of eighteen and that her father acknowledged paternity. Subsequently, Mr. Miller obtained a voluntary paternity decree from a Texas state court and Ms. Miller submitted that document with a request that the State Department reconsider her application. Ms. Miller also sought a review of her claim in federal district court, claiming that the statutory prerequisites for U.S. citizenship violated the Fourteenth Amendment's equal protection principle because of the statute's distinctions between legitimate and illegitimate children and between men and women. The secretary of state moved to dismiss her complaint and the district court agreed. In 1996, the Court of Appeals for the District of Columbia Circuit rejected Ms. Miller's constitutional claim and she appealed to the Supreme Court, which granted review.

The Court's decision was six to three to affirm the lower court and announced by Justice Stevens. Justice O'Connor, joined by Justice Kennedy, filed a concurring opinion, as did Justice Scalia, who was joined by Justice Thomas. Justices Ginsburg and Breyer filed separate dissenting opinions, which Justice Souter joined.

Justice STEVENS announced the judgment of the Court and delivered an opinion, in which the CHIEF JUSTICE joined.

There are "two sources of citizenship, and two only: birth and naturalization." Within the former category, the Fourteenth Amendment of the Constitution guarantees that every person "born in the United States, and subject to the jurisdiction thereof, becomes at once a citizen of the United States, and needs no naturalization." Persons not born in the United States acquire citizenship by birth only as provided by Acts of Congress.

The petitioner in this case challenges the constitutionality of the statutory provisions governing the acquisition of citizenship at birth by children born out of wedlock and outside of the United States. The specific challenge is to the distinction drawn by Section 309 of the Immigration and Nationality Act (INA), as amended, 8 U.S.C. Section 1409, between the child of an alien father and a citizen mother, on the one hand, and the child of an alien mother and a citizen father, on the other. Subject to residence requirements for the citizen parent, the citizenship of the former is established at birth; the citizenship of the latter is not established unless and until either the father or his child takes certain affirmative steps to create or confirm their relationship. Petitioner contends that the statutory requirement that those steps be taken while the child is a minor violates the Fifth Amendment because the statute contains no limitation on the time within which the child of a citizen mother may prove that she became a citizen at birth.

We find no merit in the challenge because the statute does not impose any limitation on the time within which the members of either class of children may prove that they qualify for citizenship. It does establish different qualifications for citizenship for the two classes of children, but we are persuaded that the qualifications for the members of each of those classes, so far as they are implicated by the facts of this case, are well supported by valid governmental interests. We therefore conclude that the statutory distinction is neither arbitrary nor invidious. . . .

It is of significance that the petitioner in this case . . . is not challenging the denial of an application for special status. She is contesting the Government's refusal to register and treat her as a citizen. If she were to prevail, the judgment in her favor would confirm her pre-existing citizenship rather than grant her rights that she does not now possess. We therefore agree with the Court of Appeals that she has standing to invoke the jurisdiction of the federal courts. Moreover, because her claim relies heavily on the proposition that her citizen father should have the same right to transmit citizenship as would a citizen mother, we shall evaluate the alleged discrimination against him as well as its impact on her.

Under the terms of the INA, the joint conduct of a citizen and an alien that results in conception is not sufficient to produce an American citizen, regardless of whether the citizen parent is the male or the female partner. If the two parties engage in a second joint act—if they agree to marry one another—citizenship will follow. The provision at issue in this case, however, deals only with cases in which no relevant joint conduct occurs after conception; it determines the ability of each of those parties, acting separately, to confer citizenship on a child born outside of the United States.

If the citizen is the unmarried female, she must first choose to carry the pregnancy to term and reject the alternative of abortion—an alternative that is available by law to many, and in reality to most, women around the world. She must then actually give birth to the child. Section 1409(c) rewards that choice and that labor by conferring citizenship on her child.

If the citizen is the unmarried male, he need not participate in the decision to give birth rather than to choose an abortion; he need not be present at the birth; and for at least 17 years thereafter he need not provide any parental support, either moral or financial, to either the mother or the child, in order to preserve his right to confer citizenship on the child pursuant to Section 1409(a). In order retroactively to transmit his citizenship to the child as of the date of the child's birth, all that Section 1409(a)(4) requires is that he be willing and able to acknowledge his paternity in writing under oath while the child is still a minor. 8 U.S.C. Section 1409(a)(4)(B). In fact, Section 1409(a)(4) requires even less of the unmarried father—that provision is alternatively satisfied if, before the child turns 18, its paternity "is established by adjudication of a competent court." Section 1409(a)(4)(C). It would appear that the child could obtain such an adjudication absent any affirmative act by the father, and perhaps even over his express objection.

There is . . . a vast difference between the burdens imposed on the respective parents of potential citizens born out of wedlock in a foreign land. It seems obvious that the burdens imposed on the female citizen are more severe than those imposed on the male citizen by Section 1409(a)(4), the only provision at issue in this case. It is nevertheless argued that the male citizen and his offspring are the victims of irrational discrimination because Section 1409(a)(4) is the product of "'overbroad stereotypes about the relative abilities of men and women.'" We find the argument singularly unpersuasive.

There is no doubt that ensuring reliable proof of a biological relationship between the potential citizen and its citizen parent is an important governmental objective. Nor can it be denied that the male and female parents are differently situated in this respect. The blood relationship to the birth mother is immediately obvious and is typically established by hospital records and birth certificates; the relationship to the unmarried father may often be undisclosed and unrecorded in any contemporary public record. . . .

Nevertheless, petitioner reiterates the suggestion that it is irrational to require a formal act such as a written acknowledgment or a court adjudication because the advent of reliable genetic testing fully addresses the problem of proving paternity, and subsection (a)(1) already requires proof of paternity by clear and convincing evidence. We respectfully disagree. Nothing in subsection (a)(1) requires the citizen father or his child to obtain a genetic paternity test. It is difficult, moreover, to understand why signing a paternity acknowledgment under oath prior to the child's 18th birthday is more burdensome than obtaining a genetic test, which is relatively expensive, normally requires physical intrusion for both the putative father and child, and often is not available in foreign countries. Congress could fairly conclude that despite recent scientific advances, it still remains preferable to require some formal legal act to establish paternity, coupled with a clear-and-convincing evidence standard to deter fraud. The time limitation, in turn, provides assurance that the formal act is based upon reliable evidence, and also deters fraud. Congress is of course free to revise its collective judgment and permit genetic proof of paternity rather than requiring some formal legal act by the father or a court, but the Constitution does not now require any such change.

Section 1409 also serves two other important purposes that are unrelated to the determination of paternity: the interest in encouraging the development of a healthy relationship between the citizen parent and the child while the child is a minor; and the related interest in fostering ties between the foreign-born child and the United States. . . .

We are convinced not only that strong governmental interests justify the additional requirement imposed on children of citizen fathers, but also that the particular means used in Section 1409(a)(4) are well tailored to serve those interests. It is perfectly appropriate to require some formal act, not just any evidence that the father or his child know of the other's existence. Such a formal act, whether legitimation, written acknowledgment by the father, or a court adjudication, lessens the risk of fraudulent claims made years after the relevant conduct was required. As for the requirement that the formal act take place while the child is a minor, Congress obviously has a powerful interest in fostering ties with the child's citizen parent and the United States during his or her formative years. If there is no reliable, contemporaneous proof that the child and the citizen father had the opportunity to form familial bonds before the child turned 18, Congress reasonably may demand that the child show sufficient ties to this country on its own rather than through its citizen parent in order to be a citizen. . . .

The words "stereotype," "stereotyping," and "stereotypical" are used repeatedly in petitioner's and her *amici*'s briefs. They note that we have condemned statutory classifications that rest on the assumption that gender may serve as a proxy for relevant qualifications to serve as the administrator of an estate, *Reed v. Reed*, 404 U.S. 71 (1971), to engage in professional nursing, *Mississippi Univ. for Women v. Hogan*, 458 U.S. 718 (1982), or to train for military service, *United States v. Virginia*, 518 U.S. 515 (1996), to name a few examples. Moreover, we have expressly repudiated cases that rested on the assumption that only the members of one sex could suitably practice law or tend bar. See *Hogan* (commenting on *Bradwell v. State*, 83 U.S. 130 (1873) and *Goesaert v. Cleary*, 335 U.S. 464 (1948)). Discrimination that "is merely the accidental byproduct of a traditional way of thinking about females" is unacceptable. *Califano v. Goldfarb*, 430 U.S. 199 (1977) (STEVENS, J., concurring in judgment).

The gender equality principle that was implicated in those cases is only indirectly involved in this case for two reasons. First, the conclusion that petitioner is not a citizen rests on several coinciding factors, not just the gender of her citizen parent. On the facts of this case, even if petitioner's mother had been a citizen and her father had been the alien, petitioner would not qualify for citizenship because her mother has never been to the United States. Alternatively, if her citizen parent had been a female member of the Air Force and, like Mr. Miller, had returned to the States at the end of her tour of duty, Section 1409 quite probably would have been irrelevant and petitioner would have become a citizen at birth by force of the Constitution itself. Second, it is not merely the sex of the citizen parent that determines whether the child is a citizen under the terms of the statute; rather, it is an event creating a legal relationship between parent and child—the birth itself for citizen mothers, but post-birth conduct for citizen fathers and their offspring. Nevertheless, we may assume that if the classification in Section 1409 were merely the product of an outmoded stereotype, it would be invalid.

The "gender stereotypes" on which Section 1409 is supposedly premised are (1) "that the American father is never anything more than the proverbial breadwinner who remains aloof from day-to-day child rearing duties," and (2) "that a mother will be closer to her child born out of wedlock than a father will be to his." Even disregarding the statute's separate, non-stereotypical purpose of ensuring reliable proof of a blood relationship, neither of those propositions fairly reflects the justifications for the classification actually at issue.

The judgment of the Court of Appeals is affirmed.

It is so ordered.

Justice O'CONNOR, with whom Justice KENNEDY joins, concurring in the judgment.

This Court has long applied a presumption against third-party standing as a prudential limitation on the exercise of federal jurisdiction. Federal courts, we have held, "must hesitate before resolving a controversy, even one within their constitutional power to resolve, on the basis of the rights of third persons not parties to the litigation." *Singleton v. Wulff*, 428 U.S. 106 (1976); see also *Warth v. Seldin*, 422 U.S. 490 (1975). Contrary to this prudential rule, the Court recognizes that petitioner has standing to raise an equal protection challenge to 8 U.S.C. Section 1409. The statute, however, accords differential treatment to fathers and mothers, not to sons and daughters. Thus, although petitioner is clearly injured by the fact that she has been denied citizenship, the discriminatory impact of the provision falls on petitioner's father, Charlie Miller, who is no longer a party to this suit. Consequently, I do not believe that we should consider petitioner's gender discrimination claim. . . .

Justice SCALIA, with whom Justice THOMAS joins, concurring in the judgment.

I agree with the outcome in this case, but for a reason more fundamental than the one relied upon by Justice STEVENS. In my view it makes no difference whether or not Section 1409(a) passes "heightened scrutiny" or any other test members of the Court might choose to apply. The complaint must be dismissed because the Court has no power to provide the relief requested: conferral of citizenship on a basis other than that prescribed by Congress. . . .

By its plain language, Section 1409(a) sets forth a precondition to the acquisition of citizenship under Section 1401(g) by the illegitimate child of a citizen-father. Petitioner does not come into federal court claiming that she met that precondition, and that the State Department's conclusion to the contrary was factually in error. Rather, she acknowledges that she did not meet the last two requirements of that precondition, Sections 1409(a)(3) and (4). She nonetheless asks for a "declaratory judgment that [she] is a citizen of the United States" and an order to the Secretary of State requiring the State Department to grant her application for citizenship, because the requirements she did not meet are not also imposed upon illegitimate children of citizen-mothers, and therefore violate the Equal Protection Clause. Even if we were to agree that the difference in treatment between illegitimate children of citizen-fathers and citizen-mothers is unconstitutional, we could not, consistent with the limited judicial power in this area, remedy that constitutional infirmity by declaring petitioner to be a citizen or ordering the State Department to approve her application for citizenship. . . .

Justice GINSBURG, with whom Justice SOUTER and Justice BREYER join, dissenting.

As Justice BREYER convincingly demonstrates [in the dissent omitted here], 8 U.S.C. Section 1409 classifies unconstitutionally on the basis of gender in determining the capacity of a parent to qualify a child for citizenship. The section rests on familiar generalizations: mothers, as a rule, are responsible for a child born out of wedlock; fathers unmarried to the child's mother, ordinarily, are not. The law at issue might have made custody or support the relevant criterion. Instead, it treats mothers one way, fathers another, shaping government policy to fit and reinforce the stereotype or historic pattern.

Characteristic of sex-based classifications, the stereotypes underlying this legislation may hold true for many, even most, individuals. But in prior decisions the Court has rejected official actions that classify unnecessarily and overbroadly by gender when more accurate and impartial functional lines can be drawn. While the Court is divided on Lorelyn Miller's standing to sue, a solid majority adheres to that vital understanding. . . .

Even if one accepts at face value the Government's current rationale, it is surely based on generalizations (stereotypes) about the way women (or men) are. These generalizations pervade the opinion of Justice STEVENS, which constantly relates and relies on what "typically," or "normally," or "probably" happens "often."

We have repeatedly cautioned, however, that when the Government controls "gates to opportunity," it "may not exclude qualified individuals based on 'fixed notions concerning the roles and abilities of males and females.'" *United States v. Virginia*, 518 U.S. 515 (1996).

One can demur to the Government's observation that more United States citizen mothers of children born abroad out of wedlock actually raise their children than do United States citizen fathers of such children. As Justice BREYER has elucidated, this observation does not justify distinctions between male and female United States citizens who take responsibility, or avoid responsibility, for raising their children. Nor does it justify reliance on gender distinctions when the alleged purpose—assuring close ties to the United States—can be achieved without reference to gender. . . .

THE DEVELOPMENT OF LAW

Rulings Dealing with Gender Discrimination and Statutory Interpretation

Case	Vote	Ruling
Oncale v. Sundowner Offshore Services, 118 S.Ct. 998 (1998)	9:0	Writing for a unanimous Court, Justice Scalia ruled that Title VII of the Civil Rights Act of

1964, forbidding sexual discrimination in the workplace, applies to same-sex harassment, no less than harassment of employees of different sexes and sexual orientations.

Gebser v. Lago Vista Independent   5:4   Held that damages may not
School District, 118 S.Ct. 1989 (1998)   be recovered for teacher–
student sexual harassment
in an implied private right of action suit under Title IX, which forbids sex
discrimination by schools that receive federal funding and is commonly
associated with bringing equality to sports programs. A bare majority ruled
that schools are not liable for such misconduct unless school officials with
authority to institute corrective measures are "deliberately indifferent" to a
teacher's misconduct. Writing for the Court, Justice O'Connor emphasized
that Title IX is unlike the Civil Rights Act of 1964, which bans sex discrimination and harassment in the workplace, because it provides for the
loss of federal funding when school officials know of and fail to respond to
misconduct and Congress, therefore, did not contemplate private cause of
action suits for sexual harassment. The four dissenters—Justices Stevens,
Souter, Ginsburg, and Breyer—countered that school districts should be
liable for teachers' misconduct on the theory that teachers are acting on
behalf of the school.

Faragher v. City of Boca Raton   7:2   Held that under Title VII of
118 S.Ct. 2275 (1998)   the Civil Rights Act an employer is subject to vicari-
ous liability for hostile-environment sexual harassment created by a super-
visor. Writing for the Court, Justice Souter held that employees need not
show that an employer knew or should have known about the sexual harassment and failed to stop it. Even if an employee did not suffer the loss of promotion or employment, a suit may be brought if the sexual harassment or
abuse was severe or pervasive. Employers, however, may offer the affirmative defenses (a) that they took reasonable care to prevent or correct sexually harassing behavior and (b) that the employee unreasonably failed to take
advantage of corrective opportunities offered by the employer. Here, Justice
Souter found that Boca Raton failed to exercise reasonable care in protecting its female lifeguards from a hostile environment of sexual harassment.
Justices Scalia and Thomas dissented.

Burlington Industries, Inc. v.   7:2   Writing for the Court, Justice
Ellerth, 118 S.Ct. 2257 (1998)   Kennedy held that employers
are liable, under Title VII of
the Civil Rights Act, for hostile-environment sexual harassment by supervisors unless they show (a) reasonable care to prevent or correct promptly sexually harassing behavior and (b) that the employee unreasonably failed to
take advantage of grievance procedures offered by the employer in order to
avoid harm. Justices Scalia and Thomas dissented.

(3) Wealth, Poverty, and Illegitimacy

By a six-to-three vote in *M.L.B. v. S.L.J.*, 117 S.Ct. 555 (1996), the Court held that states may not prevent indigents from appealing family court decisions terminating their parental rights. M.L.B., Melissa L. Brooks, could not afford to pay $2,352 for trial transcipts, which were necessary in order to appeal a decision terminating her parental rights over her two young children. In her divorce, custody of the children had been awarded to her former husband, who subsequently sought to terminate her parental rights so his new wife could adopt the children. Mississippi and a few other states make appeals in such cases dependent on the ability to pay for trial transcripts.

In a watershed ruling in *Griffin v. Illinois*, 351 U.S. 12 (1956), the Warren Court ruled that states may not deny indigents the right to appeal criminal convictions simply because they could not afford to pay for trial transcripts. Later decisions extended that ruling to other proceedings; see "The Development of Law" box in Vol. 2, Ch. 9. Although *Boddie v. Connecticut*, 401 U.S. 371 (1971), extended that principle of equal justice in a civil case, striking down a $60 filing fee for divorce proceedings, in a series of other cases in the 1970s and 1980s the Burger Court refused to further extend the principle in cases involving bankruptcy and welfare benefits.

Writing for the Court in *M.L.B.*, Justice Ginsburg emphasized the fundamental character of family life and extended *Griffin*'s analysis of due process and equal protection principles. In Justice Ginsburg's words:

> Guided by this Court's precedent on an indigent's access to judicial processes in criminal and civil cases, and on proceedings to terminate parental status, we turn to the classification question this case presents: Does the Fourteenth Amendment require Mississippi to accord M.L.B. access to an appeal—available but for her inability to advance required costs—before she is forever branded unfit for affiliation with her children? . . . For the purpose at hand, M.L.B. asks us to treat her parental termination appeal as we have treated petty offense appeals; she urges us to adhere to the reasoning in *Mayer v. Chicago*, 404 U.S. 189 (1971), and rule that Mississippi may not withhold the transcript M.L.B. needs to gain review of the order ending her parental status. . . . [W]e agree that the *Mayer* decision points to the disposition proper in this case.

In a separate concurring opinion, Justice Kennedy would have based the Court's decision solely on due process grounds. By contrast, dissenting Justice Thomas rejected both the due process and equal protection rationales for the ruling. His dissent was joined by Justice Scalia and in part by Chief Justice Rehnquist.

INDEX OF CASES

Cases printed in boldface are excerpted on the page(s) printed in boldface.

153